CONSTRUCTING URBAN CULTURE

American Cities and City Planning, 1800–1920

TECHNOLOGY AND URBAN GROWTH,

a series edited by

Blaine A. Brownell
Donald T. Critchlow
Mark S. Foster
Mark H. Rose
Joel A. Tarr

CONSTRUCTING

URBAN

CULTURE

*American Cities
and City Planning,
1800-1920*

STANLEY K. SCHULTZ

*Temple University Press
Philadelphia*

Temple University Press, Philadelphia 19122
Copyright © 1989 by Temple University. All rights reserved
Published 1989
Printed in the United States of America

The paper used in this publication meets the minimum requirements of American National Standard for Information Sciences—Permanence of Paper for Printed Library Materials, ANSI Z39.48-1984

Library of Congress Cataloging-in-Publication Data

Schultz, Stanley K.
    Constructing urban culture : American cities and city planning, 1800–1920 / Stanley K. Schultz.
        p.   cm. — (Technology and urban growth)
    Bibliography: p.
    Includes index.
    ISBN 0–87722–587–7 (alk. paper) : $29.95 (est.)
    1. City planning—United States—History—19th century.   2. City planning—United States—History—20th century.   3. Cities and towns—United States—History—19th century.   4. Cities and towns—United States—History—20th century.   I. Title.   II. Series.
HT167.S284 1988
307.1′2′0973—dc19   88–16056
                                                                        CIP

To Chris, Ben, and Jon
in thanks for the love

CONTENTS

FIGURES, TABLES, AND MAPS

FIGURES

TABLES

MAP

PREFACE

There is no absolute plan for cities, and no city can be well
planned, as the duplicate of another. . . . And yet the
beginnings made and the growths or extensions that come after,
would commonly be very different, if only there could be on
hand a little better culture, in regard to the ideas and principles
involved in the best and most tasteful arrangement of cities.

And here, exactly, is the object of our present inquiry; it is to
set on, or promote, this kind of culture—.

Horace Bushnell, "City Plans," c. 1860

CITIES ARE the accumulation of human experience. They are the
manufactured containers, the physical expressions, of human culture. In that sense, all cities are planned environments. They are
the results of cultural decisions about the most appropriate physical
uses of land and the residential distribution of people. Urban form
encapsules time and space. At any moment in time, the physical
landscape of the city reveals the countless decisions of bygone days
about the "best" uses of space—"best" means those individual or
collective values and judgments about the quality of life made by
citizens in the past, judgments that affect the lives of those in the
present—and the future. Urban forms reveal what was and was not
important to their builders and residents in any given historical moment.

During the course of the nineteenth century, American perceptions of the city underwent a profound transformation. A new urban
culture emerged to first challenge, then supplant, the traditional order of rural and small-town America. That culture arose from new

attitudes about the relationship between the physical environment and bodily, mental, and moral health. A wide variety of nineteenth-century urban reformers confronted the numerous and increasing problems of the urban physical environment and championed new technologies as solutions. Novelists, lawyers, sanitarians, landscape architects, and municipal engineers, among others, set forth plans, practices, and techniques to rehabilitate the cities of their day and to make more inhabitable the cities of tomorrow.

In most cases the planning proposals were comprehensive by the evolving standards of the day. Not every blueprint for change incorporated the range of possibilities at least mentioned in a twentieth-century city plan—new transit facilities, street layouts, public works, health legislation, land-use zoning, recreational facilities, and the like—although some plans did. Yet all reflected a growing awareness of the city as a total environment, one in which the character and quality of life depended on the character and quality of the city itself as a physical and moral container. However narrowly or broadly conceived their schemes, the nineteenth-century reformers were certain that putting their plans into practice would alter the whole urban environment, and its population. By their own lights, they were city planners striving to craft, in Horace Bushnell's words, "a little better culture."[1]

This is a book about the evolution of the new American urban culture. All nineteenth-century urban Americans participated, intentionally or unintentionally, in the emergence of that new culture. Most were unaware of their contributions, going about the daily tasks of life without consciously weighing the immediate or long-range results of their individual decisions. Still, such choices as where to erect a new house or commercial building or small manufactory helped shape the urban landscape and manifested both private and public values about the uses of urban land. There were in addition reformers and visionaries who consciously and deliberately attacked the problems of their times while planning for the future.

In exploring the changing physical landscape of urban America, I try to capture what it was like to be alive in a nineteenth-century city. I seek to explain how Americans created a new urban culture in which assumptions about the good life differed so markedly from those of previous generations. I explore the ideological and technological factors intertwined in the growth of the modern metropolis.

I ask who made conscious decisions about urban land use and how those decisions shaped and reshaped the ways in which Americans perceived themselves and their physical and cultural environment. Who were those planners whose attitudes and aspirations, ideas and practices, laid the foundations for and fashioned a new culture of planning?

For most historians, the birth of modern city planning occurred in 1909 with the First National Conference on City Planning and the Problems of Congestion, held in Washington, D.C., and with presentation of the massively detailed *Plan of Chicago* set forth by the noted architect Daniel H. Burnham. Some historians point instead to the World's Columbian Exposition in Chicago in 1893. In constructing the so-called White City as the exposition's home—a "city" that, if real and permanent, would have housed over 200,000 citizens—Burnham and the landscape architect Frederick Law Olmsted confronted all the practical problems of comprehensive planning. They had to provide for fire and police protection, water, sewer, and transportation systems, recreational facilities, and the like. That they did so while also creating a monument to civic art and architecture has led some historians to label the White City a laboratory of civic design and to claim that "the initial spur to city planning in the United States came from the spectacular Chicago Fair of 1893."[2]

I take a different tack. As I hope to persuade you in this book, "comprehensive" city planning and thinking comprehensively about the problems of the urban environment were a product of the entire nineteenth century, not just its last decade or the first decade of the twentieth century.

The nineteenth century was the American century of urbanization. For each decade between 1820 and 1860, the national population increased by over 30 percent; the urban population (i.e., people living in places with 2,500 or more inhabitants) expanded at three times that rate. Between 1820 and 1870 the number of urban places grew tenfold, and the proportion of urban dwellers in the population rose from 8 to 25 percent. Over the post–Civil War years and into the first two decades of the twentieth century, urban expansion continued unabated in every section of the United States, even in the rural South. In 1900 the Census Bureau counted 78 cities with populations numbering more than 50,000. A century of what many contemporaries called "city mania" resulted in the maturity of the

United States as an urban nation. By 1920 the majority of Americans lived in cities.

Nowhere was urban growth more evident, nor to many more ominous, than in the booming urban giants. Early in the century, the rapid rise of a New York, Philadelphia, Boston, or Baltimore appeared to threaten the harmony and stability of the largely rural and small-town nation. Later, with a ferocious determination to grow as rapidly as possible that alarmed many social observers, newer centers such as Cincinnati, Chicago, Cleveland, Kansas City, San Francisco, and Atlanta prophesied an urban future for the nation.

To most Americans during the nineteenth century, the outlines of that future were hazy at best. Americans had neither the experience nor the inclination to think about themselves as an urban or urbanizing population. As it was the century of urbanization, it was as well the American century of industrialization and technological innovation. An American born near the century's dawn and living to a ripe old age encountered a burst of mechanical inventions and alterations in the fabric of home life and work environment without precedent in his or her experience, or in living memory. While some, especially upper- and middle-class urbanites, embraced the new technologies, many others were less sanguine. Changes were unsettling at best, terrifying at worst.

All these Americans found themselves forced to think in new ways about the quality of their lives and of their environments. They had to reassess their definitions of the "good life"—and rediscover where one could live it. Over the course of decades, nineteenth-century Americans engaged in a new discourse about cities and society, a society that many believed (or feared) would become increasingly urban. Without always realizing that they had done so, Americans had started constructing and living in a new kind of urban culture.

Along the way, they invented a new social vocabulary to more clearly express their growing awareness of the intricate connections between the quality of their individual lives and that of their physical environments. Already by the 1840s and 1850s old words like "machine," "technology," and even "planning" had gained fresh meanings that signaled both caution and confidence. Caution, because for all urbanites the directions of change were unknown and the ability to control change in the interests of all citizens uncertain. Confidence, because for at least some urbanites, the city promised to become the center of American civilization.

This book is about the discourse, the people, the planners, and their cities. It advances a synthesis of the social, cultural, and intellectual origins of American city planning thought and practice. I have tried to integrate intellectual, legal, medical, and technological history to illuminate general patterns rather than to microscopically detail every facet of planning activities. As an extended essay, not a monograph, this inquiry risks overgeneralization. Readers at all familiar with any of the various parts of my story will discover much that is missing.

I have ordered this composition around several assumptions. First, what individuals wish to believe is often more significant than what is really true. Second, the task of altering attitudes customarily precedes action to affect the circumstances in which people live. Finally, systematically articulated ideas about improving the physical environment, in the United States at least, have stemmed principally from a desire to improve the moral nature of human beings.

Four themes illuminate the emergence of the new urban culture. The first section, "Imagining the City," discusses changing intellectual perceptions of the city, the nature of technology, and the quality of American civilization. The discussion moves back and forth between the real world of nineteenth-century America and the fictional world of the planned city of the future as envisioned by novelists. The second section, "Regulating the City," examines the nation's evolving legal system, ideological innovations in legal thought in response to urban growth, and the creation of a new body of urban law as central to the new culture of cities. "Sanitizing the City," the third section, explores the problems of health and disease in cities, competing bodies of medical thought about the causes of disease, and the remedies offered by urban reformers. Finally, "Engineering the City" presents the ideas and actions of those who advanced technological solutions for the problems of the urban physical environment. In particular, it traces the construction of new public works facilities and investigates the impact of public works planning on the political and administrative structure of urban government. The net results, I contend, were the maturation of a new American urban order, a deepening devotion to technology as society's savior, and a budding appreciation of the utility of social planning.

For their cooperation in my research efforts I owe thanks to the staffs of several superb libraries: the State Historical Society of Wisconsin, the Library of Congress, the Francis Loeb Library at the Harvard University School of Design, and the Massachusetts Historical Society. For generous financial support I am indebted to the Social Science Research Council, the Rockefeller Foundation, and the Research Committee of the Graduate School of the University of Wisconsin, which has never failed to answer the cry for help from this impecunious scholar. For reading and criticizing the manuscript over the years, I owe special thanks to a number of unselfish colleagues: Mark Rose, Zane E. Miller, Mark Foster, Barbara G. Rosenkrantz, James H. Cassedy, Henry Hope Reed, Jon A. Peterson, Louis P. Cain, Joel A. Tarr, Martin V. Melosi, David R. Goldfield, Thaddeus Seymour (one of my Ph.D. students and research assistants), and Clay McShane (my first Ph.D. student and the man who taught me the importance of material technology). To several individuals I am especially indebted: Charles E. Rosenberg (whose magnificent book *The Cholera Years* served as inspiration for this work), Kenneth T. Jackson (a sometime co-author on other works and a longtime friend whose courage in the face of personal tragedy, together with that of his wife, Barbara, has sustained me), Mary Lou M. Schultz (the best editor I know), Hendrik Hartog (one of the most insightful legal historians of his generation), John B. Sharpless (colleague, confidant, and friend), Martin J. Fliegel (who guided me through the most difficult shoals of my life), Virginia P. Schultz (my tenacious mother), Jane Barry (whose superb skills as a copy editor greatly improved this manuscript), and Judith A. Cochran (whose editorial advice, friendship, and word-processing skills proved invaluable). Many years ago Richard C. Wade stoked the imagination of this city boy with his own enthusiasm for the history of cities. Daniel J. Boorstin remains my model of all the word "historian" means, a person who, although he read not one word of this manuscript, hovered above every sentence. Finally, in an earlier book I thanked my sons Christopher and Benjamin for what they had taught me about childhood, family, and education. I now cannot thank enough all three of my sons—Christopher, Benjamin, and Jonathan—whose strong love, patient understanding, and unfailing support have helped their father learn something about growing up.

PART ONE

———

IMAGINING THE CITY

For here have we no continuing city,
But we seek one to come.

Hebrews 13:14

1

DREAMERS OF URBTOPIA

AT MY FEET lay a great city. . . . Every quarter contained large open squares filled with trees, along which statues glistened and fountains flashed in the late-afternoon sun. Public buildings of a colossal size and architectural grandeur unparalleled in my day raised their stately piles on every side. Surely I had never seen this city nor one comparable to it before." So observed Julian West, the narrator of Edward Bellamy's utopian romance, *Looking Backward, 2000–1887*. Propelled into the future by a quirk of nature, West marveled at the changes wrought in little more than a century. The city of the future stood in stark contrast to a late nineteenth-century Boston whose "streets and alleys reeked with the effluvia of a slave-ship's between-decks." Published in 1888, the novel quickly became one of the bestsellers of its day. Then as now, many people longed for an escape to a better life, and by Bellamy's day, criticism of America's burgeoning cities had assumed the proportions of a national literary pastime. Americans shared an ages-old cultural ambivalence about urban life.[1]

Far more than the word "country," "city" has encapsuled the worst of human faults—greed, selfishness, ignorance—and the best of human virtues—generosity, neighborliness, enlightenment. From classical times to the twentieth century, the city has served as the stage-setting for the human morality play. Neither Plato in *The Republic* nor Aristotle in his *Politics* could envision civilized society outside the boundaries of the city. More's *Utopia* and Bacon's *New Atlantis* presented a geographically isolated city as the paradigm of perfection. Eighteenth- and nineteenth-century British and American authors juxtaposed the evils of the city with the pastoral goodness of the countryside, while simultaneously displaying their fascination with the attractions of the urban scene. While pastoral

3

or arcadian works have emphasized the simplicity and nobility of rural life in contrast with the artificiality and sordidness of the city, another genre, the utopian, has stressed the ascendancy of man over nature. In the American setting, that literature usually has centered its depiction of the perfected society in the fictional city that never was, as did Bellamy's novel.[2]

The evolving values of the new urban culture paraded through the pages of what I call "urbtopian" ("city-place") fiction. Most of the stories focus on descriptions of incredible technologies of housing, transportation, sanitation, and industrial production, with character development and plot line secondary. The tales describe citizens of the imaginary cities as kindly, happy, personally and socially productive. In this increasingly popular genre, the underlying assumption is that material technology and the progress of humanity inextricably are linked.

THE TRIUMPH OF TECHNOLOGY

Americans always have wanted to put knowledge to work, usually to improve their material lot. We have shown faith in the power of technology, or "know-how," to solve pressing social and economic problems. "Know-how" entered the language shortly before the Civil War and quickly became verbal shorthand for any and all aspects of American technology. "Technology," in its modern senses, did not gain currency until the 1840s and 1850s. From the early seventeenth century, when it first appeared in English, "technology" had referred to a discourse or treatise on an art or arts as well as to the scientific study of the practical or industrial arts. It did not refer to the *practical* application of knowledge and skill to the improvement of material circumstances: early nineteenth-century Englishmen and Americans spoke of "the useful arts" when they wanted to discuss applied science. By the 1830s "technology" had gradually begun to replace that phrase. Jacob Bigelow, a Harvard professor, helped to popularize "technology" as "the augmented means of public comfort and of individual luxury" in a series of lectures published in 1829 as *Elements of Technology*. By midcentury, the word customarily meant the practical arts—engineering, medicine, invention—collectively applied to the benefit of the human condition.[3]

Earlier in the century, however, whenever Americans thought about applied science and its potential for the improvement of the human race, one word leapt to mind—"machine." Eventually, as used by an increasing number of literate Americans, the words "machine" and "technology" became interchangeable, with both underpinning hopes for the progress of civilization. "Technology" became the term employed most often by literary utopians and reformers involved in city planning schemes when they discussed the perfecting of the physical environment of the city. If we look at theoretical interpretations of the social impact of technology, we may come close to understanding what technology meant to people in the nineteenth century and why many of them elevated the machine to the national pantheon.

The nineteenth century was the first in human history in which widespread application of new machinery fundamentally challenged and changed the age-old dependence upon intensive manual labor for the production of necessities and luxuries. The machine rearranged the conditions of labor and clarified the concept of labor. No longer did the "progress of civilization" (however defined) have to rest solely upon the shoulders of manual laborers. Nineteenth-century Americans were well aware of this fact and enthusiastic about it. As a euphoric writer in the prestigious *North American Review* put the matter in 1832: "What we claim for machinery is, that it is in modern times by far the most efficient physical cause of human improvement; that it does for civilization, what conquest and human labor formerly did, and accomplishes incalculably more than they accomplished."[4]

Note that the author wrote about machinery, *not* technology per se. Later in the same year and in the same magazine, the educator and jurist Timothy Walker presented a "Defense of Mechanical Philosophy" against attacks by critics of the dawning age of machinery. Admitting that applications of new types of machinery had taken some liberties with "Nature," Walker gave a point-by-point defense of "Mechanism," the spirit of the times and the faith of the machine age. He firmly opposed the argument that new uses of machinery were creating men mechanical in head and heart, as well as in hand. Mechanism, in its triumphant march, had emancipated the minds of men; "from a ministering servant to matter, mind has become the powerful lord of matter."[5]

Walker, like the bulk of his literate fellow countrymen over the rest of the century, believed in the "permanent and continued improvement of the human race: we consider no small portion of it," he wrote, "whether in relation to the body or the mind, as the result of mechanical invention." Acceptance of the philosophy of Mechanism was a necessary and vital step toward human perfection. Of contemporaries who shared his faith, Walker noted: "They see Atlantis, Utopia, and the Isles of the Blest, nearer than those who first described them. These imaginary abodes of pure and happy beings . . . we delight to contemplate; for we regard them as types and shadows of a higher and better condition of human nature, towards which we are surely though slowly tending." Human progress and perfectibility through the triumph of technology became the watchword of the nation.[6]

Yet those who linked machinery and technology were only partly correct. Human institutions—economic, political, social, and cultural—were as much a part of the warehouse of technology as were the tools used in the production of material goods.[7]

The introduction of machine technologies transformed the work place, the work process, and the production of goods. But it also altered the ways in which people thought about themselves and their society—a change that a twentieth-century philosopher summed up in the label "technique." "Technique," observed Jacques Ellul, "certainly began with the machine," but quickly outgrew it. Technique consisted of new attitudes and angles of perception toward all facets of human experience that colored Americans' understanding of individual and collective human behavior. Shifts in the levels of technology led inexorably to the necessity of grafting a new set of cultural attitudes and expectations onto the existent social body. Technique, Ellul affirmed, "clarifies, arranges, and rationalizes; it does in the domain of the abstract what the machine did in the domain of labor. It is efficient and brings efficiency to everything." Ultimately it compelled nineteenth-century people to question the bases of their society—"its social and political structures, its art and its way of life, its commercial system." In short, it moved Americans toward social planning.[8]

Ellul's insights help explain why the antebellum orator Edward Everett attributed to the new machinery "the difference between the savage of the woods and civilized, moral, and religious man," and even the "moral and social improvement of our race." Nineteenth-century Americans committed themselves to searching for ever better technologies to improve their moral and material conditions. Without always recognizing the path they were treading, they imbued "know-how" with an almost mystical or spiritual value. Their acceptance of "technique" forged a conceptual framework that ultimately led to a confusion of means and ends.[9]

For technology, rather than being a means to an end, took on a life of its own. Henceforth, many Americans would find it impossible to imagine a better tomorrow for themselves, their children, or their children's children, outside the context of technological progress. When we refer to "the technological revolution" of the nineteenth century, therefore, we should think of far more than an acceleration of mechanical inventions or the establishment of new industrial processes. That revolution resulted in a change of world view in which the reactions, expectations, and beliefs of many Americans shifted accordingly. Change did not occur overnight; it jostled along like a wagon on a backcountry road. Still, by century's end, the triumph of technology—both in the building of a machine order and in the reordering of social perceptions—was complete.[10]

Over the nineteenth century, the United States succeeded Great Britain as the nation of inventors. The list of practical applications of new techniques and technologies in transportation, communication, industrial machinery, and household appliances lengthened with each passing decade. At the outset of the century, Thomas Jefferson had claimed confidently that mechanical inventions in the United States would develop "small scale" manufactures instead of "company establishments . . . in the towns." America, he predicted, would not emulate England and other European countries in becoming a nation of crowded cities. Events proved him wrong. Industrial inventiveness and urbanization seemed inextricably linked. From New England factory towns like Lowell in the 1820s to new industrial cities like Birmingham, Alabama, in the 1880s, the course of industrial and technological development tended cityward.[11]

Those Americans who came to fear the social impact of technology came to fear the city as well. Beginning in the late 1820s, a debate arose between critics and supporters of the new technologies and the increasing concentration of manufacturing activities in urban centers. Until the 1830s, proponents of technology employed bucolic imagery when championing the factory system. Pointing to

Lowell and other small New England textile towns, they depicted
manufacturing works set within woodland groves and handsome rural villages. Still, of Lowell in 1835, an anonymous writer could
observe that "the spirit of enterprise and improvement came, and its
touch, like that of the magic wand, had turned this seeming wilderness, not simply into a fruitful field, but into a busy, enterprising
and prosperous city."[12]

First subtly, then more stridently from the 1840s on, the social
vocabulary began to change. Critics who warned that technological
innovations were mechanizing man himself, turning workers into
mere appendages of machinery, increasingly equated city dwelling
with human degradation. A prewar generation of American fiction
writers (*not* including the urbtopians) lamented the intrusion of the
machine into the garden of pastoral America. They forecast a day
when the innocence and simplicity of rural and small-town life
would fall before the onslaught of urban industrial growth. By the
post–Civil War years the image of the city as the center of the im-
poverished human spirit had become conventional in much American fiction, poetry, and drama.[13] Many intellectual and social
leaders were beginning to dread the machine, technology, industrial
development, and the city itself as a threat to social unity and order.

Other contemporaries of the urbtopians attempted to escape the
city. Reacting against what they perceived as growing societal disorder, the communitarians ideologically, in Ellul's sense, rejected a
technique centered upon one set of technologies in favor of another.
Many of their attempts to build new kinds of communities resulted
in small-scale utopian city planning. An investigation of communal
ventures in the United States will in fact shed light on the ideas of
the urbtopian authors.

BUILDING UTOPIAN COMMUNITIES

To many nineteenth-century Americans utopia was not an impossible dream but a potential reality. Both native and foreign observers
recognized that the new nation itself was a utopian experiment
whose goal was to free humanity from the shackles of tradition by
fostering individualism within the context of a stable social order.
Gustave de Beaumont, companion of the better-known Alexis de
Tocqueville in his travels through the United States in the 1830s,

stated that "the new society in which we are . . . has no prototype anywhere." In the 1880s, the perceptive English scholar James Bryce observed that from the Revolution to his own day, "individualism, the love of enterprise, and the pride in personal freedom, have been deemed by Americans not only their choicest, but their peculiar and exclusive possessions." Alone among the nations of the world, the United States appeared to be a continuing and successful experiment in the art of transmuting hopes about human perfectibility into practical reality.[14]

Although republican government and a dynamic economy seemed to promise eventual fulfillment of the utopian vision of a free society, some Americans sought to speed up the process. Emboldened by European socialist and communist ideologies, as well as by their own revolutionary heritage, over 100,000 citizens took part in establishing communitarian settlements, small-scale "patent-office models" of utopia within the larger framework of the national utopian experiment.[15]

Between 1820 and 1920, more than 250 utopian communities sprang up around the United States. Most were short-lived. For those founded prior to 1860, for example, the average lifespan was under four years. Their importance to our story, however, lies not in their durability but in their creation.[16]

The communities ranged from religious to secular experiments, from holy commonwealths to communistic settlements. Several generations of historians have examined the subtleties and superficialities of such well-known places as Brook Farm, Oneida, and New Harmony, and such lesser-known settlements as Modern Times, Harmonia, and Celesta. The details of their wildly divergent programs need not detain us; the point is that nineteenth-century Americans fairly often had recourse to communal experiments in their eagerness to move the nation along the pathway to utopia. By 1840 Ralph Waldo Emerson could write to Thomas Carlyle that "we are all a little wild here with numberless projects of social reform. Not a reading man but has a draft of a new community in his waistcoat pocket."[17]

Most of these model communities promised a restructuring of both city and countryside in response to industrialization and urbanization. "By adopting the encompassing symbols of the model community as garden and as machine," historian Dolores Hayden commented, "the communitarians hoped to synthesize many aspects of pastoral and technological idealism which characterized American attitudes toward land and life." By locating their settlements in a middle landscape between the unfamiliar frontier and established cities, the social architects revealed their distaste for the conditions of life in the industrializing cities. Whether religious or secular in motivation, the communitarians usually tried to integrate industry with agriculture in a new kind of community endeavor. A prevalent trend, nonetheless, was to design a social and physical settlement that looked, for all the world, like an urban neighborhood more perfect than that known to contemporaries.[18]

Albert Brisbane, an American communitarian of the 1840s, expressed this goal of romantic utopianism: "Now if we can, with a knowledge of true architectural principles, build one house rightly, conveniently and elegantly, we can, by taking it for a model and building others like it, make a perfect and beautiful city: in the same manner, if we can, with a knowledge of true social principles, organize one township rightly, we can, by organizing others like it, and by spreading and rendering them universal, establish a true Social and Political Order." Plans for many of the settlements demonstrated the city planning in miniature that Brisbane envisioned. In the 1870s Charles Nordhoff's survey, *Communistic Societies of the United States*, observed of communities from Ohio to Oregon that far from being isolated homesteads, they looked "more like a small section cut out of a city."[19]

Given the prevalence of such experiments, it seems reasonable to assume that urbtopian dreamers who paraded their visions through fiction drew inspiration from the real world. The authors did not write in a vacuum. Although few stories or novels referred by name to the communitarians, many of the schemes of associationism advanced by Robert Owen or Charles Fourier found their way into the fictions of minor novelists and their more illustrious and popular counterparts.

Consider two early examples of the genre: Edward Kent's "A Vision of Bangor in the Twentieth Century" and Jane Sophia Appleton's "Sequel to the Vision of Bangor in the Twentieth Century." Published in 1848, the two tales shared a view of Bangor, Maine, as a great metropolis of the future, resplendent with magnificent buildings and rapid transit and the center of an industrial empire of cottons and woolens that stretched around the world to India and

China. One feature of urban life a century hence that drew the attention of both writers was the eating house in which all citizens took sustenance, communal buildings of the type proposed by Owen and Fourier. More important, the precepts of communalism pervaded the social order. In a direct reference rare in the genre, Appleton attributed the equal social status of women in twentieth-century Bangor "to the genius of Charles Fourier, who, by his profound insight into the evils of society, induced such changes as gave due compensation to all industry, whether in man, woman, or child. . . . True, there are no 'Associations' properly, . . . but much that that great man taught has been heeded, and men now bless his labor, and respect his name." Of less significance, although interesting as an illustration of the early devotion to technology in the genre, was Appleton's solution to the contemporary problem of filthy, unpaved urban streets: "a capital system of laying the dust by artificial showers."[20]

Yet urbtopian fiction drew on another source as well: the work of individuals even more directly involved in city platting, planning, and building. In contrast to the communalist strategy of small-scale construction, other community-minded citizens planned on a grand scale for the improvement of existing cities and the creation of new ones. The century of urbanization was, equally, the century of city plans.

PLANNING AN URBAN NATION

Skirmishes among competing town and city builders marked the conquest of the frontier by the city. Initial settlement of the Ohio valley between the 1790s and the 1830s was followed by the development of the midwestern plains between the 1830s and the 1850s, and the occupation of the Trans-Mississippi and Far West regions after the Civil War. Daniel Drake, a Cincinnati physician and an early champion of western urbanization, dared in 1815 "to speak of cities on these western waters" and to predict that villages on the banks of the Ohio would "attain the rank of populous and magnificent cities." In the 1850s the Toledo newspaperman Jesup W. Scott prophesied that "in our central plain . . . will come together the greatest aggregation of men in cities—outrivalling in splendour as in magnitude, all which past ages have produced." Within two decades similar boasts came from promoters of Denver, Seattle, and San Francisco, and other cities of the Far West.

Boosters like Drake and Scott were, to be sure, hardly disinterested prophets; they wanted to attract people and business to their particular cities and regions.[21]

Still, that such men hoped to people the continent with city dwellers highlights at least two aspects of the thoughts of those touting westward expansion. First, promoters sensed that the strongest magnet for population was the promise of a lively urban environment. Second, they knew from practical experience that urban land speculation could be enormously profitable. Local boosters, absentee real-estate speculators, railroad executives, and territorial and state politicians joined in schemes to promote new communities.

City builders and speculators alike recognized that they could not lure prospective land purchasers and migrants without some evidence that the promised settlement had been established or at least carefully planned. Easterners thinking of moving to the "Town of America" (later Cairo, Illinois) in the late 1830s, for instance, could examine a detailed plan of its present condition and future prospects (see Figure 1). In most cases of community boosterism, therefore, some sort of city design preceded land sales and construction. These ranged from the superlatively dull gridiron of James Thompson's Chicago plan (1830) and the equally uninspired Sacramento plan of 1849 to the radioconcentric design of Circleville, Ohio, in the 1830s and the even more unusual pattern of Octagon City, Kansas, during the 1850s (see Figure 2).[22]

A number of these designed communities came into existence, although rarely on the scale pictured by their promoters. Hundreds more, although the original plans are extant, remained will-of-the-wisps, leaving land purchasers with worthless investments and townsite speculators with satisfying profits. One disillusioned soul named the 1830s "the era of imaginary villages. . . . Each of these places were to be *cities*, and had some remarkable advantages that were possessed by none other. . . . A survey, and the making of a map, and the work was done to your hands. Buildings, streets, and inhabitants, were absolute superfluities."[23] From this decade on however, a town-designing and city-making mania gripped the imaginations of many nineteenth-century Americans. Both the abundance of plans and a growing awareness that planning was possible fueled the desire of an increasing number to live in congenial urban surroundings.

Such individuals stormed against their fellow citizens who seemingly denied or disregarded the need for planning. As early as 1830, for example, an anonymous writer in the *American Journal of Science and Arts* mourned that "we have yet to choose the sites of what are to be large towns and cities, in a generation or two: we have yet to plan them, with full choice as to convenience or beauty in these things." Four decades later, a similar plaint came from the landscape architect Robert Morris Copeland, who advanced a plan for renewing Boston: "We have supposed that, for some unnamed reason, planning for a city's growth and progress could only be done as it grows; . . . this is a fallacious belief."[24]

Nonetheless, the multitude of town planning ventures, especially in the West, familiarized nineteenth-century Americans with the practice of planning. Whether the town plats they saw were promotional devices or expressions of a social vision made little difference. Americans had shown themselves to be a literal-minded people prone to written expression of their most cherished beliefs and goals. The Pilgrims had their Mayflower Compact, and the Puritans their covenants with God; men of the Revolutionary generation had committed to paper the structure of governance in constitutions both state and national. Before spades ever broke soil to turn rough earth into usable streets, numerous communities marched forth from the imaginations of their designers like so many paper soldiers.

In a sense, all attempts at city designing and planning were, inevitably, utopian. Mankind could not plan for the past, only for the future. Projections of the future, near or distant, the quest for the better world of tomorrow, required rejection of the present. Even if rooted in present conditions, plans for tomorrow were always plans for *utopia*—that is, for *no place* as charted by contemporary atlases. Nineteenth-century townsite speculators, whatever the insipidity or pungency of their designs, were participants in the utopian venture of planning a new, urban nation.

In our investigation of urbtopian writings, then, we must remember that literate nineteenth-century Americans were accustomed to thinking about communities as planned enterprises. They were used to being bombarded with physical designs for promised urban developments. Fiction writers who prophesied the new world of tomorrow worked within and contributed to a culture becoming familiar with the concept and practice of planning communities. For their part the traditions of religious and socialist communalism and of new townsite design probably contributed to the popularity of urbtopian fiction. In both the real world of community construction and the idealized regions of the imagination, to at least some Americans "city" stood for human progress.

The dreamers of urbtopia and their fictional creations bear closer scrutiny in our effort to understand what the authors, and presumably much of the reading public, viewed as progress.

2

THE CITY THAT NEVER WAS

T HE CITY that never was established itself as the theme of a minor but popular literary form over the course of the nineteenth
century. Juxtaposing the squalor of contemporary cities with the
perfection of the city of the future, urbtopian fiction explored the
concerns of several generations of American writers. Historians of
American utopian fiction have concentrated on the period from the
mid-1880s to the First World War, when the genre appealed to a
broad and diverse audience. In the judgment of one literary historian, "for a decade the utopian novel was perhaps the most widely
read type of literature in America." Yet the genre was well established long before the publishing outburst of the last decade. Scholars disagree about the first publication in the United States of a
utopian romance, but stories about the perfected city appeared at
intervals before the Civil War, when controversy about the social
impact of technology and urbanization began to brew.[1]

Most writers adopted similar themes. They portrayed a future
society in which a marriage of country and city had produced a new
physical and moral environment. That environment was thoroughly
urban, economically noncompetitive, and filled with wondrous and
often fantastic material technologies. In contrast to the grimy, congested, tenement-ridden city of their own times, authors evoked a
city that was clean, spacious, and well supplied with model housing
for the masses.

Clearly such writers were responding to their cultural milieu.
But what about the writers themselves? We know more about those
who worked late in the century than about their predecessors. Still,
even an analysis concentrated on the later writers will deepen our
understanding of the emerging urban culture of the century and the

literary contributions to the evolving culture of city planning
thought and practice.

AUTHORING URBTOPIA

Literary giants like Mark Twain, William Dean Howells, and Edward Bellamy shared the urbtopian genre with literary midgets like
Mrs. Mary Griffith, Charles W. Caryl, and Cosimo Noto. Their
novels and stories were published by major houses like Houghton
Mifflin and popular magazines like *Atlantic Monthly*, by journals
like the *Lancaster County Magazine*, and by the authors themselves. Two firms specialized in the genre: the Arena Publishing
Company of Boston and Charles H. Kerr and Company of Chicago,
which brought out the "Library of Progress" series. Many of the late
nineteenth-century novels were paperbound and sold for a quarter.
The number of readers cannot be determined, but Edward Bellamy's *Looking Backward, 2000–1887* (1888) sold over 125,000 copies within its first two years, became an international bestseller
during the 1890s, and stimulated a host of detractors and admirers
to publish their own utopian responses.

On the other hand, it is doubtful that Warren Rehm's *The Practical City: A Future City Romance; or, A Study in Environment*
(1888), published under the ominous pen name of "Omen Nemo,"
attracted many readers. Still, the works tumbled forth. Between
1880 and 1900 alone, over 200 utopian titles appeared.[2]

Occasionally individuals who had achieved eminence in other
endeavors produced a single novel of note. Such was the case for
the inventor and carriage-builder Chauncey Thomas and for King
Champ Gillette, inventor and manufacturer of the safety razor.
More commonly, utopian stories came from the pens of professional
writers, whether well or little known. Although nineteenth-century
sources often lack biographical information, we can still sketch a
profile of such late-century writers as a group.[3]

Almost all were male, white, middle-aged, native-born Protes-
tants. Their responses to the social conditions of the nation were
not bound by regional experiences, because, for the most part, their
geographical distribution approximated that of the national population. Among authors who published between 1888 and 1900, some
80 percent had moved at some time from small towns or rural areas

to large urban centers; 83 percent were living in a large city at the time they wrote their fantasies. In a time period when less than 1 percent of the national population attended college, more than 72 percent of the utopian authors had done so. Their careers reflected their middle- and upper-middle-class backgrounds. A number engaged in such traditional professions as the clergy (13 percent), law (5 percent), medicine (4 percent), and education (4 percent), but heavier concentrations appear in the newer professions of business, engineering, and science (each 15 percent) and journalism (25 percent). Fourteen percent identified themselves as "political reformers."[4]

At a time when the ills of industrial cities troubled an increasing number of citizens, it is hardly surprising that the bulk of these authors, urbanites by choice or birth, focused their attentions on the urban environment. Only a handful were so hostile toward the contemporary city that they could not or would not envision a perfected urban setting, choosing instead to locate their communities of tomorrow in a rural or small-town environment. The minister and writer Edward Everett Hale, in *Sybaris* (1869), idealized the small New England community, devoid of big city troubles. In subsequent stories he elaborated his theme that the small town, or the properly conceived suburb, should be the way of the future. In William Dean Howells' *A Traveler from Altruria* (1894), most of the citizens chose to live in cooperative farm villages as their heaven on earth. "There are now no cities in Altruria, in your meaning," the hero stated, and "if it can be said that one occupation is honored above another with us, it is that which we all share, and that is the cultivation of the earth." *Solaris Farm* (1900), by Milan Edson, promised a world of small farms and small villages set in the Great Plains, a world in which each village was nearly self-sufficient. Such works, in rejecting the dream of urban perfectibility, underscore the importance of the city in the utopian thought of the era.[5]

The pre–Civil War utopian writers—whether they matched the late-century profile or not—responded no less than their successors to a perceived social crisis due to rapid urbanization by postulating a perfected city of the future. In doing so they established a set of cultural values that became conventions in the genre. Literary scholars, in explaining the publishing phenomenon of the century's last decade as an immediate response to the evils of industrial America, have overlooked or underrated the strength of the urbtopian fiction tradition. They have also done a disservice to earlier writers who saw the nation itself as an experiment in utopia and, more often than not, identified the city as the bell-jar of that experiment.

PLANNING THE CITY THAT NEVER WAS

Perhaps the earliest utopian romance printed in the United States and written by an American was *Equality—A Political Romance,* whose author, Dr. James Reynolds of Philadelphia, submitted the story to *The Temple of Reason* magazine in 1802. It appeared in book form in 1847 and again in 1863. *Equality* contained almost every feature found in the urbtopian fiction of the end of the century: universal education; the liberation of women through the abolition of marriage and family life; a restructured economic order without competitive capitalism; a central government that supplied all material goods on the basis of need; labor-saving technologies; and a political system devoid of elections, run by a kind of participatory democracy presided over by the eldest and wisest members of the community.

At first glance, readers might have considered Reynolds an opponent of cities. His protagonist is an explorer who has visited "the countries of Utopia, Brobdignag, Lilliput, &c," finally happening upon the island of Lithconia. He discovered that on Lithconia "there were formerly large towns, as in Europe; but the evils, natural and moral, which are the concomitant of great cities, made them think of abandoning them." After an earthquake and plague swept the island, destroying the large cities, Lithconians refused to return to their urban way of life.

More careful reading, however, suggests that Reynolds was not hostile toward the city per se; rather, like his contemporary Thomas Jefferson, he feared the congestion and social disorder prevalent in European cities. The perfected society envisioned by Reynolds is distinctly urban, but urban in harmony with nature. "There are no towns or markets in all the island of Lithconia—the whole is only one large city upon a grand scale," explains one of the locals. Houses stand regularly spaced along well-developed road systems. Interspersed among them are cultivated fields—truck-gardens in modern parlance—and factories with sophisticated machinery driven by water power. "The whole island may be compared to a city spread over a large garden."[6]

Here, then, is an early statement of a theme replayed time and again by urbtopian writers later in the century. The ideal environment is a city whose physical design is in harmony with nature—the "middle landscape" of later writers—a city in which design and technology join to create a perfect setting for the achievement of human equality. Within such a setting, citizens inevitably act toward one another in moral and enlightened ways.[7]

With minor alterations and additions, Reynolds' vision reappeared in "Three Hundred Years Hence," an 1836 novella by Mary Griffith, one of a handful of women utopian writers during the century. The owner of a farm in Charles Hope, New Jersey, and a member of the Massachusetts Horticultural Society, Griffith projected an agrarian democracy of the future. Strictly speaking, hers was not a comprehensive urban utopia; unlike many later writers, Griffith did not make her future world a single city or a system of cities. In it, however, cities like Philadelphia, Baltimore, and New York are as clean and comfortable as the smaller towns that dot the countryside. Travelers speed over beautifully smooth and level roads in "curious vehicles that moved by some internal machinery," through rural regions in which self-propelled machines cultivate the fields and accomplish all the tasks formerly requiring intensive human labor.

Technological innovations in building construction, paved streets, and water pipes that shoot little jets into the air to cool and cleanse the streets of "all impure smells and all decayed substances" have transformed large cities into sanitary paradises. Linked by a large bridge, New York and Brooklyn have become a single, massive city of commerce that trades with India, China, and the rest of the known world. Every American village, town, and city contains gardens and orchards in which dwellers learn "virtue" by working with nature. Government meets most of the citizens' needs, and although wealthy and poor classes still exist, no bitterness or competition divides them. Anticipating the economist Henry George's "single-tax" scheme, Griffith's state gains its revenue from "but one tax, and each man is made to pay according to the value of his property, or his business, or his labour." Finally, nearly all of the advancement toward human perfection depicted by Griffith— whether in education, religion, morals, politics, the economy, or inventiveness—are the work of women, whose climb to equality with men has liberated the entire society.[8]

In both *Equality* and "Three Hundred Years Hence," the authors treat the perfected urban environment as a given, a stage-
setting for their political, economic, and social views. Neither
writer extensively described the ideal city. This was not unusual.
Paucity of detail characterized most of the urbtopian fiction published in the United States prior to the 1870s. In *The Art of Real
Pleasure* (1864), for example, Calvin Blanchard repetitively labored
to persuade his readers of the virtues of free love. Those virtues
undergird the Universal Mutual Guarantee Company, which eventually builds a heaven on earth. Blanchard devoted little space to
the physical environment of his utopia, merely informing his readers that the world of tomorrow is one of townships centered by communities of apartment dwellers; there are no private residences
anywhere. Only the world capital is a "City of Palaces," a paradise
scantly discussed.[9]

From the 1870s on, however, following the pattern laid out by
Reynolds, the city attuned to the rhythms of nature became central
to urbtopian fiction.

THE CITY IN THE PARK

In the fictional city as conjured by most writers, tamed nature af-
fects citizens' sensibilities both aesthetically and morally. Roof gardens crown buildings, flowers and plants stand next to factory
machines, tropical gardens dot the urban landscape, and a variety of
trees beautify magnificent boulevards. One author, fancying a future
New Orleans, wrote of "those rows of chinaberry trees, alternated
with magnolias, which with their evergreen leaves, for miles give
those streets the appearance of drives through tropical forests." In
The Age of Progress (1856) by David A. Moore, the new world re-
sembles William Penn's original design for Philadelphia in the late
seventeenth century, a low-density "garden city." Moore's protagonist passes over the countryside in a mysteriously propelled air-car:
"It was one continuous, interminable city, as far as the eye could
stretch. Not compact was it, however; every building being surrounded by a small area of ground, with here and there also an
open space, of considerable extent, all covered with verdure."[10]

Every author devoted considerable attention to the open spaces
and public parks that were the hallmarks of the future metropolis.
One example will suffice. In *Utopia; or, The History of an Extinct
Planet* (1884), Alfred Cridge had his protagonist, aptly named "Psy-

cho," describe massive twin cities joined by a single bridge: "The two cities together are about as large as London, but do not contain so many inhabitants. . . . These cities together do not have half a million inhabitants, as no houses except public buildings are allowed to be over two stories in height. Here each building must have around it four times the space it occupies, besides the wide streets and avenues. In addition to this, one block in sixteen is devoted to public gardens, parks or assembling places for the people." With few exceptions, in density and the incorporation of nature the cities of the future resemble the planned suburbs familiar to twentieth-century Americans.[11]

The ubiquity of the "garden city" did not result from some historical coincidence, some casual confluence of the imagination. Nineteenth-century authors wove the prevailing attitudes and progressive ideas of their own generation into the fabric of their future societies. In designing their ideal cities, consciously or unconsciously they followed the lead of public opinion and the work of contemporary landscape architects, sanitarians, and municipal engineers (see Chapters 5–8).

C. W. Wooldridge, in *Perfecting the Earth: A Piece of Possible History* (1902), foresaw several types of cities serving different functions in his new world: the industrial city, the agricultural city, and the ideal combination of the two, "New Utopia." The last arose in this fashion: "Meanwhile the site laid out for the city of New Utopia had become a very beautiful as well as a very extensive park. . . . The site of the city of New Utopia had been treated as the canvas of a painter or the marble of a sculptor. Every suggestion tending to enhance the beauty of any part of the growing city, or to increase its convenience or the comfort or welfare of its inhabitants, was given consideration." In this case as in others, the novelist's futuristic projections were already part of planning campaigns in his own time, and well on their way to becoming realities in early twentieth-century America.[12]

THE TECHNOLOGICAL CITIES OF TOMORROW

While glorifying the powers of nature, the authors also paid homage to the powers of man. The Deity created nature; man created technology. The authors were certain that human ingenuity could harness technology to the wagon of progress.

A list of the engineering marvels that humanized the cities of tomorrow could run on for pages. Wonders included pneumatic tubes as communication and transportation devices (the first subway actually built in New York City, in 1868, was a 300-foot pneumatic tube in which a giant steam-driven fan gently blew and sucked a twenty-passenger car from one street to another); air-cars run by magnetism, electricity, or some mysterious propellant; subways and bullet-fast elevated trains; entire cities heated and air-conditioned; magnificent and permanently paved boulevards; pure water supplies; and extensive, integrated sewer systems. Some urbtopian novels not only alluded to such advances but described them (and the allegedly sound engineering principles on which they were based) in great detail. It is only a slight exaggeration to argue that in the absence of plans prepared during the late nineteenth and early twentieth centuries, we could still reconstruct the culture of city planning from a few novels. In some instances we could overlay the fictional plans with actual ones and find few discrepancies. In other cases the novelists went beyond contemporary planning practices to present ideas that foreshadowed the schemes of later planners.[13]

Between 1872 and 1878, Chauncey Thomas, an unlikely author, whiled away his leisure hours composing an urbtopian novel. The aspiring writer was one of the leading carriagemakers in New England, operating a small factory in Boston that produced custom-made carriages. Although prominent in his trade, the middle-aged man was more interested in science and technology than in making money. Almost alone among utopian novelists of the time, he was not an idealist in any sense of the word. His novel, *The Crystal Button; or, Adventures of Paul Prognosis in the Forty-Ninth Century*, reads more like a compendium of information from the pages of contemporary engineering periodicals than like a philosophical treatise on government, such as Bellamy's *Looking Backward*.[14]

Late nineteenth-century reviewers often compared the two books because both described a Boston ("Tone" in Thomas' work) of the distant future, and because Thomas' novel did not reach the public until 1890, two years after Bellamy's smash hit. Reviewers charged that the carriagemaker had tried to capitalize on the journalist's success. Thomas had in fact completed his novel in 1878, shown it to his friend George Houghton, the publisher, in 1880, and then put the manuscript aside. Bellamy's success demonstrated to both Houghton and Thomas that the public might be interested in the book after all.[15]

In *The Crystal Button* Chauncey Thomas forecast a world almost completely urbanized and hierarchically arranged from the suburb-like country village to the "cosmopolis." "Riverbanks that the beaver once overflowed by his engineering feats are now populous with towns," explains Professor Prosper, guide to the transplanted nineteenth-century engineer Paul Prognosis. "Every town of old has become a city; every city a metropolis; every metropolis a cosmopolis,—of which Tone is a fair example,—with its every human dwelling and workshop a little city in itself, towering to the sky."[16]

A comprehensive transportation network of railways, monorails, "road-vehicles," air-ships, and electrically propelled aluminum ships that turn the seas into highways traversed the world, linking the system of cities. Chemical horticulture has supplanted agriculture, while a rational method of food distribution girding the globe has eliminated any possibility of hunger. Disease no longer ravages humanity because a Department of Health has "absolute control of everything pertaining to the sanitary condition of the people, such as the purification of rivers, water supply, disposition of refuse and its useful employment, and the location and character of all places of habitation." A Department of Meteorology, through the imaginative use of electrical discharges, monitors the climate and controls rainfall. A Department of Education brings the blessings of universal education to all citizens. A "Government of Settled Forms" meets all the material needs of citizens from cradle to grave. The world has reached its state of urban perfection, says Professor Prosper, because "science, which merely means *knowing*, has now taken the place of experimenting, which means *trying to know*, and consequently implies ignorance." The "science" of engineering has reshaped the physical form of the metropolis.[17]

In a manner that would have seemed familiar to both Pierre L'Enfant (eighteenth-century designer of Washington, D.C.) and Daniel Burnham (author of the 1909 *Plan of Chicago*), the city of Tone and its suburbs extend outward from a huge central square intersected by eight radial avenues. Each avenue is two-storied, with subways running along a median strip of the lower story. Lining the surface story, reserved for pedestrians and pleasure vehicles, are monumental pyramid-shaped buildings with strips of gardens along successive terraces that, in summertime, turn each structure into "a green and blossoming hill." Constructed of glass and decorated with gilded and silvered ornaments, the gigantic buildings afford the play of air and sunshine over their surfaces and the streets as well.

Class distinctions create varied housing patterns in Tone. The pyramid apartment buildings house primarily the artisan classes of the city and average 4,000 families (or 22,000 individuals) in clean, sanitary, and attractive four-room dwellings. The structures also contain markets, shops, and dining rooms. "In brief, Mr. Prognosis, everything that heart can wish is obtainable by the dwellers of this Pyramid without ever visiting the outside world. It is simply a fully organized city, piled on end instead of being stretched out lengthwise." Describing these cities within the city, Thomas' protagonist vividly contrasts them with the disgusting working-class tenements of the author's own time. (One infers, although Thomas did not state explicitly, that Tone's professional classes dwell in low-density individual homes on the suburban fringes. His utopian city exemplifies the residential land-use patterns that would characterize twentieth-century American cities, but without the spirit of class division and competition so evident in suburban-urban relationships today.)[18]

The Crystal Button was remarkable both in its resolution of the problems facing the large industrial cities of the 1870s and in its anticipation of the land-use practices and planning thought of the twentieth century. In his urbtopian design, Thomas responded to the concern of contemporary sanitarians about sunless alleys and streets, especially in the tenement districts. He offered a solution to the problem of providing adequate housing in the face of rising central-city land values by greatly increasing the density of the metropolis. He incorporated every contemporary engineering scheme for improvements in street layout, transportation systems, water and sewerage networks, public parks, and land-use controls. In the terraced pyramid structures he anticipated the set-back architecture required under the nation's first successful zoning legislation, passed in New York City in 1916. In surrounding Tone's densely occupied, central-city high-rises with lower-density individual homes, he foreshadowed the twentieth-century planning goals advanced in such disparate visions as Le Corbusier's "Radiant City" plan and Paolo Soleri's self-contained towers.[19]

Features of urban design resembling those in Thomas' book cropped up in several other novels, notably *The Milltillionaire* by M. Auburré–Hovorrè and *The Garden of Eden, U.S.A.: A Very Possible Story* by William Henry Bishop, both published in 1895. The housing patterns depicted were strikingly similar, even though the two writers stood at opposite poles on the optimal size of the city of tomorrow.

Hovorrè predicted that the world's future population would reside in twenty cities, circular in form with an approximate circumference of seven hundred miles, each containing a minimum of one hundred trillion inhabitants. All commercial and industrial establishments would occupy the suburbs of each city, while, in the interior environs, citizens would live in luxurious caravansaries, or "Bardic Hotels" towering several thousand feet into the air and containing at least one million inhabitants apiece. "Under such a bardic regime," noted the author, "all cities become gradually transformed into immense palaces nicely intermingled with fragrant gardens and luxuriant parks—there being no dirty streets or unsightly habitations of any description."[20]

Bishop's variant of the garden city was on a much smaller scale. Harking back to the "patent-office model" experiments of earlier communitarians, Bishop proposed creating a small garden city in a North Carolina valley as an example to mankind of the way to build the new urban world of tomorrow. Intended to contain no more than 10,000 citizens, the city was to be technologically perfect and self-sufficient. Movable sidewalks and lines of electric cars connected separate districts of the city devoted to agriculture, factory production, and residential neighborhoods. The populace lived in "Domicile Blocks," buildings ten to twelve stories in height, constructed in a quadrangle shape a thousand feet wide at each end and nearly half a mile in length. Each division of a "Domicile Block" opened onto an inner garden court. The tops of the buildings, reached by high-speed elevators, supported endless series of gardens connected by covered corridors that joined all the buildings in the Block. In an appendix titled "Why Not an Eden?" the publishers claimed that Bishop's vision was not of some world in the clouds, but rather of a modern city, built according to progressive principles well understood by sanitarians and engineers.[21]

Thomas' carefully planned city, like those of Hovorrè and Bishop, emerged from the pages of his novel in verbal form. Although painstakingly described, the physical appearance and design of the city finally had to take form in the mind's-eye of the reader. Several urbtopian authors, however, relied not only on verbal detail but on graphic presentations as well. In keeping with the century's custom of using carefully prepared plats to "sell" a city, some novelists were so bold as to offer in their books physical plans for the new metropolis.

THE METROPOLIS OF THE NEW ERA

In *The Human Drift* (1894), the inventor and safety-razor magnate King Champ Gillette speculated about the new metropolis that would surely reorganize the social, political, and economic systems of twentieth-century America. Inspired by the might and beauty of the White City at the World's Columbian Exposition in Chicago in 1893, as were several other fiction writers, Gillette foresaw the world of tomorrow as a megalopolis. *"Under a perfect economical system of production and distribution, and a system combining the greatest elements of progress, there can be only one city on a continent, and possibly only one in the world."* The great city would be the heart of a vast machine spreading its steel arteries over hundreds of miles, linking the mammoth central core to regions of agricultural labor and pleasure resorts. "Metropolis" (as Gillette named his city) would be divided into industrial and residential land-use districts, with the huge central city housing the masses in an environment of "artistic beauty, grandeur, and magnificence" to which "the whole world would contribute its wealth and treasures."

Like Thomas and others before him, Gillette solved the housing problem by concentrating the population in grand apartment houses or hotels (see Figure 3). Built in circular form, these buildings were to stand "twelve hundred feet [apart] from centre to centre"; the buildings themselves, "about six hundred feet in diameter," would be distributed "on a determined plan that would give an average equal population to the square mile throughout the city." Structures soared skyward among avenues, walks, and gardens, so that the city was "a beautiful park throughout its whole extent" (see Figure 4). Metropolis would contain about sixty million people, although Gillette argued that with its regularity of planning, it would make no difference if the city housed a million or one hundred million citizens. In essence, Gillette advocated a cellular city resembling the organically planned environment called for by twentieth-century planners like Victor Gruen (compare Figures 5–6).[22]

Stressing the necessity of comprehensive city planning, the inventor insisted on perfect sewerage, water distribution, cooling and heating, "electric telephonic communication," and transportation systems. As for the fear that city planning would lead to monotony—as expressed, for instance, in Anna Bowman Dodd's earlier novel *The Republic of the Future* (1887)—Gillette was adamant. "It does not follow that if a city were laid out regularly, it would necessarily become monotonous from sameness. Although the buildings and population would be equally distributed, and each building designed to accommodate about the same number," he claimed, "here all similarity would end. . . . Each and every building of 'Metropolis' would be a complete and distinct work of art in itself." To drive home his point, Gillette urged his readers: "Imagine for a moment these thirty odd thousand buildings of 'Metropolis,' each standing alone, a majestic work of art,—a city which, with our present population, would be from sixty to seventy-five miles in length, and twenty to thirty in width,—a never-ending city of beauty and cleanliness, and then compare it with our cities of filth, crime, and misery, with their ill-paved and dirty thoroughfares, crowded with the struggling masses of humanity and the system of necessary traffic. And then compare the machinery of both systems, and take your choice; for I believe the only obstacle that lies in the way of the building of this great city is man."

If humanity only possessed the will, Gillette was certain that the city of tomorrow could arise within twenty-five years. Sharing in what had become the grand American conceit, Gillette equated a technologically and physically perfected urban environment with the advancement of human progress. The industrial baron knew that the ideally planned city of the near future would transform the mean, competitive spirit of his age into one of universal cooperation among peoples, creating "a new and perfect civilization and an environment made beautiful by United Intelligence and Material Equality."[23]

Two equally grandiose schemes also merit our attention. *New Era* by Charles W. Caryl (1897) and *Perfecting the Earth: A Piece of Possible History* by C. W. Wooldridge (1902) had in common militaristic sentiments, the means of constructing model cities, proposed layouts, and the social, economic, and political organization of their new urban societies. Both writers attested their familiarity with the works of Edward Bellamy, but neither openly attempted to expound and extend Bellamy's views. Both, however, conceived of their new order of human affairs as arising from the intelligent use of an "industrial army," much as Bellamy had done in *Looking Backward* (1887) and *Equality* (1897).

Caryl's was the most intriguingly precise urbtopian novel of the century. Identifying himself as a practical and successful businessman, the president of a Colorado mining company, Caryl nonetheless seemed to possess the soul of an architect or engineer. In the layout of his model city (see Figure 7), with concentric circles zoned for various uses surrounding a central civic area, the author gave precise widths of streets and avenues, heights and dimensions of buildings, and lot sizes, as well as exact costs of construction. Although he shared with other late nineteenth-century novelists a general notion of designated land-use patterns, Caryl was far more rigorous than most in his descriptions of urban zoning.

Each "New Era Model City" consists of 239 circles or zones serving particular functions. The inner zones, from 1 to 33, contain administration buildings, parks, commercial and light manufacturing structures, educational centers, amusement palaces, and "the finest and most complete hotels and office buildings in the world." Circles 34 to 221 hold residences ranging from expensive individual mansions to inexpensive apartment buildings of varying sizes and population density, with each circle in turn surrounded by small-scale business districts containing schools, churches, clubhouses, and shopping emporiums. Circles 222 and 223 are given over to heavy industry. Circle 224 provides a warehouse and railroad district. Circles 225 to 235 house "those who perform crude, coarse and common kinds of work, or are only learning, or have been taken on probation or trial." Finally, circles 236 to 239 hold the houses and fields of gardeners and farmers. Advanced technologies of transportation and sanitary engineering link and service all the zones, making the model city "the complete centre of everything magnificent, delightful, useful and desireable that will contribute to making the lives of those who may be so fortunate as to secure a home within its limits the most perfect, prosperous and happy that will be possible here on earth." These fortunate citizens would number between one and five million.[24]

In a reversal of late nineteenth-century land-use tendencies, Caryl made his inner residential zones the homeplace of society's elite classes. The circles that radiate outward from the core segregate other social classes by occupation (see Figure 8). The social structure has the character of a mighty, well-disciplined army. Presiding over the society are the officers of the "New Era Union," a cooperative organization in theory but in practice a paternalistic hierarchy. "Generals," the most elite group, have the technocratic abilities to serve as presidents, executive officers, and directors of the city's administrative departments. Next in the meritocracy come "majors" (general managers of departments), followed by "captains" (professionals), "lieutenants"(industrial foremen, musicians, and artists), "sergeants" (skilled mechanics, accountants, and successful salesmen), "privates" (the semiskilled), and, finally, "recruits." The last rank includes unskilled laborers in industry and agriculture, domestic servants, and all those who want to take up residence in the model city but first must prove their worthiness.[25]

Caryl's new social order must have appealed mightily to many of the successful entrepreneurial and industrial capitalists of his own generation. Beset by labor strife and union organization, besieged by social reformers who condemned the human costs of industrialization, and bewildered by economic fluctuations, many late-century businessmen yearned for a stable social order led by men like themselves. For such men the military metaphor was seductive. What better way to conceive of society than as an army of disciplined men and women united in a crusade for progress?

Whether Caryl knew it or not, the physical features of his plan and the ways in which they controlled and directed the civic behavior of citizens mirrored the ambitions of some of his contemporaries. His civic center, parks, parkways and boulevards, zoned industrial districts, and surrounding belt of agriculture, all linked by rapid transit facilities, were almost identical to the notions of contemporary "City Beautiful" and "garden city" planners. Allowing for slight variations in scale and design, we could overlay Caryl's plan with a typical "City Beautiful" plan of the period or with sections of Burnham's *Plan of Chicago* and discover numerous similarities (see Figure 9). Even more striking was the likeness between Caryl's "New Era Model City" and the "garden cities of tomorrow" plans published by Ebenezer Howard, an Englishman, in 1898, the year after Caryl's novel appeared (compare Figure 7 with Figure 10). Once again, the fancies of an urbtopian novelist and the supposedly more practical ideas of professional planners shared a common vision.[26]

Finally, we must consider the contribution of C. W. Wooldridge, a physician who offered his own unique notions in *Perfecting the Earth*. Alone among the urbtopian novelists of the period, Wooldridge projected an urban world that contained not one, but three, types of cities, each fulfilling a different function. Nearly alone among his fellows, he established his urban society not in the distant future, but little more than a decade hence.

In 1913, in the aftermath of a great world war, the United States finds itself faced with the critical problem of what to do with a standing army of over half a million men and a growing army of unemployed civilians. The military commander-in-chief, General Theodore Goodwill, a man of imagination and foresight, proposes and receives congressional approval for a plan to make the army self-supporting, to make army life wholesome, to use the army "in constructive work for the public benefit," and to lead soldiers grad- ually into civilian citizenship. To accomplish these aims, the gen- eral puts the army to work constructing three new cities, each a model of its kind. He intends each to be a laboratory experiment whose success will spark imitation and lead the rest of the nation and the world to build their own perfect urban centers.[27]

The first city, named Fort Goodwill, is to be an industrial center with huge factory districts zoned apart from commercial and resi- dential sectors. The community is not expected to be self-sufficient, but for short-term purposes there are agricultural lands at its edges. At the center of the model residential district (Figure 11) is a square for public buildings. Radiating outward are four main thorough- fares. With adjustments for special conditions of topography, each district contains parks and playgrounds, with standardized, mass- produced houses set back from parkways that thread together the entire block unit. In turn, each unit is connected to others in the city by subways, by thoroughfares along which travel rubber-tired automobiles, and by bicycle paths, bicycles being the favored form of transit in the community. Like other urbtopias Fort Goodwill is a clean, hygienic city, serviced by an elaborate water and sewer sys- tem. In short, Wooldridge's neighborhood block units both hark back to the unit plan of eighteenth-century Savannah, Georgia, and foreshadow the "superblock" idea advanced by Clarence S. Stein, among other planners, a few years after the novel's publication (Fig- ures 12–13).[28]

The factories of Fort Goodwill produce the heavy machinery and parts necessary to construct the second and third model cities. Although erected on the same basic design as Fort Goodwill, Mount Ceres has arisen in a different geographic region, since it is to be an agricultural city. In contrast with the several millions of the industrial center, Mount Ceres will eventually house a maximum of

100,000 citizens. The third community, New Utopia, combining the best features of the industrial and agricultural cities, is to serve as the showcase of Wooldridge's new urban world.

The functionally geometric plans of Fort Goodwill and Mount Ceres give way, in New Utopia, to aesthetically curvilinear streets, among which stand grand public buildings, attractive apartment houses, and occasional small homes. As Wooldridge described it, "the city is a park, the buildings being worked in with prime reference to perserving its beauty as a park, while furnishing all possible conveniences to their inhabitants." For the most part, the people of New Utopia are citizens who have retired from active life, whose children have grown up and moved into homes of their own. In modern parlance, New Utopia is a retirement community constructed to meet the needs of the elderly, a fictional prototype of today's Sun City, Arizona.[29]

Wooldridge's vision was unique in projecting an urban world with a regional system of specialized cities. Smaller towns, connected to one another and to major cities, gradually spring up throughout the land. After some twenty years of urban construction, the military army disbands, the government dissolves, and the nation evolves into a perfected urban society: "During these years whatever remained of the ancient regime has passed away. The Cooperative Commonwealth is perfected." Every citizen receives whatever material goods and public services he or she desires. No habitation is "shabby or unsightly"; no person lives in poverty or the fear of poverty; "the whole land is like a landscape garden."[30]

Although we do not know how familiar Wooldridge was with the ideas of contemporary professional city planners, his arrangement bore a remarkable resemblance to current arguments for regional planning. Ebenezer Howard, as we have noted, had just suggested a similar system in his *Garden Cities of Tomorrow*. During the 1920s, more than two decades of debate about the virtues of regional planning would result in the formation of the Regional Planning Association of America, whose reports glowed with the enthusiasms so prominent in the physician's conception of *Perfecting the Earth*.[31]

■

The emerging urban culture of nineteenth-century America stimulated the writers of urbtopian fiction, who in turn helped construct the culture. These writers were active participants in the growing tradition of urban reform that became such a marked characteristic of nineteenth-century American society. Reacting to a multitude of problems accompanying the country's rapid urbanization and identifying varying causes for them, most authors agreed that the cure lay not in abandoning, but in perfecting, an urban way of life. Whether they called for small or large cities, garden cities or industrial communities, isolated cities or an urban network, the novelists concurred in prophesying an urban world for the near or distant future. Most equated technological progress with the progress of the human spirit. Most predicted that both forms of progress would arise from a physically perfected urban environment. Whatever their sources of inspiration, most American utopian writers dreamed of the city that never was.

Those dreams, of course, stood in stark contrast to the reality of the city that was. Whatever visions men and women might have of the morrow, they had to cope with the conditions of the day. Often, the pages of fiction dovetailed with the real-world plans and practices of landscape architects, sanitarians, and civil engineers. Yet the latter had to act within the boundaries of nineteenth- and early twentieth-century U.S. society—within the framework of American law.

The nation's legal system was a form of social organization. It was also part of a broad set of social technologies. The law served both as a cultural expression of the beliefs and aspirations of society's members and as an array of social and political tools designed to cut across and channel those beliefs and aspirations. Shifting cultural values and goals, however, required the forging of new tools. A principal part of nineteenth-century Americans' construction of a new urban culture was an effort to change the nation's legal system. Urban Americans refurbished old legal doctrines to create modern urban law. Interwoven with the emerging urban culture was a new legal culture both shaped by urbanization and shaping it in return. Schemes and dreams, plans and projects, whether modest or ambitious, could only proceed at a pace permitted by the legal system.

PART TWO

———

REGULATING THE CITY

Is it not lawful for me to do what I
will with mine own?

Matthew 20:14

3

THE LEGAL LANDSCAPE

URING THE nineteenth century, as Americans occupied a continent and expanded a nation, they also expanded the social reach of law. Nowhere was faith in law more evident, nor conflict over its social reach more frequent, than in the nation's growing cities. To reach the provinces of nineteenth-century city planning, civic improvers had to traverse the legal landscape of America. Law embodied the competing ideologies and social aspirations of generations of urban Americans. Modern definitions of private rights and public purposes literally arose from city streets.

Municipal power to dictate the uses of urban land is not absolute; nor has it ever been. From the earliest days of settlement in the New World to the present, most Americans have sanctified private property ownership and the right of the individual to exercise complete control over the uses of personal property. A cornerstone of the earliest national land-use plan—the Northwest Ordinance of 1787—and of the Fifth (1791) and Fourteenth (1868) Amendments to the federal Constitution was the guarantee that no agency of government could seize private property without just compensation, due process of law, and reasonable evidence that the general welfare of the community demanded such action. The state could chip away at this cornerstone when, and only when, it could prove that a vital public purpose underlay taking an individual's property.

The legitimacy of government taking of property posed perplexing questions in nineteenth-century law. Even demonstrable public purposes, such as construction of a public water-supply system, collided with the tradition of private property ownership. From city to city, state to state, and within the national constitutional arena, widely divergent interpretations of public necessity versus private rights filled the pages of statutory law books, judicial decisions, and legal treatises.

In pursuit of municipal control over private property rights, competing interpretations traveled two parallel highways. One road followed the doctrine of eminent domain, the other that of the police power. An important difference between the two was that unlike eminent domain, government application of the police power in order to "take" a person's property for public use did not require just compensation. Along the way, the paths of nuisance and negligence doctrine intercepted and eventually merged with the two main highways. In any case, sanitarians, landscape architects, engineers, and other groups of urban reformers found that all roads led to and through the temple of law.

Unfortunately, the tale is not tidy. We cannot trace a linear and logical expansion of the police power doctrine at the expense of eminent domain proceedings. Too many economic, political, and social interest groups jockeyed for advantages and clashed with one another throughout the century, and proponents of rapid economic expansion often carried the day over the protests of the defenders of private property rights. Still, the outcome was never certain. Municipal officials undertaking planning and public works projects allegedly in the "public interest" were blocked more than once by private citizens who had resorted to legal action.

PRIVATE PROPERTY, PUBLIC INTERESTS

The term "eminent domain"—the governmental power to "take" private property for public use—was an American coinage. It did not appear as such in the English common law that formed the foundation of jurisprudence in eighteenth- and early nineteenth-century America. Apparently the first American to use the phrase was the attorney general of South Carolina, in a 1796 case. Although the phrase was new, however, the concept was not.[1]

Eighteenth-century discussions of English law addressed the extent to which the state could interfere with the rights of private property. In John Locke's theory of property, ownership springs from two founts: man mixes his labor with the resources of Nature; and Civil Government recognizes and protects the results as rights. Through exercise of this responsibility, the state gains legitimacy as standing above the quibbles and quarrels of individuals, and becomes the arbiter of petty property disputes. The *Commentaries on the Laws of England* by Sir William Blackstone, the most widely read and influential source of American jurisprudence for nearly a century after its publication in 1765, took Locke one step further.

Blackstone argued that civil society not only recognizes and protects property but also creates it. All property ownership, blessed by both natural and societal law, therefore exists at the sufferance of the state. At the same time, Blackstone declared, nature's law dictates that "every man has, or ought to have, by the laws of society, a power over his own property." Property rights are inviolable. Even for the welfare of the whole community, civil law cannot sanction violation of an individual's property rights without payment. "Besides," Blackstone stated, "the public good is in nothing more essentially interested than in the protection of every individual's private rights, as modeled by the municipal law. . . . The legislature alone can, and indeed frequently does, interpose, and compel the individual to acquiesce. But how does it interpose and compel? Not by absolutely stripping the subject of his property in an arbitrary manner; but by giving him a full indemnification and equivalent for the injury thereby sustained. . . . All that the legislature does is to oblige the owner to alienate his possessions for a reasonable price." Here entered the idea of eminent domain, if not the phrase itself.[2]

The colonial assemblies and municipal legislatures of early America systematically regulated certain kinds of property use. Boston, New York, Philadelphia, Charleston, and other cities commonly passed ordinances that established a "fair market" price for various goods; dictated the kinds of materials to be used for construction; and controlled the locations of enterprises that might prove to be nuisances, such as slaughterhouses, tanneries, and gunpowder manufactories. Rarely, however, did either the assemblies or municipal legislatures authorize the taking of private property for public use. With land for development relatively abundant, there was little need.[3]

In an era of government that taxed little and performed few services in return, that restraint was understandable. When legislatures did approve takings, usually for laying out streets and roads or for construction of a dam or grist mill, they seldom compensated private individuals for property loss. Despite the stirring of new demands for governmental activities on behalf of the general welfare, questions about government's responsibility to pay property owners

for any infringements of their rights arose only where a complete
physical appropriation of land had occurred.[4] Such cases were rare.
New roads, for example, usually ran along the top of the land without deep cuts in the earth or elevation of the road surface.

When "public necessity" demanded it, therefore, the state could
generally "take" property without worrying about court-ordered
compensation. The justification rested upon the common law tradition that all property ownership was subject to the sovereign. A
Pennsylvania case in 1795 succinctly summarized that view: "The
despotic power as it is aptly called by some writers, of taking private
property when state necessity requires, exists in every government;
the existence of such power is necessary; government could not sub-
sist without it."[5]

Yet this judicial position collided with Blackstone's sanctification
of private property ownership. Disagreements between state legislatures and the courts over eminent domain "takings" and the right of
compensation began to surface. As cities grew in size, population,
and level of economic development over the first half of the nineteenth century, requirements of compensation became more bur-
densome. City fathers and private developers alike, eager to provide
"public" works, increasingly found their efforts balked by statutory
and judicial requirements of compensation for private property
taken in the public interest. Uncommon at the century's dawn,
such requirements became commonplace in most states between the
early 1800s and the 1830s. State legislatures applied the compensation principle most vigorously in cases where communities *physically* invaded private property in the name of the general welfare.[6]

"Property" had two dimensions, one tangible, one intangible.
Tangibly, it meant, for example, not only one's piece of land or
tools of trade but also the price at which one sold goods or the materials one used to build a house. It meant the street fronting an
individual's home or place of business, the stream that powered a
mill owner's apparatus, the road or highway that connected one
community of private property owners to another. The intangible
dimension was the package of legal rights and responsibilities that
accompanied tangible property. How to wrap or unwrap this package would prove to be a vexing question for nineteenth-century
Americans, especially for those anxious about the growing trend of
government "taking" private property for public use.

"Taking" was a chameleon word, its legal hues depending on the situation. At varying times it could mean physically injuring private property; destroying it; asserting legal although not physical control over its uses; denying an individual full possession of the property; depriving a person of sole use of the property; invading the property without entering upon it (for instance, by allowing smoke from a nearby manufactory to waft across the land); and even hindering in some small way an individual's access—for example, by installing a sewer system beneath the street fronting his or her property.

Whatever their meanings at any precise moment, "property" and "taking" were vessel words into which and from which legal logicians poured the precepts of eminent domain. Attempts to define "eminent domain" occupied much of the time and energy of state legislatures and courts during the first half of the nineteenth century. The phrase gained currency through the writings of Chancellor James Kent of New York during the 1820s and through usage by the famed Massachusetts jurist Lemuel Shaw in the decades that followed. The new technologies of turnpikes, canals, and railroads encouraged a number of suits challenging the right of the state to sanction the taking of property in any fashion by private developmental corporations, even when authorized to do so by a state government. In an 1834 decision denoting a newly constructed railroad a "public work," Shaw ruled that under the power of eminent domain, the state could, with fair compensation, allow appropriation of private property for public purposes. Five years later, the justice handed down a decision that clarified the doctrine, with far-reaching effects on the growth of Boston and, eventually, other cities as well.[7]

The facts were simple. In the 1820s the Commonwealth of Massachusetts had chartered the Boston Water-Power Company, granting it a vast section of low-lying land bordering the Back Bay. In return, the company was to supply water power through a mill dam project for factories yet to be built in the area. In the early 1830s the government authorized the Boston and Worcester Railroad to lay a line over part of those lands. Claiming that the state had invaded its exclusive franchise and substantially reduced the value of its land, the water company sued. Shaw admitted the loss of land value while also deciding that the state had not "taken" the franchise, since the land physically was not destroyed. Construction of a railroad was a "public use" of the land, the justice declared; "there can be no doubt, that land granted by the government, as well as any other land, may be taken by the legislature in the exercise of the right of eminent domain, on payment of an equivalent. Such an appropriation," Shaw held, "therefore is not a violation of the contract by which property, or rights in the nature of property, and which may be compensated for in damages, are granted by the government to individuals."

Partly in response to the decision, the Boston Water-Power Company shifted its attention from supplying water to speculating in real estate. Over the next decade local sanitarians succeeded in convincing the city that the marshy and flooded lands of the Back Bay posed a major threat to Bostonians' health. The power company began to sell its lands to developers and to the city; land-fill operations transformed the area. Eventually, the West End of Boston emerged as a newly planned and fashionable neighborhood for the city's elite. Although this result was unintended, an eminent domain action had resulted in at least a partial victory for the supporters of economic development and planned land usage in the public interest.[8]

As we might expect, changing applications of the eminent domain doctrine entangled a number of competing interests. The dilemma lay within definitions of "public interest" and "public purpose." At its core, the debate pitted against one another differing attitudes about the desirable pace of urban growth and the role of government in fostering or restraining development.

On one side of the issue stood defenders of vested interests who feared that the Jacksonian ideology of egalitarianism might render all private property subject to eminent domain takings by legislative whim. The accelerating pace at which states and municipalities were demanding internal improvements and public works presaged ever-increasing infringements upon private property rights. The leading constitutional lawyer Daniel Webster, who had argued the same point in the famous Charles River Bridge case (1828–1830), warned the Supreme Court in 1848 against too broad an interpretation of the "novel" doctrine of eminent domain. Webster predicted that if the legislature and its agents "are to be the sole judges of what is to be taken, and to what public use it is to be appropriated, the most leveling ultraisms . . . may be successfully advanced." The

Court ignored his argument. Its ruling in *West River Bridge Co.* v. *Dix* confirmed a sweeping application of eminent domain for all public purposes, a position firmly advanced by Lemuel Shaw nearly a decade earlier.[9]

On the other side of the eminent domain debate were lined up all those who wanted to extend the efforts of municipal corporations to bring some semblance of order to the chaos of uncontrolled urban growth. Opponents of the principle of compensation included many public officials, private entrepreneurs hoping to secure state authorization and subsidies for their schemes, and planning reformers. All were eager for inexpensive economic development. If a municipal corporation or a state-authorized private corporation had to pay damages for every change in the grade of a street, for every block of rail lines, or for every section of a water or wastewater system, vitally needed public improvements would go wanting. The costs of development—planned or unplanned—would simply be too high.

American law never fully and clearly resolved the eminent domain debate. In a society splintered by contending economic and political interests, no final resolution was possible. Yet two consistent trends appeared. First, between the 1830s and the 1850s an increasing number of state legislatures wedged eminent domain provisions into their constitutions. Most gave the state greater authority to "take" private property if it offered just compensation. Second, an increasing number of state judges widened the boundaries of the "public interest" and "public purposes" as expressed in public works construction. At the same time, they began to narrow the field of actions requiring compensation by government.[10]

Along the way, and often so imperceptibly that many justices seemingly failed to recognize the ramifications of their decisions, they redefined the nature and uses of property. Perhaps they unwittingly succumbed to what one historian, writing in an altogether different context, called "the brute dominance of . . . issues" that caused courts to redefine "both 'reasonable' and 'due process.' " In their own day, the "brute" forces at work were the pace of economic development and growing middle-class demands for public works construction to improve the physical quality of the urban environment. At any rate, consciously or not, judges restaked the legal fences of private and public property ownership. As they did so,

American courts altered the common law of nuisance and developed a new doctrine of "consequential damages." Both would have a significant impact on the legal structure of the emerging urban culture.[11]

THE CONSEQUENCES OF NUISANCE

At the beginning of the nineteenth century, the terrain of private and public nuisance law was an almost uniform plain. Distinctions existed, but only an occasional dune of legal interpretation clearly demarcated the one from the other within the confines of common law. Private nuisance law dealt with actions taken on one's own property that affected the use of another person's land, such as interference with drainage or production of offensive smells or smoke. A public nuisance—such as damming a river or obstructing a street—interfered with the rights of many people.

Both branches of the law stood as barriers against unwarranted invasion of private property rights. At the same time, both permitted governmental control over individuals' use of private and public property. With the passage of time and in response to changes in the urban landscape, an increasing number of American judges came to emphasize the latter aspect. Down through the Civil War years, courts gradually sorted out the limits of private and public nuisance doctrines. They broadened the public nuisance stream and lengthened the reach of state control over uses of real property. Eventually, that newly expanded stream would merge with others in the realm of the police power doctrine.[12]

At the heart of both private and public nuisance law lay the maxim *sic utere tuo, ut alienum non laedas*: loosely translated, "use your own property in such a way as not to injure that of another." In his *Commentaries* Blackstone had emphasized that if a person's use of his property caused *any* damage to the property of another, he was liable for compensation, even if he had used his property in a completely lawful manner. If a man suffered injury, he could sue for damages. Rarely did American courts follow the strict interpretation that *any* and *every* action that caused hurt, inconvenience, or damage to the property of another automatically constituted a nuisance. Rather, they treated as nuisances only those activities that fell under common law principles. This meant, in turn, that interpretations of nuisances were rarely consistent from state to state, or even within a given state.

Courts found it difficult if not impossible to precisely define the laws of nuisance because common law enforcement often varied from jurisdiction to jurisdiction. As the leading nineteenth-century commentator on nuisance law explained: "In the very nature of things, there can be no definite or fixed standard to control every case in every locality. The question is one of reasonableness or unreasonableness in the use of property, and this is largely dependent upon the locality and its surroundings." During the first half of the century, the evolution of a "reasonableness" doctrine in various local and state courts signaled significant shifts in the application of private and public nuisance law to land-use decisions.[13]

In the preindustrial city, application of both private and public nuisance doctrines was relatively straightforward. As urban commerce and manufacturing boomed, however, strict application of common law in this area became a hindrance to economic development. Eager to grant state legislatures and municipal corporations leeway in encouraging physical growth and economic expansion, judges looked for ways to reduce or eliminate excessive nuisance litigation. Courts invoked the public nuisance doctrine to allow local governments to do things that would have made private individuals liable under the common law of nuisance. So long as the resulting nuisance was common to the public at large rather than falling upon a specific individual, the government was protected from nuisance suits. The result was an assertion of state sovereignty over some of the rights of private property ownership.

During the first half of the nineteenth century, American courts rarely required municipal corporations to pay nuisance damages for actions authorized by a legislative statute. Judicial reluctance to interfere in such matters both underscored the sovereign power of state legislatures and underwrote the ability of city governments to engage in some public works construction.

The range of activities allowed was fairly broad. When New York City limited docking at private wharves or hindered access to them by improvements of waterway (1827), courts were unsympathetic to nuisance injury claims. When Boston officials ordered the land-filling of a creek that had been polluted by drainage from a recently built municipal sewer line (1831), the court denied damages. When local governments closed down sections of a major street for repairs or for construction of rail lines (1850, 1851), nuisance suits brought by outraged property owners failed. So matters went. In earlier times private citizens would have successfully challenged such public action; now the courts simply turned a deaf ear.[14]

The law was adapting to the changing requirements of land use in a rapidly growing city. The state case of *Lexington & Ohio Rail Road* v. *Applegate* (1839) was typical. A number of local businessmen sued to prevent a railway from running its horse- and steam-cars at the excessive speed of six miles per hour down the main street of Louisville. They alleged loss of business profits, a lowering of house rents, annoyance, inconvenience, and hazard to the general public. The complainants were willing to have the court stop the traffic by declaring it either a private or a public nuisance.

The court proved unwilling to do either. The state legislature, it observed, had authorized the location and construction of the rail lines and the city's collaboration with the railroad company. The loss of profits and rental income might be merely a result of "the translation of . . . business, by the cars, to other portions of the city." That was "a common case in commercial cities; and will always occur . . . from . . . public improvements for facilitating travel and commerce." In a thriving city all property was "subject to any consequences that may result, whether advantageously or disadvantageously, from any public and authorized use of the streets." Although "in ages that are gone" such public works as transit lines might have been nuisances, that was no longer true. The court proclaimed that "the onward spirit of the age must, to a reasonable extent, have its way. The law is made for the times, and will be made or modified by them." Molding a new legal environment in response to the "brute" force of economic development, many judges permitted and even encouraged municipal corporations to plan and carry out public or quasi-public works for the presumed general welfare.[15]

The same courts expanded the power of municipal corporations to apply public nuisance law to certain kinds of land use. When urban residents used their property in a manner that appeared to threaten the comfort, safety, health, or morals of the general public, most courts upheld the city government's right to abate (put an end to) that use as a public nuisance. Several examples illustrate that growing trend.

Relying upon both current medical theories of disease causation and the obvious increase in population density, for instance, New York judges upheld the right of municipal corporations to declare privately owned cemeteries urban nuisances (1827). The court rejected the argument that the antiquity of land use as a cemetery prevented government interference. A once "remote and inoffensive" use of land, the court affirmed, "may become otherwise by the residence of many people in its vicinity; and . . . it must yield to by-laws, or other regular remedies for the suppression of nuisances." The following year a Massachusetts court allowed Boston officials to prevent a private company from hauling offal (food garbage) through city streets without a license. The court asserted that "minute regulations are required in a great city, which would be absurd in the country." On similar grounds of public health regulation, another court permitted a city government to summarily label certain privately owned, decaying buildings "nuisances" and tear them down to guard against the spread of disease (1836). Within a sometimes confusing covey of limitations, courts allowed city governments to fashion a crude set of land-use controls. [16]

As pre–Civil War courts refined and refurbished the doctrine of public nuisance law, hints of the judicial system's willingness to stretch nuisance law even beyond its newly flexible boundaries began to appear. Prior to the case of *Commonwealth* v. *Tewksbury* (1846), most courts applied public nuisance doctrine negatively as a cure for existing ills in cases in which a citizen's use of his or her property impaired "the public rights and interests of the community." But in the seemingly trivial *Tewksbury* case, involving a man fined for having removed gravel and sand from his own beach, Lemuel Shaw showed a readiness to promote public nuisance law as a preventive measure. Citing the *sic utere* doctrine as a basis for limitation of the absolute rights of private property ownership and usage, Shaw observed that changing conditions of the urban physical environment ultimately determined whether a particular use of property would be harmless or harmful. Government had a responsibility to ensure the comfort, health, and safety of the city's population. The law could not confine vital community interests to the mere restraint of a nuisance already committed. It was proper, Shaw stated, for the legislature "to interpose, and by positive enactment to prohibit a use of property which would be injurious to the public, under particular circumstances." [17]

The presence of either a nuisance or a *potential* nuisance justified state intervention. It demonstrated that an owner had failed in his social duty to use his property in a "reasonable" manner. Judicial determinations harmonized discordant uses of private and public property in booming cities. In effect, they made judges after-the-fact land-use planners. Shaw's decision established a precedent for the application of public nuisance law that encouraged municipal corporations in their efforts to regulate the actual and potential uses of property and to plan for a less chaotic urban environment.

Concurrent with new applications of older common law nuisance principles, a growing number of pre–Civil War jurists created a novel doctrine of American law called "consequential damages." The theory had emerged early in the nineteenth century to protect private citizens from liability when improving their own property. If, while erecting a building on his own land, and assuming due care, an individual caused indirect injuries to a structure on adjacent property, he did not have to compensate his neighbor. By the 1820s courts had raised the doctrine as an umbrella to shelter various governmental activities.[18] In 1823 the Massachusetts Supreme Court invoked it in a case that would become an often-cited precedent.

Callender v. *Marsh* hinged upon Boston's right to improve the quality of city streets without having to reimburse private property owners for any injuries caused in the process. The plaintiff charged that the city's regrading and reconstruction of the street fronting his house had endangered its foundation, thereby causing him great expense to "render it safe and convenient of access, as before." In essence the court responded, "That's unfortunate, but that's progress." It held that when public improvements were at stake, it would not require just compensation to "one who suffers an indirect or consequential damage or expense, by means of the right use of property already belonging to the public."[19]

Other state courts followed suit. In 1828 the New York Supreme Court revealed that in certain situations it would conceive of property as an intangible bundle of legal interests to be either protected or ignored. When a property owner incurred loss as a consequence of governmental action legitimately undertaken in the public interest, "it is *damnum absque injuria* [damage or loss without injury], and it is to be bourne as a part of the price to be paid for the advantages of the social condition. This is founded upon the principle that the general good is to prevail over partial individual convenience." There was no doubt about the appeal of this utilitarian philosophy to many Americans both within and without the legal fraternity. Certainly numerous judges ground their grist through this mill.[20]

By 1850 the New York Supreme Court could note blithely that it was "a very common case, that the property of individuals suffers an indirect injury from the constructing of public works." The following year Pennsylvania Chief Justice John B. Gibson, whose influence spread far beyond the boundaries of his jurisdiction, began to enforce the principle that to prevent excessive damage awards, it was necessary to remove constitutional support for certain kinds of compensation. Some citizens began to fear that no private property was sacred. In *O'Connor v. Pittsburgh* the justice affirmed the city's authority, for planning purposes, to change the grade level of a street, although by so doing it destroyed the value of a church. In light of the public purposes involved, Gibson stated, this injustice was unavoidable. Eminent domain simply could not pertain. Similar holdings soon surfaced in other states. A process decades in the unfolding seemed near completion.[21]

POLICING THE CITY

Nineteenth-century American law never clearly and formally established boundaries for the exercise of the old branch of law known as the police power. Between the 1820s and the Civil War, federal constitutional law gradually delegated authority for its use to state legislatures—but not to cities. Although an increasing number of judges appeared willing to stretch the limits, pre–Civil War state courts, as well as the Supreme Court, often fluctuated between extreme latitude and excessive restriction with respect to municipal corporations' use of the police power. City officials trod cautiously in the fields of land-use regulation and planning for future urban growth. Every attempt to invoke the police power was open to judicial scrutiny. What kinds of "reasonable" efforts to promote the health, safety, and comfort of the citizenry permitted a city government to control private property use, *without* compensation to the owner, for "public purposes"? Put another way, how far could a municipal corporation go in policing the city? The confusion about which city actions would require compensation to private property owners under eminent domain were compounded by shifting perceptions and use of the word "police."[22]

In common nineteenth-century parlance, to "police" the city meant to prevent actions that threatened public order, safety, health, or convenience, and to promote means of securing them. When an educator, for example, referred to public schools as the best "police" his city could have, he was touting an institution intended to promote order and obedience among the citizenry. When a local public health official moved to prevent a malaria epidemic by quarantining ships coming into the harbor, he was trying to "police" the public health. Over the decades of rapid city growth between the 1820s and the 1860s, new problems confronted city officials and private citizens alike. Sanitarians, physicians, landscape architects, engineers, merchants, industrialists, and city boosters, no less than many individual householders, clamored for expansion of municipal services. For the sake of public health standards, street improvements, the provision of water and sewer systems, the recruitment of professional police and fire departments, and dozens of other amenities, a growing number of urbanites championed a stronger than traditional involvement of local government in the daily concerns of city life. In all instances, citizens were calling for more efficient policing of the city. The law, however, did not always keep pace with public demand.[23]

In the language of the law, two terms were intertwined: "police" (or, as it often appeared, "internal police") and "polity." From the eighteenth century until the Civil War years, legal scholars and judges employed these terms interchangeably. Both English and American law approved of executive, legislative, and judicial actions intended to maintain public morals and order, to preserve domestic tranquility, and to promote public convenience, safety, and health. Within this broad universe of meanings, two more technical definitions gradually surfaced.

First, "police" frequently referred to the affairs of a single community (as opposed to the "polity" of a nation) and to the derelictions of individuals. In these instances, writers labeled police authority as a "civil" or "municipal" power. Second, the domain of "police" action extended to "restraining the turbulent passions of mankind, the dispensing of justice, and the supporting of order and regulation in society." In this second sense, the term came to refer specifically to formal societal arrangements to secure that domain.

Noah Webster's *American Dictionary of the English Language* (1828) defined "police" as the administration of laws and regulations of a city, incorporated town, or borough. Francis Lieber's monumental *Encyclopaedia Americana* (1835) noted that in common usage in England and the United States, " 'police' is applied to the municipal rules, institutions, and officers provided for maintaining order, cleanliness, &c." Although these technical definitions seem straightforward, in policing the city throughout the century, the officials of many a municipal corporation had to wade through a morass of persistent legal ambiguities. [24] As Chief Justice Lemuel Shaw of the Massachusetts Supreme Court observed in 1851: "It is much easier to perceive and realize the . . . sources of this power, than to mark its boundaries, or prescribe limits to its exercise." In 1873 the U.S. Supreme Court stated that by its very nature the doctrine was incapable of exact definition. Reviewing nineteenth-century statutes and decisions in an extraordinarily influential book in the early years of the twentieth century, Ernst Freund proclaimed the police power an ever-evolving expression of contemporary social, economic, and political conditions and asserted that it must remain "elastic." A later scholar was even more blunt, calling the police power the "dark continent" of American law, "the convenient repository of everything for which our juristic classifications can find no other place." [25]

Nineteenth-century city governments, state legislatures, and the courts struggled to perceive and predict the limitations on cities' efforts to control their present and future development. The only consistent direction that cities could expect from the courts was the general proposition that any valid police power enactment had to be responsive to present social or economic conditions. Yet courts varied widely in their judgments on the nature of those conditions. Only gradually did a more or less coherent body of legal decisions emerge from the welter of police powers litigation. [26]

Invocations of the police power took three forms: (1) response to harm already inflicted upon one property owner by another; (2) regulation of certain uses of property to prevent one individual from harming another's property; and (3) efforts to protect the community at large from injurious uses of private property. Legally, all these uses sprang from the confluence of three sources—a presumed tradition of English common law, the "overwhelming necessity" concept, and the *sic utere* doctrine of nuisance law. The edges of these three streams often overlapped. For our purposes, however, it will be convenient to examine them as though they flowed independently and then to consider how, in merging together, they influenced the legal climate of opinion in urban America.

Late eighteenth- and early nineteenth-century state cases and statutes commonly used the term "police" when upholding the right of a city to control certain kinds of property use. A Pennsylvania case of 1799, for instance, affirmed Philadelphia's right to forbid, as a fire hazard, construction of wooden buildings in certain districts of the city. The court ruled that under its charter the city could regulate its own police. In that same year the Common Council of New York City, fearing a recurrence of the yellow fever epidemic that had raged the previous summer and eager to avoid tedious lawsuits to force private citizens to remove offensive filth from city streets, urged the legislature to grant broader regulatory powers to the municipal corporation. The sources of the "afflicting pestilence" were local, stated the Council's report, and the legislature should place discretionary power "in the hands of the immediate representatives of the city, who already have the police of it committed to them." The legislature agreed, and in 1803 the city established a Department of Scavengers, employing men at public expense. Other typical police regulations dealt with the location and placement of cemeteries within city limits and the storage of gunpowder in populated areas. Nearly every ruling in favor of such regulations relied upon justifications traditional in English common law, often citing Blackstone's well-known statement about the "due regulation and domestic order of the kingdom."[27]

So familiar and repeated were references to the common law underpinnings of the police power doctrine that late nineteenth-century treatise writers accepted their antiquity as an article of faith. But they were only partly correct. As interpreted and applied by judges, the police power was essentially a nineteenth-century invention.[28]

There was one principle in English common law, however, that American courts did employ to strengthen and widen the urban foundation of regulatory law. At the dawn of the seventeenth century, English jurists discovered a "natural law" doctrine that they incorporated into common law—"overwhelming" or "overruling" necessity." Normally, when a city "took" private property for an alleged public benefit it had to compensate the owner under eminent domain law. Social and economic crises, however, could overrule the normal course of the law. In such instances, the supreme law was not the protection of individual property rights, but promotion of the general welfare of all citizens.

Thus, when an epidemic ravaged a community in nineteenth-century America, elected officials could order the destruction of a slum that they believed harbored the disease, without fearing that the courts would force them to pay compensation to the slumlord. When fire threatened lives and property, city fathers could order the leveling of a privately owned building or warehouse to create a firebreak without worrying about just compensation. As a treatise writer succinctly put the matter, in any "great calamity, the private property of any individual may be lawfully taken, used or destroyed for the relief, protection, or safety of the many, without subjecting the actors to personal responsibility. In these cases, the rights of private property must be made subservient to the public welfare." Extreme conditions permitted extreme responses, for which cities would not incur financial liability. Such responses were at most temporary expedients. Still, that American courts, usually eager to protect private property rights, permitted them at all lent support to the noncompensable regulatory powers of cities. As a strand of police power doctrine, the concept of "overwhelming necessity" presented urban America with an opportunity to broaden regulatory authority over various kinds of land uses. Of greater potential still was the law of public nuisance. [29]

Early nineteenth-century uses of the police power were in many ways interwoven with the law of public nuisance. Down through the 1850s, numerous cases that strengthened the threads of police power regulation arrived in the courts in the guise of nuisance suits. State courts gradually codified common law nuisance principles under the sovereign police power authority accorded to state legislatures. Over and over again, judges offered the common law principle of *sic utere* as justification for a regulation of private property usage that later courts would customarily file under the police power of the state. As the codification proceeded, slow but significant changes occurred in application of nuisance doctrine and, therefore, in the scope of the police power itself.

Traditionally, in common law, courts wielded nuisance doctrine as an "after the fact" tool. Only after a person's use of his property had done some harm to that of a neighbor did the law intervene, prevent further usage of that sort and perhaps order compensation. A man might dam or divert water from a stream running across his own and neighbors' property, thereby denying others their customary access. A man living in a sparsely populated area might extend his fences into a public roadway, thus limiting his neighbors' normal flow of traffic. A property owner's burning garbage might produce loathsome smells that interfered with a neighbor's enjoyment of his own property. Each man had created a nuisance. In such cases nuisance law as applied was retrospective and conservative. Courts employed the doctrine to prevent changes in the use of property by individual owners.

Such common, and usually narrow, applications of nuisance law sufficed as long as the physical environment remained fairly uncluttered. In America's booming antebellum cities, however, such retrospective action was cumbersome or useless. Had courts allowed every person upset by a neighbor's use of property to file suit, they would have found themselves swamped. An increasing number of property owners became reluctant to attempt action when the court costs of doing so began to outweigh the potential rewards. Moreover, for both city leaders eager to promote urban development and private entrepreneurs eager to secure state blessings and the profits available through the provision of services, the traditional boundaries of nuisance law were too restrictive.

To handle the difficulties, and to mediate rising tensions between the cherished ideology of individual opportunity and equality and the changing realities of the urban economy, judges tended to follow two courses. First, a court could simply refuse to recognize the legal right of an individual property owner to bring a nuisance suit. For example, a Boston shopowner, irritated that the city had granted a horse-car company a franchise to run a line down his street, challenged the action as a nuisance affecting his personal use of his own property. In effect, the court said "nonsense," and ruled that since the street itself was city land and since many individuals owned property fronting it, the man did not have sufficient legal standing to bring such a suit. Second, in cases of farther-reaching importance, judges melded nuisance law with an expanded police power doctrine. Beginning in the 1820s and continuing down to the Civil War years, courts increasingly interpreted nuisance actions as subsumed by the state's right and duty under the police power to promote economic development and to protect the rights not only of individuals, but of all citizens of the community. Rather than a relic of common law antiquity, the police power was a judicial creation of the pre–Civil War decades. Urban leaders and activist judges, more eager to foster change than to prevent it, fabricated American police power law. [30]

CRAFTING THE POLICE POWER

Early hints of the new direction the courts would take came during the first decades of the century in a series of cases involving riparian water rights. Although such examples may seem a far cry from decisions involving urban land and public works, the legal logic and reasoning underlying them provided precedents for other cases. The widespread erection of dams and mills led to some of the earliest and most significant battles about the relationship between property law and economic development. In those clashes, the champions of economic improvement more often than not triumphed.

The courts were moving away from the traditional common law principle that particular uses of water over a lengthy period of time gave an individual property owner a legal right to enjoy such uses unimpaired, unchallenged, unchanged. While still citing the *sic utere* maxim, judges began to modify and broaden its social reach, applying it in light of their own readings of the wider social context within which individuals used their property. Through their decisions, a number of judges directly altered social policy.

Attention to the societal conditions that retarded or fostered economic development beneficial to the community gradually replaced the old common law emphasis on the sanctity of individual property and the need to keep one person's use of property from injuring another. The principle received clear exposition in *Tyler* v. *Wilkinson* (1827), perhaps the most influential early decision about water rights. "The law here, as in many other cases," stated the court, "acts with a reasonable reference to public convenience and general good, and it is not betrayed into a narrow strictness, subversive of common sense, nor into an extravagant looseness, which would destroy private rights. The maxim is applied, 'Sic utere tuo, ut non alienum laedas.' " The novel judicial balancing act, at least in this case, played to an audience that applauded economic development. [31]

The widening pool of water rights decisions quickly overflowed into disputes about city regulation of privately owned urban property. The year 1827 was a banner year in the transition from narrowly applied nuisance law to more flexible police power regulation. In Louisiana, a New Orleans ordinance that reserved to the city primacy in health care came under fire from entrepreneurs denied the profit-making opportunity to build a private hospital on private land. With the public health possibly at stake, judges proved willing to grant considerable authority to municipal officials. The state supreme court made it clear that "the right of individuals to the possession and enjoyment of things" stemmed not from natural law but from municipal law, which in turn, arose from prevalent social conditions. In New York City, Trinity Church challenged an ordinance prohibiting burials in private grounds in certain sections of the community. The state supreme court upheld the city's regulatory authority, pointedly arguing that changes in population size and dwelling density required changes in traditional patterns of land use. A third case, *Vanderbilt v. Adams*, showed most directly the leeway that courts were ready to permit government in exercising the police power.[32]

Under authority from the state legislature, the City of New York enacted a series of bylaws that regulated ship-docking at privately owned wharves in the harbor. Dock owners, already in fierce competition with one another to profit from increased commercial traffic, reacted angrily against the new controls. One owner refused to obey a direct order from the harbor-master to make room at his wharf for an incoming steamer. In response, city officials attempted to impose a financial penalty. A lawsuit ensued. Only by the very broadest interpretation of the *sic utere* maxim could one sustain an argument that the wharf owner was using his private property to anyone's injury. The owner's refusal posed no immediate threat to public health, safety, or morals, traditionally the grounds upon which courts upheld the legitimate use of police regulations. The only portion of the "public welfare" in question was the city's right to control the use of private property, in this instance to impose some semblance of order on a commercially crowded harbor. Yet the court found for the city.

The statute employed by the city, the court ruled, "appears to be a necessary police regulation, . . . although it may, in some measure, interfere with individual rights." It was "necessary for the purpose of protecting the rights of all concerned." The justices cited the density of population and commercial traffic in the city and harbor. Changing social conditions demanded changes in the power to regulate. "Every public regulation in a city may and does, in some sense, limit and restrict the absolute right that existed previously," they observed, but there was nothing wrong with that. "Police regulations are legal and binding, because for the general benefit." Having taken this utilitarian stance, the court moved one step beyond it, implying a sort of "trickle-down" theory of "community" in which an individual's best interests derived from and depended on law's serving the best interests of the entire community. Police powers rested on the "duty of the supreme power to protect all by statutory regulations, so that, on the whole, the benefit of all is promoted. . . . But this is not considered as an injury. So far from it, the individual, as well as others, is supposed to be benefited." That reading of urban regulatory authority was hardly the stuff of traditional nuisance doctrine. It was, instead, material for a novel police power construction in American law.[33]

Later courts never questioned, and frequently cited, the reasoning of *Vanderbilt* v. *Adams.* Yet the justices hearing the case had ventured into relatively unfamiliar terrain. They stood on safe ground when upholding the sovereign power of the state to grant regulatory authority to the municipal corporation of New York. But when they stretched the *sic utere* maxim to cover the specific facts at issue, when they justified the city's action as directed toward the "general benefit," and when they reasoned that changing social conditions permitted new types of urban policing of property use, the judges knew that they were crossing a legal frontier. Note the tentativeness of their language—"appears to be a necessary police regulation"; "the individual . . . is supposed to be benefited." But the language of later opinions was far from tentative. Between the early 1830s and the onset of the Civil War, various state courts explored the new terrain, placing guideposts in their passage.

The most definitive expressions and expansions of the urban police power occurred in Massachusetts. Three cases—*Baker* v. *Boston* (1831), *Lumbard* v. *Stearns* (1849), and *Commonwealth* v. *Alger* (1851)—stood above the field of many that confirmed police power authority. In the first, Justice Wilde of the state supreme court validated the city's right to landfill a sewage-polluted creek without paying compensation to property owners who used the stream for navigation. Following *Vanderbilt* logic, Wilde said of the plaintiff: "The law presumes he is compensated by sharing in the advantages arising from such beneficial regulations." The second case underscored the authority of cities to engage in public works construction, in this instance, a publicly regulated water supply. Chief Justice

Lemuel Shaw affirmed that "the supply of a large number of inhabitants with pure water is a public purpose," regardless of
inconvenience or injury to individual property owners. The same
justice's *Alger* decision became one of the most widely discussed and
frequently cited cases in the history of constitutional law.[34]

The facts of the case were simple. On his own property, Mr.
Alger built a wharf jutting into the Boston Harbor. The new structure did not impede navigation at all, but it did extend beyond a
boundary line established by the city under authority of the legislature. City officials viewed Alger's actions as a direct affront to their
authority and that of the state. Alger saw the municipal ordinance
as an invasion of his right to do whatever he pleased with his own
property. When the case reached the state supreme court, Alger's
attorney argued that the police power was a power only to regulate,
not to destroy, private rights, and certainly not to do so without
compensation to the owner for financial loss. Lemuel Shaw did not
agree. This was not a mere riparian rights case. This was not an
eminent domain case. Nor was it a common law case of nuisance.
Shaw revealed an eagerness to move well beyond the *sic utere*
maxim. At stake, Shaw believed, were both the capacity of cities to
govern, at least in part, their own process of growth and, also more
significantly, the sovereign authority of the state legislature:

We think it a settled principle, growing out of the very nature of well
ordered civil society, that every holder of property . . . holds it under the
implied liability that his use of it may be so regulated, that it shall not be
injurious to the equal enjoyment of others having an equal right to the
enjoyment of their property, nor injurious to the rights of the
community.[35]

How would the court decide the appropriateness of any particular
piece of police power regulation? According to Shaw, the court had
to examine the social conditions that had presumably inspired it.
The law had to keep up with the commercial, industrial, and physical development of the cities. As he defined it, the police power
should not redress previous wrongs as much as it should address
ways of promoting the public welfare in the present and for the future. In fairness to all, legislative responses to urban change had to
establish definite and understandable rules, but individuals could
not decide for themselves which regulations of property use were

reasonable. "All property in this commonwealth, . . . is derived directly or indirectly from the government, and held subject to those general regulations, which are necessary to the common good and general welfare. Rights of property, like all other social and conventional rights, are subject . . . to such reasonable restraints and regulations established by law, as the legislature . . . may think necessary and expedient." The sovereign authority of the legislature was undeniable. Not surprisingly, Shaw ruled in behalf of the city.[36]

Other judges soon followed Shaw's lead. In a frequently cited Rhode Island case a few years later, the court spoke directly about the necessary flexibility of the police power:

This power exists in great part for the very purpose of changing the [common law] adjustment [among property and community rights] from time to time, as the relative circumstances of the community and individuals may require. Our regulations of internal police and of trade, [are] adapted by positive law to our condition, and changed by it according to our changing circumstances.[37]

By the end of the 1850s, a number of American courts had insinuated strength and muscle into the maturing body of police power law. With some degree of confidence, urban leaders could anticipate increasing opportunities to flex those muscles. Broadening interpretations of traditional nuisance doctrines, the recent development of the "consequential damages" principle, and reevaluations of eminent domain law had opened a door through which the police power could stride. City officials could not foresee that immediately after the Civil War, judges and writers of legal treatises would try to enfeeble the police power and close the door.

They did know, however, that despite the eagerness of some courts to embrace the police power, municipal corporations did not yet control their own destinies. Alongside the legal trend toward a more flexible urban law marched a judicial commitment to enforcing the sovereignty of state legislatures even at the expense of hobbling the cities' police powers. When trying to invoke the police doctrine in the "public interest," local governments were often hindered by limitations within their corporate charters. The evolution of the city as a municipal corporation during the nineteenth century breathed life into the eminent domain and police power species, eventually forcing both to adapt to a new urban environment and a new urban culture.

4

THE LAWFUL CITY

At the vital center of city making in the nineteenth century stood the temple of land-use law. Public health regulations, street layouts, park constructions, transportation networks, water and sewer systems—these and other subdivisions of city making were uninhabitable by those who lacked legal authority over the uses and purposes of urban land. Chief among the reasons for this was the legal status of the city as a municipal corporation. The eighteenth-century conception of local autonomy deriving from a charter granted by the crown withered under nineteenth-century notions about sovereignty. Authority to create, modify, or destroy corporations came to reside in the legislative power of state governments and the judicial system's review of that power. For city-makers eager to exercise autonomy in land-use regulation, evolving judicial definitions of the nature of the corporation often sired confusion rather than clarity. [1]

Eighteenth-century courts treated the law of corporations as unified. Private business enterprises, state-run banks, churches, schools, town governments, all fitted into "one legal bag." [2] In theory, the state chartered all corporations to further public purposes. But as the number of privately funded corporations multiplied following the American Revolution, questions arose over the "public purposes" served by businesses obviously founded for the personal profit of their investors. Eager both to unleash economic growth and to guard investors' property from state control, judges answered those questions by opening the bag, separating the corporate items into two categories, and applying different rules to each. To one side they placed enterprises they called "private corporations"; to the other, "public" ones. Over the first half of the nineteenth century, courts looked at the "private" corporations and found more

59

and more reasons to adopt a hands-off policy. At the same time, using new legal bonds, they began to tighten their hold on city governments. They publicized the municipal corporation.

PUBLICIZING THE MUNICIPAL CORPORATION

In any modern sense of the term, "municipal corporation" is an American invention. Denoting an incorporated town or city with specific legal powers and obligations, it entered common usage around the middle of the nineteenth century. "Municipal" had a more venerable lineage. Although the Latin root of the word meant "city," legal parlance applied a much broader definition. From the sixteenth to the early nineteenth century, "municipal law" in both England and North America referred to the sovereign legal system of an individual state as distinguished from international law. Thus, through the 1830s Americans commonly used the term to refer not only to the law of a city, but also that of the individual state. Hendrik Hartog has emphasized the significance of that usage: "The idea of a 'municipal law' thus encompassed two central notions of nineteenth-century public law in America: the uniformity of law within a jurisdiction and the supremacy of the state as a source of power and authority."[3]

Between 1820 and 1860 American jurists crafted a new body of law, the law of municipal corporations. Responding to tumultuous economic growth, courts began to distinguish between property used to fashion collective economic progress and property used to protect individual security. Displaying a preference for societal uses of property that were "dynamic rather than static," judges nevertheless recognized a responsibility to secure individual property rights against unwarranted intrusion by government. The critical questions were: When and under what circumstances could a municipal corporation legitimately intrude on such rights? When and how should the law hedge the social reach of a duly-chartered corporation?[4]

When a city government's land-use regulations and public works policies clearly violated the property rights of one or more citizens, many courts had difficulty deciding the extent to which those actions genuinely advanced the general welfare. Judges were forced to explore the limits of authority bestowed upon all corporations by the state. To facilitate their decisions, courts manufactured a distinction between private and public corporations.

From the *Dartmouth College* decision in 1819 through the 1850s, courts affirmed a unique "public" status for what they came to call the "municipal corporation." Public corporations might exercise some private interests, stated Massachusetts Justice Joseph Story in the *Dartmouth* case, "but strictly speaking, public corporations are such only as are founded by the government for public purposes, where the whole interests belong also to the government." The clearest early expression of this new attitude came from New York's Chancellor Kent during the 1820s. "Public corporations are such as are created by the government for political purposes, . . . they are invested with subordinate legislative powers to be exercised for local purposes connected with the public good, and such powers are subject to the control of the legislature of the state." Underlying those seemingly artless words was what lawyers called a legal fiction. "Created by the government": Kent knew that was a fiction, that most municipal governments had erected whatever authority they enjoyed on the foundations of local compromise, not legislative fiat. "Local purposes connected with the public good": one might expect that those in the best position to determine that "good" were members of the local public. Such was not to be.[5]

A state legislature could undercut and overturn whichever powers a municipal government employed for "local purposes connected with the public good." In 1835 New York Supreme Court Justice Samuel Nelson, echoing what by then had become conventional wisdom, pointed out that a municipal government corresponded to a private business only in sharing with it the title "corporation." A sound economic policy of sheltering "the private property of the corporators" from state intrusion underlay the charter of a private business. Towns and cities, however, were political institutions incorporated "for the good government of the people" and as such subject to a kind of legislative control that the state could not exercise against a private corporation.[6]

Although most courts before the 1850s only occasionally curbed local autonomy, they had segregated the legal status of private and public corporations. In fashioning the new structure of municipal corporations, judges had guaranteed that state representatives who challenged the local authority of city governments would receive the blessings of the law.

During the pre–Civil War years the process of publicizing the municipal corporation had at least two marked effects on land-use planning practices. First, for a variety of public works endeavors, city officials gained new flexibility in dealing with private property owners. Courts viewed city governments as "clothed with legislative powers and prerogatives to a certain extent, and . . . fully empowered to adopt measures of police, for the purpose of preserving the health and promoting the comfort, convenience, and general welfare of the inhabitants within the city." Second, city officials quickly discovered that private property owners stood ready to challenge nearly every action of theirs in court, and that the courts' insistence upon the sovereignty of the state legislature over the municipal corporation sometimes restrained the latter's freedom of action. A citizen irked by proposals for a sewer line in the street abutting his property, for example, might sue the city to halt construction. If he could argue successfully that the city lacked proper authorization from the state legislature, he might scuttle several years worth of careful planning. City fathers learned to be wary of precipitous action, regardless of the benefit to the "general welfare," lest they find themselves hauled into court.[7]

The developing law of municipal corporations had both an energizing and an enervating impact upon proponents of various kinds of land-use controls. New legal conceptions of the municipal corporation alternately heated and chilled the climate of opinion about the potential of city planning. A spate of mid-century court decisions revealed the complexity of issues raised by urban efforts to plan in the public interest. A fascinating case in point was *Sharpless* v. *The Mayor of Philadelphia* (1853).

SHARPENING THE LEGAL SWORD

Believing that recent advances in transportation technology in Boston, Baltimore, and New York City had locked their own community into a life-and-death struggle for commercial survival, Philadelphia leaders hurried to enter the city in the railroad race. This avenue of public works activity encompassed a kind of land-use regulation and "taking" of private property different from that involved in raising the grade of a street or building water and sewer lines. Yet the issues posed in the case lay at the core of all types of planning and public works construction by municipal corporations.[8]

In 1852 the Pennsylvania legislature authorized the City of Philadelphia to acquire shares in two railroad companies. One company's line was to terminate slightly outside the city limits. The other's was to start almost 350 miles from Philadelphia, link up with an already existing line from the City of Brotherly Love, and extend its commercial reach further west. Four local property owners filed suit against the city to prevent the purchase, protesting that as taxpayers they would have to bear an unwelcome and unlawful burden. They asserted that the municipal corporation had no state-authorized right to coerce them into a contractual venture of which they disapproved. Arguments advanced by both the majority and the minority opinions of the court plumbed deeper levels, however, than mere taxpayers' disgruntlement. Writing for the majority, Justice Black claimed that "this is, beyond all comparison, the most important cause that has ever been in this Court since the formation of the government. The fate of many most important public improvements hangs on our decision."[9]

The issues raised in *Sharpless* hinged upon American legal definitions at least half a century in the making. Another half-century would pass after the decision before courts had crafted consistent and predictable responses to those problems. For convenience sake we will examine the case briefly under two headings: the "practical" issues, which weighed the immediate force of the law upon urban public works, and the issues of "principle," which focused primarily on questions of legal definition.[10]

In "practical" terms, both the majority and the minority opinions in *Sharpless* considered four problems. First, could a municipal corporation, through the power of taxation, coerce its citizens to support the construction of public works? Justice Black said "yes"; Justices Lowrie and Lewis, dissenting and offering their own rather convoluted interpretations of the power to tax, said "no." Second, which segments of the urban population received benefit, and which injury, from a municipal corporation's promotion of public works? Both majority and minority opinions preferred to skirt this tricky political and economic question. Third, should the state, or a local government authorized by the state, involve itself in mixed-enterprise projects—that is, those that mingled public and private investments? The majority pointed out that mixed-enterprise projects had gone unchallenged in Pennsylvania since they had first come into vogue in the late eighteenth century. The minority tried to distinguish between projects that genuinely benefited the "public interest" and those that principally served one class of the citizenry bound together by investment in *private* enterprise. Cities, they argued, henceforth should not engage in mixed-enterprise under-takings of so-called "public" works. The fourth problem proved the most difficult.

Was the range of a municipal corporation's authority in the planning and construction of public works limited to its geographic boundaries? If not, how far beyond its legal borders could a city government reach to secure the health, safety, welfare, and prosperity of its citizens? Justice Black levied no limits. Justice Lewis did. Although little-noticed at that time, Lewis' opinions clearly articulated the position of contemporaries who believed that municipal corporations had gained too much autonomy in exerting control over property owners' uses of urban space. His argument would become conventional judicial wisdom over the last three decades of the nineteenth century. It warrants our attention.

Admitting that the legislature could create municipal powers, Lewis nonetheless stated that cities had to confine the exercise of those powers to *"local* and *governmental objects.* There has been no usage or custom under which the people of particular districts can be embarked in *extra territorial adventures* against their will." He then affirmed:

The paving and lighting of streets of a large city, and supplying it with wholesome water, are necessary to the comfort, safety, health, and even the existence of its inhabitants. If suitable paving materials cannot elsewhere be obtained, . . . if the wells and springs of water within the city are insufficient in quantity or quality, it . . . may construct works for the purpose at *any necessary point,* either within or beyond its territorial limits. The test of its power is the *object to be obtained.* . . . It is no part of the duties of municipal corporations . . . to construct distant railroads. . . . If they may do this it is impossible to assign any limits to their powers. They may establish lines of steamers across the Atlantic and Pacific Oceans, and commercial agencies and extensive mercantile houses throughout the world: they may build hotels within and beyond their limits. . . . The manufacturing interests are equally within the range of municipal powers, because they are necessarily connected with commercial prosperity. These authorities may therefore, on the same principle, erect extensive manufacturing establishments. They may thus take control of every branch of industry. Like Aaron's rod, municipal enterprise may swallow up all private enterprises. It may thus extinguish separate and individual rights of property, and bring everything into common. What is this but a *Fourier establishment* upon a magnificent scale? The system of the *Socialists* may have its advantages, but no man can constitutionally be *compelled* to embark in it. [11]

Taken at face value, Justice Lewis' musings appeared entirely reasonable. They seemed to grant city governments ample authority to plan and construct necessary public works. Contained within the body of the argument, however, were stringent limitations on the use of that authority. The judge rejected far more than municipal involvement in a regional railroad line.

By implication, he wanted to restrain local governments from engaging in any activities that might interfere with private enterprise. If private entrepreneurs could and would provide vitally needed services, municipal corporations must not compete with them. In his own day, the catalogue of such services was lengthy. Sewer construction, horse-car lines, street cleaning, supplies of fuel for heating and lighting, repair of docks and wharves, building heights, lot size and building placement on lots, water supply in the poorer sections of Philadelphia—all were the province of private enterprise. Lewis would defend that province against municipal control.

No city could adequately deliver services—even the limited ones Lewis would countenance—when imprisoned within its own boundaries. Economies of scale were essential. But eager to elevate private property over public necessity, Justice Lewis ignored the obvious. Over the last several decades of the nineteenth century, many American courts adopted his position, even though for some reason his views did not appear in the official court record. Nonetheless, many a later court decision helped to hammer his *Sharpless* dissent into a sharp-edged sword wielded against municipal corporations.

Like the "practical" matters, the "principles" of the case revolved around four questions. First, did a municipal corporation's investment of tax dollars for so-called public works constitute an illegal taking of private property? Although offering different reasons, both the majority and the minority opinions said "no," following the by-then accepted definition of taking as *physical* invasion of property. Second, how far could definitions of "public purpose" go in treading upon the property rights of private citizens before calling forth the doctrine of eminent domain and its requirement of just compensation? Here the majority and minority concurred: "as far as is necessary"; but they disagreed vigorously about what was necessary. Again on separate grounds, both sides stated that in this particular case eminent domain should not apply. Third, and more broadly, should the state adopt a positive and active role in economic policies involving the property rights of private citizens?

"Yes," pronounced Justice Black; public investment in public works was a legitimate function of government. "No," thundered Justices Lowrie and Lewis, upholding the theory of limited government. Finally, the *Sharpless* decision turned to the most crucial principle of all.

Ultimately, the ability of cities to improve their present environments and to plan intelligently for the future depended upon their sinews of sovereignty. If strong, municipal corporations could shape their own destiny. If weak, they might bend and break beneath external forces. *Sharpless* directly confronted the question: what degree of sovereignty, if any, did a municipal corporation possess? A quarter of a century earlier, the majority and minority opinions would probably have gone in opposite directions. In 1853 the two merged. Accepting without question the recently developed law of municipal corporations, both sides prostrated the city before the power of the state.

Justice Lewis left no room for doubt. "Municipal corporations cannot destroy or affect the rights of property. They are mere creatures of the government, instituted for governmental purposes alone. They may be established without the consent of the inhabitants within their limits, and may be abolished at the pleasure of the power that created them. They have no permanent existence for a single day."[12]

Some fifteen years later, a relatively obscure Iowa judge named John F. Dillon handed down a decision that eventually led to a doctrine known as "Dillon's Rule." That "rule" identified and synthesized a variety of symptoms of the allegedly diseased condition of municipal corporate law. What we might call the "Dillon syndrome," a body of attitudes and opinions long in the making, permeated legal thought and judicial decision making over the last decades of the nineteenth century and the first ones of the twentieth. No single individual did more to shape American urban law, or the new urban culture, than the Iowa justice.

THE DILLON SYNDROME

In 1868 John F. Dillon, then chief justice of the Iowa Supreme Court, attempted once and for all to distinguish the authority exercised by municipal corporations from that retained by state legislatures. Dillon ruled that "municipal corporations owe their origin to, and derive their powers and rights wholly from, the legislature. It breathes into them the breath of life, and without which they cannot exist. As it creates, so it may destroy. . . . [Municipal corporations] are the mere tenants at the will of the legislature." Nearly forty years later, in *Hunter* v. *City of Pittsburgh* (1907), the U.S. Supreme Court adopted the Dillon Rule as its own. Of the powers of municipal corporations, the Court declared that "the State, . . . at its pleasure, may modify or withdraw all such powers . . . expand or contract the territorial area, unite the whole or a part with another municipality, repeal the charter and destroy the corporation. All this may be done . . . with or without the consent of the citizens, or even against their protest." In 1923, with *City of Trenton* v. *State of New Jersey,* the Court completed the business. It held that municipalities were in no way entitled to the constitutional protection granted all other corporations. From a legal standpoint, state sovereignty over cities was final.[13]

Roughly between the Civil War decade and the first decade of the twentieth century, courts throughout the land retreated from ground occupied during the pre-Civil War years. Having granted cities considerable, if not always consistent, flexibility in land-use regulations, judges turned toward strengthening their own control over all kinds of regulatory legislation. Judicial scrutiny of both municipal and state legislation intensified, and the courts' case loads grew. Judicial decisions blurred the recently developed distinction between eminent domain and legitimate use of the police power. New state constitutions—for instance, the Illinois constitution of 1870—required government to pay eminent domain compensation for a host of actions previously regarded as noncompensable. This in turn limited the willingness or ability of municipal corporations to plan and construct new public works and to regulate private uses of property in ways intended to benefit the general welfare. In a Wisconsin case that reached the U.S. Supreme Court in 1870, Justice Samuel Miller rejected the argument that "in this country . . . a municipal corporation, without any general laws," could by police power declaration force the removal of a structure as a nuisance. To allow such an intolerable action, stated the judge, "would place every house, every business, and all the property of the city, at the uncontrolled will of the temporary local authorities."[14]

"Temporary local authorities"—that was a timely and pertinent concern. The character of local politics, rarely harmonious in the

past, had become increasingly cacophonous and volatile. The rise
of urban political machines, based largely on coalitions among the
working classes, recently arrived immigrants, and the poor, had incurred the wrath of middle- and upper-class reformers intent upon
governing communities in an efficient, businesslike manner. Cities
increasingly were battlegrounds between machine politicians who
wanted above all to foster growth and expand public works and reformers who wanted to keep costs down and growth stable and predictable. At their core, the battles were over competing visions of
the urban future and over which groups should benefit the most
from urban development. In democratic America it was inevitable
that courts would enter the fray as the final arbiters. It was perhaps
also inevitable that, as the most vulnerable, fragile, and newly created of legal institutions, the municipal corporation would suffer in
this war of attrition.[15]

To dismiss Dillon's opinion as simply an expression of hostility
toward cities would be unfair. Rather, as a legal scholar who viewed
the law more as conservator of things as they are than progenitor of
things as they might be, he sought a balance between opposing
forces, a climate of stability. His treatises, speeches, books, and law
review articles proved central to the process of consolidating a consistent definition of the role of municipal corporations in American
society. That his views found such a receptive audience was but a
reflection of a widespread societal response to the rise of urban giants during the post-Civil War years, a suspicion (heightened into a
certainty in many corners of American society) that big city life bred
evils.

Born in rural New York in 1831, Dillon grew up in Davenport,
Iowa. He received little in the way of formal education. At age sev-
enteen he embarked upon the study of medicine in the offices of a
local physician. He later attended lectures at the medical school in
Keokuk and in 1850 earned a medical degree at the Davenport
branch of the University of Iowa's College of Physicians and Surgeons. He had aimed at general medical practice in rural Iowa, but
an injury made it impossible for him to ride the circuit on horse-
back. Returning to Davenport, he undertook self-tutoring in the
law. Without formal legal training or apprenticeship in a law office,
he nonetheless gained admission to the bar in 1852.

He entered politics that same year. In 1858 he gained election as
judge of Iowa's seventh judicial district. In 1862, running on the

Republican ticket, he rose to the state's supreme court. In 1869 President Ulysses S. Grant named Dillon a U.S. circuit court judge for the newly formed eighth judicial circuit. For the next ten years he sat on the federal bench, resigning in 1879 to accept a professorship of law at Columbia College. He left that post in 1882 and until his death in 1914 practiced corporate law throughout New York State. Among his clients he numbered the Missouri Pacific Railroad, the Union Pacific Railroad, Western Union Telegraph, and the business interests of Jay Gould, one of the Gilded Age's most notorious capitalists.

In 1892 his colleagues elected him president of the American Bar Association. Two years later he published *The Laws and Jurisprudence of England and America*. For our purposes, however, his most significant contribution came earlier, in 1872.[16]

His *Treatise on the Law of Municipal Corporations* was the first, most comprehensive, and most influential catalogue of legal thought and practice on the subject. The initial edition ran to some 800 pages in its attempt to graft onto the growing American body of urban corporate law the old English municipal system. As judicial activism broadened enforcement of eminent domain legislation while constricting regulation under the police power, Dillon's compendium expanded. The fifth and last edition of the treatise, published in 1911, required five thick volumes.

Challenges came from celebrated contemporaries, including Judge Thomas M. Cooley, the attorney Amasa Eaton, and the legal scholar Eugene McQuillin (who published his own multivolume *Treatise on the Law of Municipal Corporations* in 1911). In his fifth edition, Dillon gleefully observed that these scattered counterattacks had won little judicial acceptance. In 1923 the historian William Munro observed in a widely read and highly regarded book that the Dillon thesis was now "so well recognized that it is not nowadays open to question." We might fairly regard John F. Dillon as the father of the modern law of municipal corporations.[17]

Yet we might, with equal justice, regard his work merely as the capstone of some forty to fifty years of judicial opinions. Dillon cited state courts' decisions dating back to the 1820s in support of virtually every one of his arguments. In the late 1820s, for example, Chancellor James Kent had stated categorically that "as corporations are the mere creatures of the law, established for special purposes, and derive all their powers from the acts creating them, it is perfectly just and proper that they should be obliged strictly to show their authority for the business they assume, and be confined in their operations to the mode, and manner, and subject matter prescribed." Kent's strict-construction interpretation of legislative intent presaged Dillon's attitude toward the municipal corporation. Perhaps we should think of Dillon not as the father of municipal corporate law, but as a midwife presiding over a lengthy and painful delivery.[18]

In any event the Dillon syndrome spread throughout the body of American municipal corporation law. Central to the syndrome was the "Dillon Rule": any and every action taken by a local government lacked legal authority unless expressly granted by a state legislature, or proved necessary to the fulfillment of a specific goal defined by the legislature. The duty of the law was to clear away all ambiguities about "whether the legislature intended to confer the authority in question." "Any fair, reasonable (substantial) doubt," he proclaimed, "concerning the existence of power is resolved by the courts against the municipal corporation, and the power is denied." Courts (meaning individual judges, of course) had to defend the private property rights from attacks by overzealous mayors and city councils, however much city fathers might protest that their only concern was the "general welfare." The above-mentioned ambiguities had arisen from the half-century-old judicial practice of viewing municipal corporations as curious mixtures of public and private spheres of interest. For too long, Dillon charged, courts had fabricated false distinctions between a city's governmental and proprietary functions. He intended to end such foolishness.[19]

Dillon accepted and approved the earlier nineteenth-century notion, articulated by Chancellor Kent and others, that state legislatures "created" the city as *government* by drawing up a charter. Prior to the existence of that piece of paper, citizens living together in a community presumably could not govern themselves in reasonable and effective ways, at least not in ways recognized and certified by American law. Only the charter, whatever hodgepodge of rights and responsibilities it contained, breathed legitimate life into the city as a government. In that role, properly bound in the use of its authority by legislative charter, a city could and should undertake specific "public" functions such as laying out streets, constructing commercial facilities, erecting schoolhouses, and the like. That much Dillon conceded. But "properly bound" was a key phrase. He defined "public" functions almost solely in negative terms: as actions that did not interfere with or encroach upon private enterprise. It was precisely the judicial tolerance of such encroachment that irritated the Iowa judge.

In their myopic inability to correctly distinguish between a city's proprietary and governmental activities, previous courts had stumbled into a blind alley. Viewing the city as a private property owner, Dillon argued, antebellum courts had stated that a city might own and change the uses of lands as streets, cemeteries, docks and wharves, schoolyards, and other types of public property. That much was acceptable; unfortunately, past courts did not stop there. Under the law of common nuisance and a misconstruction of police power doctrine, courts had allowed the city the privilege of regulating property or taking it from private citizens without compensation. Such actions, thought Dillon, often caused two equally undesirable results. They led municipal corporations into profligate investments in private business and into the competitive provision of services "better left to private enterprise." They also unduly and unnecessarily entangled the courts in a thicket of disputes between private citizens impaired in the use of their own property and the city itself, which, appropriately under the law, enjoyed the constitutional protections accorded to private property owners. That a city should retain *any* private identity as a proprietor the judge found "difficult exactly to comprehend."[20]

Dillon formulated his rule to dispel the ambiguities generated by previous court decisions. At first glance, it appeared carefully crafted. Looked at more closely, the rule stood or sometimes wobbled on four uneven legs. Two were assertions of legal principles; two were assumptions that sprang from Dillon's personal and social convictions.

His first assertion was that the law had to restrict cities to the performance of purely "public" functions by enforcing a narrow interpretation of their powers. This would prevent both short- and long-term dominance of city government by private business interests and, at the same time, protect private economic activities from being overwhelmed by governmental interference. Dillon called on state legislatures to exercise more control over urban activities and on the courts to develop uniform, objective criteria with which to measure the lawfulness of urban conduct. He proposed to interpose the courts between city fathers and state legislatures, allowing judges to determine the legitimacy of city activities under legislative authorization and identify the potential long-term consequences of such authorization. "The courts, too," he asserted, "have duties, the most important of which is to require these corporations, in all cases, to show a plain and clear grant for the authority they assume to exercise; to *lean against constructive powers*, and, with firm hands, to hold them and their officers within chartered limits." The law must shorten the reach of city government into the lives of private citizens.[21]

The second legal principle, following logically from the first, labeled the state control of cities "absolute." The judge's belief in the rectitude of state legislators (as opposed to that of city officials)—naive as it may seem to us—was unshakable. Admitting that state control was subject to political tempests, he argued nonetheless that it was purely "public" (a mystifying distinction).[22]

Some dissenters argued that urban officials administered a government whose local interests somehow stood apart from those of the state as a separate and higher entity. Although a state legislature had the constitutional right to control or alter the privileges and responsibilities of local governments, such writers maintained that to do so without the willing consent and cooperation of local officials was unusual and unwise. As the New Jersey Supreme Court put the matter;

> Almost invariably in practice municipal charters have been granted or altered by the legislature, in accordance with the expressed will of the corporators. The exceptions are very rare. They have occurred in seasons of high excitement; they cannot be reconciled to sound principle. They are to be regarded as beacons to be shunned, not as precedents to be followed.[23]

Dillon remained firm. The state must retain total control over cities. In turn, it must submit itself to judicial oversight of that control. The authority of the state, Dillon declared, "is supreme and transcendent: it may erect, change, divide, and even abolish, at pleasure, as it deems the public good to require." Judges bore the responsibility of forcing state legislatures to exercise their sovereignty whenever some wavered from performance of their duty. Even such time-honored activities as city investment in transportation systems would, if not covered by specific state statutes, be declared illegitimate. And if a state legislature authorized a particular municipal action, the courts would have to decide whether it genuinely met the test of serving the "public good." In practice, both in Dillon's day and subsequently, courts rarely opposed a state legislature's definition of a "public use." Foreknowledge of that, however, would not have altered Dillon's conviction. As far as he was concerned, decisions about the propriety and legality of local government actions rested in judges' hands.[24]

Dillon's third point was that local urban governments were, by their very nature, not to be trusted to act in the public interest. He denounced the city governments of his day as inefficient and corrupt, and the larger the city, the more likely it was, in his view, to be governed by men of inadequate moral character. "The usefulness of our municipal corporations has been impaired by evils that are either inherent in them or that have generally accompanied their workings"—for two reasons. First, "men the best fitted by their intelligence, business experience, capacity and moral character, for local governors or counsellors are not always, it is feared,—it might be added, are not generally—chosen. This [is] especially true of populous cities." Second, "those chosen are too apt to merge their individual conscience in their corporate capacity. Under the shield of their corporate character, men but too often do acts which they would never do as individuals."[25]

In presenting this rationale for his legal principles, the justice revealed his distrust not only of those elected to urban public offices, but of the electorate itself. In the best tradition of American republican ideology and English common law, Dillon sought a social balance among the elements of power, liberty, and virtue. Public virtue stemmed directly from the private virtues of individuals. Any vices practiced by private citizens threatened to flood the vaults of public virtue. Society, through its constitutional, legal, and governmental safeguards, had to stand constantly on the alert against subversion. It was clear to Dillon that present-day city governments posed the major threat to the delicate balance necessary for public virtue. Nor was he alone in his suspicion and fear. Denunciations of vicious municipal governments, political bosses, immigrant voting blocs, and urban populations riddled with crime, disease, and poverty were commonplace in Dillon's America. Moral and political reform movements flourished during the late nineteenth century and culminated in the so-called progressive movement of the early twentieth century. Dillon breathed that air and vented his anxieties against municipal corporations.[26]

The fourth leg supporting the judge's rule was the assumption that an objective, rational form of government was desirable and possible. Such a government could and would protect private property against abuse by both runaway democracy (evident in the activities of too many municipal corporations) and too-powerful private economic interests (exemplified by the burgeoning corporations and trusts of the period). Dillon subscribed to the American tradition of governance by a disinterested and presumably benevolent elite: "It is a duty of perpetual obligation," he proclaimed, "on the part of the strong to take care of the weak, of the rich to take care of the poor." The judge rejected any legislation or judicial decision that overly rewarded the wealthy while overly punishing the poor. Government had to serve as a broker among competing interest groups. For Dillon, society was an organic being whose separate parts could and should cooperate in a rational manner directed toward the health of the entire body. It was also a business: "In many of its more important aspects a modern American city is not so much a miniature State as it is a business corporation,—its business being wisely to administer the local affairs and economically to expend the revenues of the incorporated community." When we learn how to apply business methods to the structure of municipal government and the conduct of urban affairs, the cities will be on the right road.[27]

John F. Dillon devoted much of his legal life to proclaiming the necessity of major changes in the structure and functions of municipal corporations. In decisions from the bench and in his learned writings, he called for truly "public" city governments, acting in the best interests of all citizens, protecting the rights of private property, ensuring at least minimal levels of safety at the lowest possible dollar cost. City government and city planning were too important to be left to the whims of urban dwellers. Mistrusting the intentions of local officials and the intelligence of the urban electorate, Dillon declared the courts the appropriate and final arbiter in the broker state. "From this vantage point," in the words of Hendrik Hartog, "Dillon's Rule becomes an appropriate moral gesture, a way of compelling the legislature to take responsibility for the actions of an errant child. The city was not to be set loose on the streets of public action and expenditure freed from the constraints of its parent. The law would compel the legislature to superintend its charge." Of the law's ability to discharge such an important task, the judge had no doubt. The law, Dillon intoned, was "the beneficence of civil society acting by rule, in its nature . . . opposed to all that is fitful, capricious, unjust, partial or destructive."[28]

Dillon's Rule, and his views in general, were enormously influential in the post-Civil War attack on the police power. For many urban leaders, those years were confusing times. A number of state and federal courts curtailed certain uses of the police power and redefined others. Yet that power did not lack defenders among those eager to reshape the physical city and willing to reshape the lawful city if necessary. Counterbalancing the attacks, some courts revived the police power doctrine to promote the health, safety, comfort, and morals of urban Americans.

RETRENCHING, REDEFINING, AND REVIVING THE POLICE POWER

Legal and social circumstances made the period from the late 1860s to the *Pennsylvania Coal Co. v. Mahon* decision in 1922 one of retrenchment for the urban police power. The Fourteenth Amendment (1868) provided that no state could deprive a citizen of life, liberty, or property without due process of law; the laissez faire concern to protect the rights of private property from governmental intrusion absorbed the judiciary. Together, the two shaped an era in which state courts and the U.S. Supreme Court erratically, but with increasing frequency, narrowed the police power authority of state legislatures and their delegation of that authority to municipal corporations. Courts hacked away at the regulatory authority of local and state governments to control private economic activities and jealously protected property rights vested in private enterprise.[29]

A decision of the early 1870s set the tone. In *Watertown v. Mayo* (1872), the Massachusetts Supreme Court affirmed that the law "will not allow rights of property to be invaded under the guise of a police regulation for the preservation of health or protection against a threatened nuisance; and when it appears that such is not the real object and purpose of the regulation, courts will interfere to protect the rights of citizens." That same year, in a case involving the construction of the extensive Riverside Park in New York City, the State Supreme court held that private land could be taken for public use only when the city followed due process under eminent domain.

Subsequently, a series of park cases in New York City, Albany, Boston, St. Louis, and Chicago underscored that point.[30]

A significant number of decisions limiting the police power by requiring just compensation centered on railroads running over and above city streets. State courts began to expand the older definition of taking property for public use from a *physical appropriation* of land to an *interference* with a private owner's access to and use of his property. In cases where the building of a street railroad did not alter the grade of a street, as in New Orleans, courts often upheld the right of the city to grant construction rights under the police power. Temporary obstruction of private property was acceptable; for the "public good" owners had to endure such "inconveniences." But where elevated tracks restricted the use of streets in front of a private property and hindered the free flow of light and air, as in New York City, or where construction of the tracks raised the grade of a street and limited its use for other purposes, as in Buffalo and Rochester, the courts required just compensation.[31]

Perhaps the major nineteenth-century statement limiting the police power in favor of eminent domain came from Oliver Wendell Holmes. In an 1889 decision that presaged his views in the *Pennsylvania Coal* case, Justice Holmes, writing for the Massachusetts Supreme Court, explained that the difference between the police power and eminent domain

is only one of degree; most differences are when nicely analyzed. At any rate, difference of degree is one of the distinctions by which the right of the legislature to exercise the police power is determined. Some small limitations of previously existing rights incident to property may be imposed for the sake of preventing a manifest evil; larger ones could not be, except by the exercise of the right of eminent domain.

By opening the door to judicial nitpicking, Holmes both reasserted the authority of the courts over state legislatures and city halls and set the stage for various twentieth-century limitations on the urban police power.[32]

While the courts were retreating from certain antebellum applications of the urban police power, a generation of legal writers began redefining the scope of that doctrine. Their treatises appear to have strongly influenced their contemporaries on the bench. Beginning with Thomas M. Cooley in 1868 and concluding with Ernst

Freund in 1904, most drew careful distinctions between legitimate exercise of the police power and its arbitrary or capricious use by state legislatures or municipal corporations.[33]

Although differing on which to tug tightly, which to hold more loosely, these writers selected three fundamental lines of argument to rein in what they perceived as a runaway urban police power. First, they restated and reapplied the old *sic utere* doctrine to restrict regulations under the police power to circumstances that visibly threatened the public's safety, morals, comfort, or health. For example, a city could regulate the speed of railway cars passing over its streets or public grounds, but it could not extend that police regulation to control the activities of a private railroad corporation. Second, they fashioned constitutional restraints, principally invoking the contract clause of the Constitution and the due process clause of the Fourteenth Amendment. Third, they limited both a state's use of eminent domain procedures to acquire land for so-called public use and the range of instances in which a city might avoid just compensation through police power declaration. Although a handful of writers opposed or qualified these major trends, the courts rarely heard their voices, relying instead on the arguments of the redefiners for support of their own laissez faire inclinations.[34]

Yet the last great treatise of the period advertised the eventual demise of laissez faire. In 1904 Ernest Freund, a University of Chicago law professor, published *The Police Power: Public Policy and Constitutional Rights*. He claimed that the essence of the power was that every individual had to submit to restraints in the exercise of his liberty or property rights. The state took property under eminent domain because it was useful to the public, and under the police power because it was harmful. At the same time, he qualified, and in certain instances rejected, the *sic utere* doctrine as the mainstay of police power regulations. Past courts, he warned, had gone too far in subjugating the police power to the contract clause. The police power was inalienable and could not be bartered away by state legislatures, municipal corporations, or the courts, and the degree to which the contract clause "restricts the operation of the police power has never been precisely formulated." In a sense, he urged a return to pre-Civil War utilitarianism, using the power flexibly to effect the greatest good for the greatest number of people. Applications of the police power had to keep pace with rapidly changing circumstances. He promised that close examination "will reveal the police power not as a fixed quantity, but as the expression of social, economic and political conditions. As long as these conditions vary, the police power must continue to be elastic, i.e., capable of development." For Freund, the two main characteristics of the power were that "it aims directly to secure and promote the public welfare, and it does so by restraint and compulsion."[35]

"Promote the public welfare"—that was Freund's most significant contribution to the several-decades-old debate about the reach and limits of the doctrine. He brought the discussion back to its origins and retraced the evolution of police power theory in the courts of Lemuel Shaw and other antebellum justices from a *negative* doctrine applied to nuisances and community self-protection to a *positive* one aimed at promoting the general welfare of urban Americans. When Ernest Freund eliminated the negative and accentuated the positive characteristics of the police power, he was marching in step with at least one strain of judicial decisions over the previous quarter-century. For in the midst of treatise writers' redefining and courts' retrenching, some judges went about the business of reviving and expanding certain uses of the police power. These judicially sanctioned uses proved crucial to city planning efforts.

After the Civil War, and especially from the early 1870s on, state and federal courts permitted and often encouraged legislatures and municipal corporations to regulate uses of urban land to benefit public health, safety and civil order—sometimes even with the approval of treatise authors dedicated to laissez faire policies. Rapid expansion of the urban police power was associated with the provision of water supplies, sewer systems, street lighting, and street railroads and the enactment of new building codes that restricted certain types of construction while fostering others. One contemporary noted that "health laws in the different states, and statutes governing car companies, telephone companies, electric-light companies, elevators and other business in which there is a public interest to be protected, have greatly extended the sphere, limits and force of police powers." Without a favorably disposed legal and judicial climate, those efforts would not have succeeded.[36]

Wherever the public health and morals entered, the police power was almost certain to follow. Listen to the most conservative of the treatise writers, Christopher Tiedemann: "The streets of a city are never deserted at any hour of the night; and the presence in the city of evil designing persons, together with the difficulty of locomotion in the dark, makes it highly essential to the safety and comfort of the inhabitants of a city that its streets be properly lighted at nights." Or, again: "the corporation may, by virtue of its power to make and maintain streets, and by the power conferred upon it to do all necessary acts for the protection of the health of the community, construct sewers, drains and culverts in or upon the soil of the street, not only without compensation being made to the adjacent owners, but at their expense." A growing number of U.S. Supreme Court decisions agreed, helping to broaden specific applications of the police power to promote the general welfare. Still, the expansion most applicable to city planning efforts occurred on the state level. A handful of examples will suffice.[37]

One of the earliest and most significant outcomes of the waterworks cases was a lengthening of the urban reach in attempts to provide adequate and pure water supplies. By the early 1890s—much earlier in some states—court decisions had guaranteed that a city possessed the power to appropriate private property *beyond the city limits* to establish a system of waterworks. Those decisions had an enormous impact on provisions of other kinds of public utilities, including transportation, sewer systems, and electric lines. They also reinforced decisions that allowed cities to acquire land beyond city limits for park planning purposes. Finally, they encouraged planners to explore means of exerting control over suburban subdivisions that one day might become urban neighborhoods through annexation or consolidation and would certainly grow as part of the greater metropolitan area. By the early twentieth century, a number of planners presented schemes covering a metropolitan region, not just the city proper. The best known of these was the Chicago plan of 1909.[38]

In litigation over the uses of city streets—paving, laying water, gas, or sewer lines, and railway construction—courts were generally holding in favor of city authority by the last decade of the century. Similarly, courts tended to support the new building codes springing up around the nation. An 1891 Maryland case stated the matter concisely: "This is purely a police power, and we think it clear, this ordinance was passed in the exercise of *that power*. . . . The main purpose of the ordinance is to give the commissioners power to *control* the erection of *new buildings*, so that wherever such building, either by the character of the materials out of which, or the manner in which, it is proposed to be built, its location in the town, or the character of the business proposed to be carried on therein, would in their judgment be *detrimental* to the town, they may prevent its erection by refusing a permit." A few years later, the Massachusetts Supreme Court was even more blunt. In upholding a Boston ordinance governing the height and mode of building construction as a proper police power exercise, the court affirmed: "The right to make such regulations is too well established to be questioned." Private citizens challenged both decisions. In Maryland, the state court reversed itself; the Boston case made its way to the U.S. Supreme Court, which ruled in favor of the city's police powers.[39]

After a century of small beginnings, confusions, clarifications, retrenchings, redefinings, revivals, defeats, and successes, a more or less coherent body of urban law had emerged. At least in public health matters (broadly construed), the courts had opened the police power door wider. By the end of the nineteenth century, planning enthusiasts had also learned that whatever the legal principles espoused by treatise writers and courts, special legislation important to their goals more often than not remained the province of local decision making. That in itself was a measure of how far urban law had gone over the course of the century. Although the legal system still operated in a contradictory and confusing fashion, by the early years of the twentieth century city planning enthusiasts found ample reasons for hope. For many, that hope would become reality some years later in the most important decision ever involving the urban police power.[40]

In 1926 the Supreme Court decided a case called *Village of Euclid* v. *Ambler Realty Co.* Legal scholars tend to overuse the word "landmark," but in this instance the term is appropriate. The Court's decision stamped a constitutional seal of approval on municipalities' invocation of the police power to direct and control private uses of land. A local government need only demonstrate that its use of the police power was a "reasonable" effort to promote the health, safety, and comfort of the general public.[41]

From one legal standpoint—the convoluted evolution of police power doctrine—the decision appeared predictable and perhaps even historically consistent. From another—the doctrine of state sovereignty—the decision disclosed that shifts had occurred in the strata of judicial assumptions. The physical, economic, and social landscape of large American cities had matured considerably since the days of *Sharpless* and Dillon's Rule, generating a host of fresh challenges to conventional legal wisdom. A new generation of self-styled progressive urban reformers had articulated a philosophy of more direct government involvement in local affairs. Many judges had adopted the Freund view of the socially elastic nature of the police power. The *Euclid* decision revealed the extent to which some justices were willing to stretch the doctrine.

That case, and its immediate background, are the endpoint of our story about law, the municipal corporation, and the new urban culture.

A GEOMETRY OF PLANNING

In late November 1922 Associate Justice of the U.S. Supreme Court Oliver Wendell Holmes wrote a letter to his English friend of nearly half a century, Sir Frederick Pollock. Amidst literary observations about the commentators on Shakespeare and overly poetic translators of the Holy Bible, Holmes mentioned his recent decision in *Pennsylvania Coal Co. v. Mahon.* Holmes could not understand the dissenters: "everybody seeming to have misgivings about another [case] on the police power which I believe to be a compact statement of the real facts of the law and as such sure to rouse opposition for want of the customary soft phrases." In a subsequent letter, Holmes enclosed a copy of his decision and the dissent by Justice Louis Brandeis. Responding a few months later, Pollock observed "that if Brandeis' dissent were right the Fourteenth Amendment would be eviscerated: and your opinion exposes the fallacy of stretching police power to that extent in a very convincing fashion."[42]

As a conservative defender of private property, Holmes customarily held that whenever government wanted to control uses of private property by the owners, it should invoke its eminent domain powers. Thus, when reviewing his draft opinion on another case, his colleagues had to persuade him that "the petty larceny of the police power" was an injudicious phrase. In the *Pennsylvania Coal* case, writing for the majority of the court, Holmes was terse: "The general rule, at least, is that while property may be regulated to a certain extent, if regulation goes too far it will be recognized as a taking. . . . We are in danger of forgetting that a strong public desire to improve the public condition is not enough to warrant achieving the desire by a shorter cut than the constitutional way of paying for the change."[43]

In this instance the potential loss involved a single private house whose foundation might collapse if the company mined coal beneath adjacent land that it owned. The state legislature had prohibited, within city limits, any mining that might damage or destroy public or private structures. Employing the regulatory provisions of the police power doctrine, it had curtailed previously existing rights of property. In Holmes's view, the legislature had stretched its police powers too far. It had "taken" private property unconstitutionally from the coal company. Dissenting from the majority, Brandeis echoed a nineteenth-century line of reasoning that clearly separated the police power and eminent domain. He observed that every property regulation imposed by the police power deprived the owner of some rights. "But," he cautioned, "restriction imposed to protect the public health, safety, or morals from danger threatened is not a taking. . . . The state merely prevents the owner from making a use which interferes with paramount rights of the public." Such regulation did not require compensation.[44]

In one sense *Pennsylvania Coal* was an anomaly, the sole case in which the Supreme Court decided that an urban police power regulation actually was a "taking" of private property that required compensation under eminent domain proceedings. At the same time, the case served as the penultimate scene in a historical morality play that had run for many decades. "The fallacy of stretching police power," "customary soft phrases," "protect the public health, safety, or morals from danger threatened"—these phrases encapsulated opposite viewpoints in a longstanding dialogue in American law. The play's closing lines—*Euclid*—were uttered four years later.

The significance of *Euclid* lay not in its breathing life into zoning ordinances but in its authentication of the use of the police power. At face value, the issue involved nothing more than the disposition of sixty-eight acres of undeveloped land in a suburb of Cleveland. Serviced by the Lake Shore and Nickel Plate railroads on its northern border, the Village of Euclid (incorporated in 1903) stretched eastward from the edge of Cleveland for about three and one-half miles along the shore of Lake Erie. Although it had a population of nearly ten thousand, the village consisted into the early twenties mostly of farm land. The disputed acreage lay on the westerly edge of Euclid, between the Nickel Plate tracks and, about a third of a mile to the south, Euclid Avenue, a major commercial thoroughfare that ran from the center of Cleveland through an industrial, metropolitan community of more than a million people. Once it reached the eastern edge of Cleveland's central business district, however, the avenue gradually changed from a commercial to a purely residential street. Over a distance of a half-mile or more, set back from the avenue by double rows of trees, wide lawns, and magnificent gardens, and uninterrupted by cross streets, stood the imposing mansions of the wealthy. Labeling it "Millionaire's Row" and "Prosperity Street," contemporaries judged it the nation's most beautiful urban avenue. In 1911 a Cleveland real-estate firm, Ambler Realty Company, started to purchase land in the village, content to bide its time until Cleveland's industrial expansion eastward drove prices up and the land could be developed as factory sites. By the early 1920s the time appeared ripe. The Village of Euclid, however, had other ideas. [45]

In 1922 Euclid's mayor, taking advantage of new state enabling legislation, appointed a commission headed by James F. Metzenbaum, a village resident and a Cleveland lawyer, to draft a zoning ordinance. After six months of deliberation, including scrutiny of the 1916 New York City zoning legislation—the nation's first comprehensive ordinance—the village adopted its own scheme. That ordinance (closely following New York's) divided Euclid into height, area, and use districts that restricted the location of businesses, industries, and residences, the type of housing, the size and height of buildings, and the lot areas to be built upon. The hierarchy descended from single-family houses through two-family and apartment houses to mostly unrestricted industrial districts—six zones in all.

Ambler objected most strongly to the zoning of the area between Euclid Avenue and the railroads. On the south side of the avenue, nestled against and along a rolling ridge, were the homes of some of Cleveland's most prominent citizens. Undeveloped land stretched northward to the Nickel Plate line. On both the east and west sides of the disputed sixty-eight acres, Ambler and other developers had already sold lots with residential deed restrictions and had begun construction of houses. Now they wanted to build factories on the land in between. For at least a portion of that land, the village said "no." The ordinance divided the sixty-eight acres into three use districts. The first strip, fronting the north side of the avenue, was to contain only single-family and two-family dwellings. The second allowed apartment buildings. The third strip, holding the bulk of the acreage running northward to the railroad, permitted business and industrial establishments. In its suit, Ambler alleged a loss of several hundred thousand dollars if it could not develop its entire parcel for commercial and industrial purposes.[46]

As the case wound its way through the Ohio district court system and eventually to the Supreme Court of the United States, municipal officials and city planners across the nation eagerly awaited the outcome. Prior to the Supreme Court's acceptance of the case, the highest courts of eight states had already upheld the constitutionality of zoning. More than four hundred cities across the country, containing some 27 million citizens, feared that the outcome of the *Euclid* case might destroy their carefully laid plans for land-use control and development. Metzenbaum recalled that "it was recognized from coast to coast, that a defeat in this case, would cause all zoning ordinances in successive order throughout the land to fall, like a row of dominoes stood on end."[47]

The preamble to Euclid's ordinance stressed that the village was in a state of emergency, seeing its safety and health threatened by land uses inconsistent with its proposed plan of development. The mayor testified that "during all these many sessions that lasted for those many months, as to the relationship of the proposed map and ordinance to the safety, health and general welfare of the municipality, the health and welfare of the community was really the only question that was taken into consideration, and it was only along those lines that this Ordinance was gotten up and this map made out." Ambler responded that there were no socially reasonable grounds for the zoning classifications other than aesthetics.[48]

The issue was drawn. The village wanted to maintain its present character and avoid being swamped by the tides of metropolitan growth that had transformed many a small Lake Erie community into a grimy, industrial suburb. The realty company wanted to protect its investment, to make a reasonable profit, and to allow the "natural" flow of urban economic expansion to run its course. Invoking the eminent domain doctrine, the company sought appropriate compensation for damages, charged that the village had "taken" its land in violation of its Fourteenth Amendment rights, and demanded that the court strike down the legislation.

Judge David C. Westenhaver of the U.S. District Court for the Northern District of Ohio did so in January 1924, declaring that Euclid's ordinance violated both provisions of the Ohio constitution and the Fourteenth Amendment. The village could legally control the uses of Ambler's property only through its condemnation power under eminent domain and payment of just compensation. Westenhaver explicitly rejected Euclid's statement that it had properly employed its inherent police power right to promote the general health and safety of the entire community. "If police power meant what is claimed," noted the judge, "all private property is now held subject to temporary and passing phases of public opinion, dominant for a day in legislative or municipal assemblies." Clearly, Westenhaver observed, the authors of the ordinance understood neither the police power doctrine nor the true nature of property.[49]

The judge was confident that he knew the proper value and use of the land in question. With equal certitude, he discerned the "real" purpose behind the village's zoning legislation. Not content merely to render his decision, Judge Westenhaver expounded his social philosophy. The true object of Euclid's ordinance

was to place all the property in an undeveloped area of 16 square miles in a strait-jacket. The purpose to be accomplished is really to regulate the mode of living of persons who may hereafter inhabit it. In the last analysis, the result to be accomplished is to classify the population and segregate them according to their income or situation in life. . . . The true reason why some persons live in a mansion and others in a shack, why some live in a single-family dwelling and others in a double-family dwelling, why some live in a two-family dwelling and others in an apartment, or why some live in a well-kept apartment and others in a tenement, is primarily economic. It is a matter of income and wealth. . . .

The judge's tone and words made it clear that he would not approve an ordinance whose purpose was "furthering such class tendencies."[50]

Make no mistake: Westenhaver was no agitator for a redistribution of income, but a staunch defender of the status quo. He unquestioningly accepted the doctrine that the hidden forces of the marketplace should determine the direction of urban growth. Much

of Cleveland's Euclid Avenue was a thriving commercial thoroughfare; all evidence, stated the judge, showed that this should be "its
natural, obvious, and ultimate use within and beyond the village of
Euclid." Citing an earlier Supreme Court case as authority, the
judge delivered a truism: "There can be no conception of property
aside from its control and use, and upon its use depends its value."
The village of Euclid proposed an "unreasonable" use of property
within its borders. Stating that the property in question was private
property whose proposed usage did not fall under police power provisions, the judge declared Euclid's ordinance null and void. Despite the passage of time and changing circumstances, the spirit of
Dillon's Rule appeared as strong as ever. Appearances, though,
proved deceiving. [51]

The elders of Euclid were incensed at the district court decision,
as were advocates of planning and zoning around the nation. Westenhaver had realized that his would not be the final word, prophesying at the beginning of his decision: "This case is obviously
destined to go higher." On 27 January 1926 the Supreme Court
agreed to hear it. Although Metzenbaum presented the village's arguments, Edward Bassett, an early member of the National Conference on City Planning and the father of New York City's zoning
legislation, and Alfred Bettman, a Cincinnati lawyer and nationally
prominent leader of the planning and zoning movements, advised
him. The National Conference on City Planning, the National
Housing Association, the Massachusetts Federation of Town Planning Boards, and the Ohio State Conference on City Planning filed
amicus curiae briefs on Euclid's behalf. Newton D. Baker, former
reform mayor of Cleveland and secretary of war under Woodrow
Wilson, argued the case for the Ambler Company as he had done
before the district court. [52]

A LITTLE EUCLIDIAN SOCIAL GEOMETRY

The village's brief tried to elevate the problem to a lofty plane. The
issue "is really freed from the question of reasonableness or unreasonableness of the particular restriction and the subject really nar-
rows down to the sole and completely *legal* and *fundamental*
question as to whether there be a *constitutional power* to enact such
ordinances as the one in question." At stake was not the use of sixty-
eight acres, but the future of all zoning ordinances throughout the

nation—indeed, the future of all city planning efforts. Ambler's arguments, by contrast, struck toward the narrowest possible view. The real question "is whether Ordinance No. 2812 of the Village of Euclid, as amended, is a valid police regulation of the property of the appellee in the village." The realty company contended that "under the guise of the police power," the village had attempted regulations "which are unreasonable and confiscatory." In other words, in the absence of due process the village had cost Ambler money. But, not wanting to leave the matter there, the realty company borrowed a leaf from Judge Westenhaver's social homilies.

The community, Ambler asserted, simply wanted to enforce its "eccentric and supersensitive taste," to preserve the village council's "ideas of beauty," to forever "embed a fly in amber," at the expense of "natural" business expansion and at a high social cost to the lower-income members of the community. "By the obvious necessities of the case the territory between the two railroads will be industrially developed. All the people who live in the village and are not able to maintain single-family residences . . . are pressed down into the low-lying land adjacent to the industrial area, congested there in two-family residences and apartments and denied the privilege of escaping for relief to the ridge or lake." It made no social sense, urged Ambler, that "the lots on which the fewest people live are required to have the largest free area for light and air while those in which the most people live have minimum requirements for ventilation and light." Not only had the wealthy of Euclid deprived honest businessmen of their due profits; worse, they had literally denied the honest working people of the community their place in the sun.[53]

During the years immediately preceding *Euclid*, the Supreme Court had vigorously displayed its distaste for social legislation, especially in cases of government regulation of private property. Between 1920 and 1926 the Court had declared unconstitutional under the due process clause more economic and social legislation than in the previous fifty-two years of the Fourteenth Amendments's existence. Yet in the *Euclid* case the Court did a dramatic about-face. By a vote of six to three, it upheld the validity of the ordinance. It did so after an initial decision to uphold the lower court's ruling and after taking the extraordinary action of agreeing to rehear the case when Alfred Bettman appealed to his friend from Ohio, Chief Justice William Howard Taft.[54]

The Court reviewed the facts of the case from the district court record and found no reason to dispute them. Writing for the majority, Justice Sutherland agreed that the normal and reasonably expected use of Ambler's land along Euclid Avenue would be for general trade and commercial purposes, with the remaining acreage being developed for industry and trade. Nevertheless:

Until recent years, urban life was comparatively simple; but with the great increase and concentration of population, problems have developed, and constantly are developing, which require, and will continue to require, additional restrictions in respect of the use and occupation of private lands in urban communities.

Even half a century ago, wrote Sutherland, regulations that now appear necessary and wise would probably have fallen as arbitrary and oppressive. The meaning of constitutional guarantees never varies, but "the scope of their application must expand or contract to meet the new and different conditions which are constantly coming within the field of their operation. In a changing world, it is impossible that it should be otherwise." Regarded by contemporaries as a strict constructionist, Sutherland customarily ruled in favor of private enterprise. His invocation of social conditions showed that judicial assumptions about the urban use of the police power had changed dramatically over recent years.

Like jurists before him, Sutherland found that he could not determine the limits of the police power. The line that separated legitimate from illegitimate uses "varies with circumstances and conditions." If separating industrial establishments from residential areas was a proper exercise of the police power, Sutherland observed, it would not be easy to find a sufficient reason for denying that power, even though its use might divert the flow of industrial development from its normal channels. Clearly, drawing from nuisance doctrine, many past courts had sustained the police power right to exclude from residential areas offensive trades, structures, and industries likely to create nuisances.

Finally, the justice noted that no serious difference of opinion existed about the validity of past legislation setting the heights of buildings or construction materials, eliminating overcrowding, or dictating open space on lots to minimize the dangers of fire or collapse. He reviewed investigations by previous zoning commissions and state court decisions that broadly sustained the police power of zoning. Without knowing how much weight to give Euclid's social arguments, Sutherland nonetheless concluded that "at least, the reasons are sufficiently cogent to preclude us from saying, as it must be said before the ordinance can be declared unconstitutional, that such provisions are clearly arbitrary and unreasonable, having no substantial relation to the public health, safety, morals, or general welfare."[55]

The decision elated the advocates of zoning. Metzenbaum recalled that there was "rejoicing from coast to coast." Secretary of Commerce Herbert Hoover, whose special advisory committee had promulgated a standard state zoning enabling act in 1924, ordered copies of the decision for distribution the day after it was handed down. Before a year had passed, Pennsylvania, Texas, and New Jersey joined the swelling ranks of states with zoning legislation or zoning amendments to their constitutions. Courts in many states ruled that they would leave zoning details to the discretion of city councils as long as ordinances reasonably spoke to promotion of community health, safety, morals, and general public welfare. By the end of the twenties, three-fifths of the nation's urban population, dwelling in nearly eight hundred cities, lived under some type of zoning controls. Zoning's—and planning's—triumph appeared to be assured.[56]

Such was not to be the case, at least not for city planning. Its most ardent advocates had insisted since the inaugural National Conference on City Planning in 1909 that zoning was only one component of comprehensive planning. At the end of the twenties, Alfred Bettman reiterated that "the zone plan is that part of the city plan which relates to developments on private property, whereas the other parts of the city plan relate to public developments. The relationship of the two is so obvious and so integral, that there can be but one answer to the question of whether a good zone plan can be made without making it a part of a more comprehensive plan. There surely cannot." That was precisely the theme of his brief in support of Euclid's zoning ordinance before the Supreme Court. But as planning enthusiasts soon and sadly discovered, the authority to zone districts of a city for particular land-use purposes did not necessarily lead to comprehensive city planning. In their eagerness to employ the newly approved use of the police power, cities hastily enacted zoning legislation unfettered by comprehensive city plans.

Most of the zoning ordinances that now sprouted in city after city actually snarled rational planning efforts.[57]

The young urban philosopher Lewis Mumford, describing zoning as "the legal agent of intelligent city planning," warned against the widespread illusion that "zoning is an automatic relief for all the evils of unregulated or badly regulated city development." Zoning legislation principally served the interests of speculative financiers, he charged, perpetuating "the one function that all American cities have traditionally looked upon as the main end of human activity, namely, gambling in real estate." Rarely, in his opinion, did good city plans accompany the passage of zoning laws or emerge from their presence:

In sum, the zoning ordinances today have, like the city plans that were spawned between 1900 and 1910 [the heyday of "City Beautiful" plans], chiefly a decorative value. Used realistically, used in the best interests of the whole community, they would upset the speculative pyramid upon which American city development rests. Their present use is to keep that pyramid in equilibrium; and while this is their task, their practical applications are narrow, uncertain, and ineffectual.[58]

Coming at the issue from a businessman's point of view, George H. Coffin, Jr., head of the Los Angeles Realty Board, made much the same point: "Certain realtors and professional promoters seek the zoning of residential property for business in order to exploit it, pocket the false value created by the establishment of a business zone and depart, leaving a trail of depleted residential value in their wake." Although Coffin did not refer specifically to Euclid, the village's subsequent development supported his charge and held a note of irony. Following the hoopla of the 1920s, the community quietly evolved into a largely industrial suburb of Cleveland. Over time the village rezoned Ambler's original sixty-eight acres. By the end of the 1950s, General Motors owned the land. Whether at birth or in maturity, zoning and planning seldom walked hand-in-hand.[59]

Those able and willing to admit the shortcomings of zoning were few. Largely ignored also was Judge Westenhaver's prophecy. Whatever intent underlay his social geometry, the justice forecast a use of the police power that reached beyond regulation to regimentation of the entire social order. Reflecting upon an earlier Supreme Court zoning decision, Westenhaver remarked: "The blighting of property values and the congesting of population, whenever the colored or certain foreign races invade a residential section, are so well known as to be within the judicial cognizance." Time underscored his point. Skin color and ethnic heritage, no less than wealth or income, would become valid reasons for zoning legislation. "To regulate the mode of living"; "to classify the population and segregate them according to their income or situation in life"; "furthering such class tendencies"—those were his predictions.[60]

The warnings of this judicial Cassandra, like his restrictive interpretation of the police power doctrine, fell on deaf ears. However cautiously worded, the Supreme Court's approval of Euclid's social geometry seemed sweeping enough to warrant its widespread adoption by municipalities across the nation. By 1926 the decades of attempts to highlight the shadowy reach of the police power appeared at an end. After nearly a century of wrangles over eminent domain and police power doctrines, public works and planning enthusiasts seemed to have won. The next fifty years,—beyond the scope of our story here—would reveal the limitations of the victory.

Nevertheless, a body of urban law had evolved to serve as a blueprint for the construction of the rising city culture. As that body of law took shape, so did several new professions bent on challenging and coping with the changing physical and cultural environments of the cities. At the forefront of urban reformers intent on creating a culture of planning stood sanitarians, landscape architects, and municipal engineers. The new professionals hailed each new legal decision as one more step along the road to bettering their cities. They gradually found their way through the corridors of the temple of law, but devoted far more time and energy to learning about the nature of the urban system through surveys and investigations. On the basis of their findings as well as their own value judgments, they proposed new techniques and new technologies to improve the public health and public morals of urban Americans. They became intent on sanitizing the cities.

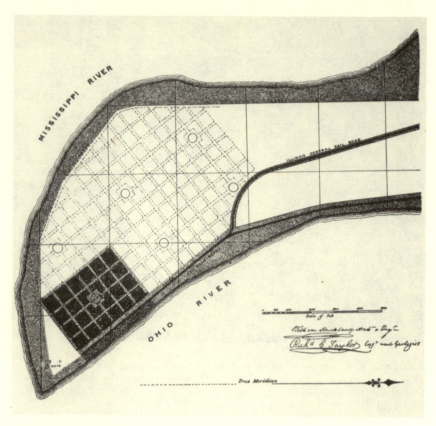

FIGURE 1. Plan of Cairo, Illinois, by William Strickland, 1838. In John M. Lansden, *A History of the City of Cairo, Illinois* (Chicago, 1910). Courtesy State Historical Society of Wisconsin.

FIGURE 2. Early radio-concentric plan of Circleville, Ohio; first laid-out in 1810. From a painting by G. W. Wittich (1870) in Williams Brothers, *The History of Franklin and Pickaway Counties, Ohio* (Cleveland, 1880). Courtesy State Historical Society of Wisconsin.

FIGURE 3. Gillette's proposal for huge apartment houses or hotels to house the population of Metropolis. King C. Gillette, *The Human Drift* (Boston, 1894). Courtesy State Historical Society of Wisconsin.

FIGURE 4. Gillette's plan for the garden-like environment surrounding the residential quarters of the citizens of Metropolis. In Gillette, *Human Drift*.

FIGURE 5. Cellular distribution of buildings in Gillette's Metropolis, with apartment houses in groups of six, served by educational buildings (A), amusement buildings (B), and food storage and preparation buildings (C). In Gillette, *Human Drift*.

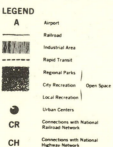
FIGURE 6. "Metropolis of Tomorrow" proposed by Victor Gruen, 1964, in his *The Heart of Our Cities: The Urban Crisis: Diagnosis and Cure* (New York, 1964). Printed with permission of Simon and Schuster.

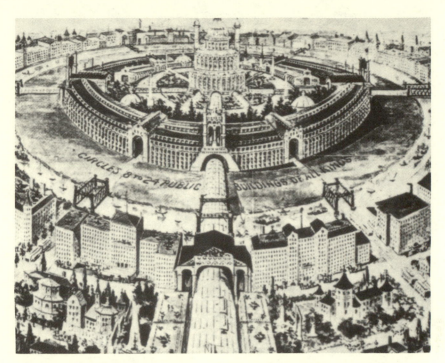

FIGURE 7. Sketch of center of "New Era" Model City. In Charles W. Caryl, *New Era: Presenting the Plans for the New Era Union to Help Develop and Utilize the Best Resources of This Country* (Denver, 1897). Courtesy State Historical Society of Wisconsin.

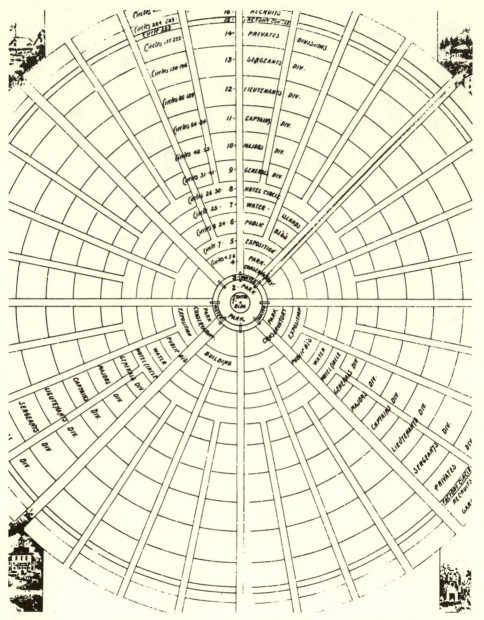

FIGURE 8. Concentric Circle Plan of "New Era" Model City. In Caryl, *New Era*.

FIGURE 9. View of the proposed civic center plaza and buildings. In Daniel H. Burnham and Edward H. Bennett, *Plan of Chicago* (Chicago, 1909). Courtesy State Historical Society of Wisconsin.

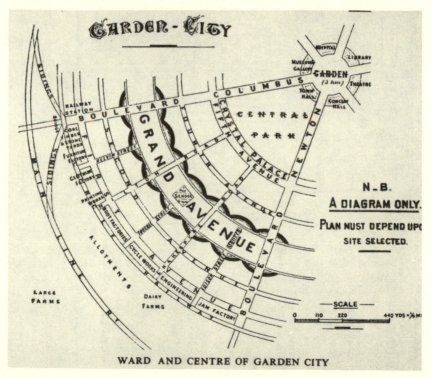

FIGURE 10. Center section of Ebenezer Howard's "Garden City." In his *Garden Cities of To-Morrow* (London, 1902). Courtesy State Historical Society of Wisconsin.

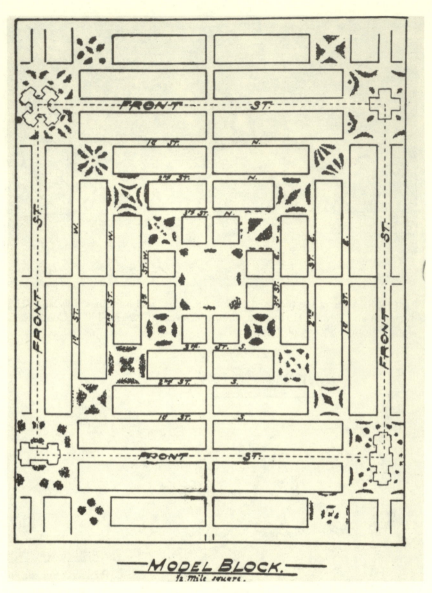

FIGURE 11. Model residential block, a neighborhood unit plan which anticipated the "superblock" design favored by numerous twentieth-century urban planners. In C. W. Wooldridge, *Perfecting the Earth: A Piece of Possible History* (Cleveland, 1902). Courtesy State Historical Society of Wisconsin.

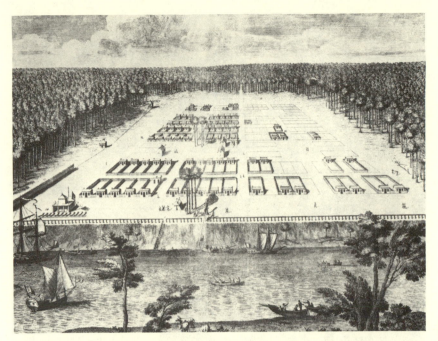

FIGURE 12. Neighborhood unit plan of Savannah, Georgia, 1734. Drawn by Peter Gordon. In *A View of Savannah as it stood the 29th of March, 1734* (London, 1734). Courtesy State Historical Society of Wisconsin.

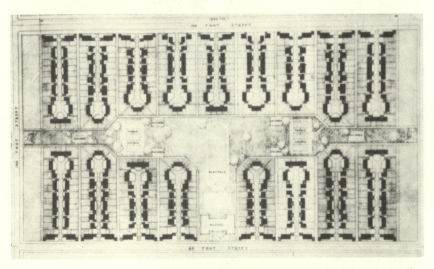

FIGURE 13. Theoretical study of "superblock," 1928, which became the basis of the Radburn, New Jersey Plan. In Clarence S. Stein, *Toward New Towns for America*, rev. ed. (Cambridge, Mass., 1957). Reprinted with the permission of the M.I.T. Press.

FIGURE 14. Dead horse in city street, 1850s. In author's personal collection.

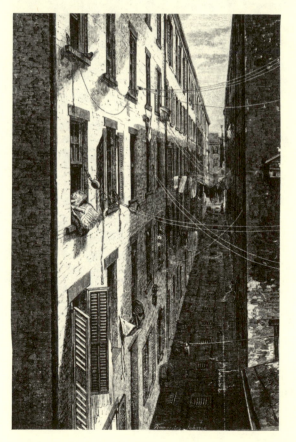

FIGURE 15. View of "Gotham Court," typical wooden tenements, New York City, 1860s. In *Report of the Council of Hygiene and Public Health of the Citizens' Association of New York, upon the Sanitary Condition of the City*, 2d ed., (New York, 1866). Courtesy Middleton Health Sciences Library, University of Wisconsin-Madison.

FIGURE 16. *View of Central Park, New York City, 1863,* Drawn by John Bachman, published by F. Heppenheimer. In author's personal collection.

FIGURE 17. Sunday recreation in Forest Park, St. Louis. In *Annual Report of the Park Department. City of Saint Louis. . . 1901.* Copy in author's personal collection.

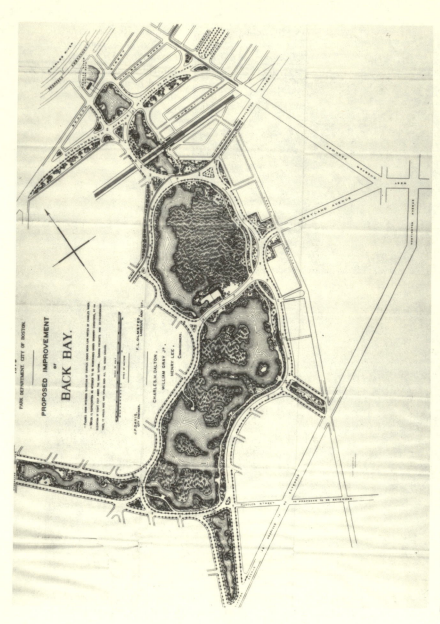

FIGURE 18. Olmsted Plan for Back Bay Fens, Boston, 1879. In *Annual Report of the Boston Park Commissioners, 1879* (Boston, 1879). Copy in author's personal collection.

FIGURE 19. The "Wonderous Dreamland" of the White City, Chicago, 1893. In *The Magic City: Massive Portfolio of Original Photographic Views of the Great World's Fair and Its Treasures of Art, Including a Vivid Representation of the Famous Midway Plaisance*, vol. 1, no. 2 (Philadelphia, 1894). Copy in author's personal collection.

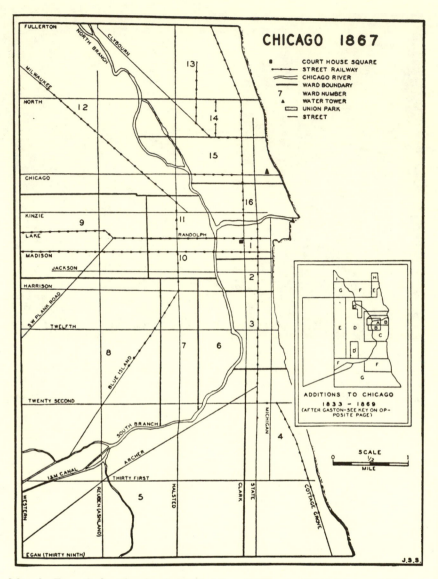

MAP 1. From Rufus Blanchard, *Guide Map of Chicago,* 1867 (Chicago, 1867). Copy in author's personal collection.

PART THREE

SANITIZING THE CITY

They that be whole need not a physician,
but they that are sick.

St. Matthew 9:12

5

THE UNHEALTHY CITY

CONSIDER TWO CITY dwellers. Although fictional, their lives are composites of the experiences of thousands of nineteenth-century urban Americans. They are workingmen, home owners, family men.

The first, a carpenter residing in Pittsburgh in the 1840s, is about to leave home for the day's work. After making a trip to his backyard privy and filling the water bucket for his wife from a nearby pump, he steps into the street fronting his house and sinks into the mire brought by last night's rain. Shaking a sodden mixture of dung, garbage, and mud from his boots, he heads down the street, dodges two omnibuses converging from opposite directions, and threads his way among passersby, horse-drawn wagons, and children walking to school. Although the morning is sunny, a pall of dust from unpaved streets and coal soot from small manufactories darkens the air; he coughs when taking a deep breath. Gazing at the school-bound youths, he reflects on the recent death of the youngest of his four children: "Typhus," the doctor had declared. The carpenter had accepted her death as God's will and as a familiar fact of life. With equal resignation, he accepted the stench and filth of his surroundings. He would, if asked to predict the future, express certainty that tomorrow would be like today, and that his city, though becoming larger and more populous, would remain smelly, dirty, and disease-ridden. He might not like it, but he anticipated no great change in the rhythms of his life.

By contrast, look at our second subject. He is a steel mill foreman in the same city in 1910. Like his grandfather, he lives in one of the better working-class districts. Unlike him, our foreman enjoys the amenities of indoor plumbing, clean water, gas for indoor lighting and cooking, and paved streets relatively clear of refuse piles reeking of manure. The air he breathes is often soot-filled, and on his journey to and from work aboard an electric trolley, he passes through rotting neighborhoods. But he expects the local health board to attack these problems soon. Last year's massive street-cleaning campaign had demonstrated what the city fathers could accomplish when pushed into action. This morning's newspaper quotes the superintendent of public health as promising an extensive citywide survey of housing and sanitary conditions. Although he worries about his children's health, he knows that typhoid fever, yellow fever, and cholera no longer freely stalk the city's streets, at least not in his neighborhood. To be sure, his community is no hygienic utopia. Thousands of his fellow citizens still live with poverty, filth, and disease as their daily lot. Yet, considering the improvements within his own lifetime, he looks forward to a cleaner and healthier tomorrow for his children and his children's children.

Over the years from the 1840s to the first decade of the twentieth century, a major shift in attitudes, expectations, and policies had occurred. How, over the span of a single lifetime, did such a momentous change take place?

THE RISE OF MORAL ENVIRONMENTALISM

The answers point to several independent but concurrent sources. First, debates within the medical profession about the nature, causation, and transmission of disease among urban populations gave rise to new theories about the physical environment that gradually became conventional wisdom. Second, urban critics discovered connections between the quality of the physical environment and the bodily and moral health of citizens, leading to new investigations of the sanitary problems of cities undergoing transition from commercial to industrial manufacturing centers. Some of the investigators pooled information and joined in demands for more governmental action. A new profession, that of the sanitarian, slowly evolved, becoming fully professionalized after the Civil War years. Third, urban businessmen, city boosters, and local politicians started to voice concerns about the impact of contagious diseases on urban economic growth. Later in the century, a fourth element emerged. New medical techniques joined with new technologies of public works construction to publicize the possibility of achieving healthier cities. Throughout the century these forces merged, giving rise to sanitary campaigns to clean up the cities of the present while planning new physical environments to ensure the cleanliness (and, many believed, the godliness) of the cities of the future.

Each deserves our attention. But first we have to explore certain intellectual caverns of nineteenth-century thought.

Underlying the sanitary campaigns, as well as other reform efforts, was an attitudinal bedrock that surfaced as part of the eruption of the century's new urban culture. A striking characteristic of nineteenth-century urban reform campaigns was the moral tone of their public rhetoric. Critics of the changing conditions of life in the cities began to abandon the old religious concept of innate depravity and turned toward a new explanation of human ills and evils. We might call this new set of assumptions about human nature the gospel of moral environmentalism. It carried the conviction that if one altered the physical environment, the moral seasons were certain to change as well.

Especially from the early 1830s on, urban reformers attacking a host of different social problems increasingly relied upon environmental explanations of the causes of human degradation. One of the pioneers of modern urban social work, Joseph Tuckerman, observed that "in all times cities have been the centers of the moral corruption of countries," and would so continue until men found a scientific way to break the environmental cycle of poverty. The Unitarian minister William Ellery Channing, whose writings and sermons circulated widely throughout antebellum urban America, asked: "Why is it that so many children in a large city grow up in ignorance and vice? Because that city abandons them to ruinous influences, from which it might and ought to rescue them." The generation of educational reformers who created the nation's first urban public school systems likewise trumpeted the strains of moral environmentalism. "In the byways and crowded streets of a city, where poverty casts its victims into heaps, and stows them away in cellars and garrets, . . . it often happens that the surface disease of coarse and untamed manners is aggravated and made virulent by moral distempers within," noted Horace Mann. In the changed urban landscape, with its growing tenement and slum districts—hotbeds of disease and vice—Mann claimed, not even "the purest virtue can secure happiness, or an immunity from danger." He warned that "the favored classes may think they occupy favored apartments in the ship but, if it does founder, the state will go down with the steerage." Whether discussing the insane, the infirm, or the criminal classes, practitioners of medicine and "moral science" (an early form of psychology) too stressed that the physical environment all but determined human moral behavior.[1]

Moral environmentalism suffused the social vocabulary of the new urban culture taking shape in antebellum America. To be sure, not all observers of the bustling cities accepted it; nor did all those reformers urging environmental explanations articulate them to the exclusion of all other arguments. But the seductiveness of the concept for many urban reformers was undeniable. Appeals to reason, moral behavior, and religious dogmas failed to alter human actions substantially. Those who believed in human nature as the root of social misbehavior had little recourse but prayer, hope, and, as often pursued, punitive legislation.

Those who believed that nurture could overcome nature, however, reveled in the courses of action open to them. If the physical environment strongly influenced moral behavior, genuine social change was possible. Human action could alter the face of the city and reshape the moral health of the urban populace.

THE PERILS OF POLLUTION

One could not walk the streets or breathe the stultifying atmosphere of a classroom, retail store, small factory, or even one of the better homes in a growing nineteenth-century city and remain unaware of the insults to health daily encountered by all classes of people.

Aroused citizens, no less than preachers of the gospel of moral environmentalism, vigorously complained about five particular perils: epidemics; the unsavory condition of city streets; the ways in which cities disposed of garbage, wastewater, and animal wastes (human and otherwise); increasing air pollution; and the seemingly sudden appearance of slum housing districts.

The clearest threats to health were the waves of epidemics that irregularly yet frequently swept American cities. Although contemporaries were unable to compile precise morbidity and mortality statistics for every city, the figures they did have were frightening. Over the first six decades of the century, urban death rates from all diseases apparently rose dramatically. Between 1815 and 1839 the average annual death rate of all citizens in Boston, New York, Philadelphia, and New Orleans combined was 28.1 per thousand of population; from 1840 to 1860 the rate climbed to 30.2 per thousand. If one looked at the cities individually, the figures were even more startling. Cholera claimed nearly 150 victims per thousand residents of New Orleans in 1832; yellow fever killed more than 80 per thousand in 1847; together the two diseases took more than 100 per thousand in 1853. In 1849 more than 55 people per thousand died of cholera in Chicago; five years later typhoid fever and cholera killed more than 60 per thousand. In the nation's largest city, the crude death rates rose from around 21 per thousand in 1810 to over 37 per thousand by the close of the 1850s, a jump of nearly 80 percent. Similar reports involving pneumonia, smallpox, tuberculosis, scarlet fever, and intestinal disorders came from other cities over the period. [2]

Of the *daily* problems confronting city dwellers, few were more obvious than the condition of the streets. In the late 1840s Chicago's muddy streets and sidewalks were covered by wooden planks: "Under these planks the water was standing on the surface over three-fourths of the city, and as the sewers from the houses were emptied under them, a frightful odour was emitted in summer, causing fevers and other diseases, foreign to the climate." Not infrequently "a loose plank would give way under the weight of a passing cab, when the foul water would spurt into the air high as the windows." In New York, as a newspaperman put it, "with the exception of a very few thoroughfares, all the streets are one mass of reeking, disgusting filth, which in some places is piled to such a height as to render them almost impassable by vehicles." In Charleston, the South's social capital, a committee complained in the late 1850s about the omnipresent filth and refuse, "with the morning sun beating down on it and disengaging the foetid emanations from streets, alleyways and courts, the poisonous gases of putrifying animals and vegetable matter passing into the atmosphere to the injury of every section of the city, and all classes of society." [3]

Garbage collection remained a province of private companies and was spotty at best. Despite ordinances in many cities requiring property owners to clean their frontage areas, urban streets stood thoroughly mired. New York "householders swept as often as they pleased; and for the matter of being carried away, the dirt often remained in heaps several days; or rather the heaps were trodden and scattered about again; and required to be swept and collected anew." In southern cities at mid-century, turkey vultures and cattle served as inexpensive garbage collectors. Even into the 1860s herds of swine roamed the streets of Cincinnati and New York performing similar scavenger duties.[4]

Stratagems for dealing with these problems filled the pages of sanitarian publications during the 1860s and 1870s. Lamenting the waste involved in dumping garbage and offal into the sea, a New York sanitarian, Jackson S. Schultz, suggested in 1875 that with their daily refuse the 60,000 families of Manhattan could each support one pig. He proposed that the city furnish swill barrels into which householders could dump their garbage, lease or buy an island in Long Island Sound, assign to work there "such able-bodied paupers as are now eating the bread of idleness," and there shelter and feed 60,000 swine. The results, he predicted, would be the removal of scavenger swine from city streets, a cost-efficient refuse collection system, and a ready supply of fresh pork for every urban family. To the objection that "no doubt hogs would eat city garbage and dead horses, but who would eat the hogs?" Schultz responded that Americans were already eating garbage-fed swine and that hogs "were made constitutionally to become the scavengers of mankind." His plan did not bring home the bacon.[5]

For the better part of the century, most cities across the nation rid themselves of garbage, refuse, wastewater, and human wastes in ways their eighteenth-century predecessors would have found familiar. Nearby farmers purchased a considerable amount of the cities' garbage, street sweepings, stable manure, and offal for use as fertilizer and animal feed. As late as 1880, for example, Boston sold farmers over 26,000 loads of offal (400–500 cubic feet per load) a year. San Antonio burned "street dirt" within the city limits; Houston used it as land-fill for "low places in the suburbs"; Topeka sold it to farmers; Kansas City threw it into the Missouri River to float away; San Francisco dumped it directly into the bay; and Galveston city workers buried it at night beneath the sands of the public bathing beach.[6]

Urbanites did not consider wastewater a recyclable resource. They poured it on the ground or into a dry well or cesspool. Nineteenth-century cesspools were a far cry from the modern watertight containers. Customarily they were holes in the ground lined with broken stones or chunks of brick. Continuous seepage of polluted wastewater was common.[7]

Disposal of human wastes proved a more difficult problem. In some communities householders dumped their wastes into cesspools. More commonly, they deposited excrement in privy vaults located in the dirt cellars of houses or in backyards. Like the cesspools, the privies leaked their contents into the soil, saturating and polluting urban lands. Nor were the vaults' capacities extensive. They had to be cleaned or replaced frequently. Earlier in the century, when urban land was relatively abundant, many citizens simply filled up the vaults, covered them with dirt, and dug new ones. Later, that practice no longer sufficed. Most cities passed legislation requiring householders to pay private entrepreneurs to empty the privy vaults periodically. By mid-century, a few of the largest cities either assigned city employees or contracted with private firms to clear the vaults at public expense.[8]

Whether privately or publicly paid, workmen either cleaned the vaults by hand, employing shovels and buckets, or, as the century wore on, used a pumping mechanism inappropriately called an "odorless-evacuator." After emptying the vaults, they carted away the wastes, leaving behind opened vaults whose odors were less than appealing and, since the barrels were rarely tightly hooped and the workmen were usually careless, waste trails. To lessen the latter nuisance, most cities enacted ordinances stating that privies should be cleaned only at night, apparently in the hope that by dawn's early light property owners would have swept up the wastes in front of their homes or businesses. Yet the waste trails remained. In seaports and cities near lakes and rivers, privy cleaners often dumped their loads directly into the water; elsewhere, they would haul their cargo beyond the city's boundaries and simply deposit it on the land. Sometimes nearby "truck" farmers purchased the wastes for use as fertilizer. Given the practice of nighttime emptying, these wastes became known as "night soil." As late as 1880, a cosmopolitan city like Brooklyn, with over 25,000 privy vaults in use, reported the application of 20,000 cubic feet of "night soil" each year to "farms and gardens outside the city."[9]

Disposal of human excrement was merely part of the problem. Horses remained the principal source of transit power throughout the century. Owners of horses who died in harness quite often simply cut the traces and left the dead beasts to rot in the streets for days or weeks until collected by a city offal cart (see Figure 14).

Early in the present century Chicago yearly removed almost 10,000 horse carcasses from its streets. Even more troublesome were the tons of manure clogging the streets. Sanitary experts estimated that each healthy city horse dropped an average of twenty-two pounds of manure a day. In a city like Milwaukee, with a horse population of 12,500 in 1907, the streets received 133 tons of manure per day, an average of three-quarters of a pound of manure for every resident. In addition to boosting the fly and mosquito populations, posing a health hazard, and fouling the air, animal excrement made the simple act of crossing a street an unpleasant adventure. Inadequate or nonexistent paving only made things worse, especially during the wet seasons, when human and animal traffic churned dirt streets into manure-filled mudholes. [10]

While the disposal problems of wastewater and human and animal excrement mounted, so did concerns about a perceived and perceptible rise in air pollution. Although medical science could not prove the harmful effects of polluted air, a growing number of mid-century reformers suspected that foul air and inadequate circulation increased the incidence of various diseases. Allegedly harmful miasmas or vapors arose from swampy or damp places, backyard privies, and the streets; and the air was further "vitiated" or "poisoned" by poor circulation in the ever more crowded urban environment. The iron hooves of horses pulverized the garbage and manure of the streets into a fine dust that soiled clothing and choked lungs. As the number of small manufacturing establishments increased, so did the soot and smog in the atmosphere. A major iron and steel city like Pittsburgh or a railroad center like Chicago experienced heavy air pollution. But even a smaller community like Atlanta, with its guano and fertilizer plants and its slaughterhouses, suffered. [11]

Among all the perils of environmental pollution, burgeoning tenement and slum districts provoked the greatest amount of public discussion, which reached a high pitch in the late 1840s and the 1850s. The sudden influx into the cities of large numbers of unskilled native workers and foreign indigents put heavy demands on the supply of available housing. Real estate owners and speculators seized the opportunity to meet the housing needs of the newcomers and, at the same time, line their own pockets. They transformed former mansions, warehouses, and abandoned factories into crowded and unsanitary living quarters. Boardinghouse owners subdivided their buildings into immigrant flats rented by the week at costs far exceeding their quality. In alleyways speculators erected new structures, three and four stories high, with twenty to thirty tiny apartments lining narrow, sunless passages (see Figure 15).

The foulest slums arose on whatever vacant spots remained behind or beside old buildings. The tenements, sheds, and shanties utilized every inch of space. The immigrant poor squeezed into attics less than three feet high, and into cellar apartments lacking both light and fresh air. Boston investigators in 1849 described the Broad Street-Fort Hill district as "a perfect hive of human beings, without comforts and mostly without common necessities." There, crammed together "like brutes, without regard to sex, or age, or sense of decency," investigators observed "grown men and women sleeping together in the same apartment, and sometimes wife and husband, brothers and sisters, in the same bed." Could there be any doubt, wondered sympathetic Bostonians, that "under such circumstances, self-respect, forethought, all high and noble virtues soon die out, and sullen indifference and despair, or disorder, intemperance and utter degradation reign supreme?" Not only did they offend middle-class sensibilities, but there appeared to be little doubt about the health hazards posed by the tenements.[12]

Growing concern about the slums, air pollution, waste disposal, the condition of city streets, and especially epidemics contributed to changing public expectations about the role of government in citizens' daily lives. When voting on expenditures for public improvements—common schools or street paving, for instance—many mid-century urbanites proved reluctant to expand governmental intrusion into the private sector. But the realm of public health saw an increasing tendency to expect and even demand some sort of action by local government. One example was the creation of public health boards. Yet that very example illustrated many of the difficulties encountered by reformers eager to clean up the unhealthy city of the present and to plan the healthier city of tomorrow.

HEALTH BOARDS AND CITY POLITICS

Periodic epidemics were in large measure responsible for such health ordinances and local health boards as existed in American cities prior to the Civil War. Most local health laws, carryovers from the eighteenth century, dealt with smallpox or quarantines of one type or another. Before the enactment of a comprehensive public health act in New York City in 1866, no American city possessed a systematic health code. Still, boards of health had come into being: New York led the way in 1796, followed by Baltimore (1798), Boston (1799), Charleston (1815), New Orleans and Philadelphia (1818), and Providence (1832). By the eve of the Civil War, some type of agency designed to monitor or eliminate health nuisances existed in most large urban centers.[13]

For the most part, despite their ostensibly broad powers, the boards were impotent. In New York and most other large cities, they were the playthings of party politics. Usually, the boards consisted of the mayor and some or all of the city councilmen, so that membership revolved with each election and administrative continuity was rarely possible. Most urban Americans placed little faith in the disinterested benevolence of their elected officials, and with good cause. In mid-century New York City, for example, a journalist suggested that the best way to get the board of health to enforce street-cleaning ordinances was to collect funds and bribe the city councilmen. When cholera struck that metropolis in the early sixties, Mayor Fernando Wood refused to call together the health board on the grounds that the aldermen who served on it were more dangerous to the city than was the disease itself.[14]

Mid-century Chicago, like many smaller communities, depended on unpaid volunteers for enforcement of scanty sanitary ordinances. Only in a crisis like the onslaught of an epidemic did those whose "public opinion" mattered—the urban elites of business and professional men—encourage the boards of health to engage in broad preventive medicine measures. Then, almost any action that might rid the city of pestilence gained approval. When the crisis ended, the "public" expected the boards to dissolve (which happened in many cities) or at least to recede into the background, emerging occasionally to exercise some control over the water supply, the burial of the dead, or the piles of filth in the streets.[15]

Rarely did the boards include physicians, although some served as occasional advisors. Politicians concerned primarily with self-preservation and fearful of confessing their own inadequacies were loath to take advice from their medical consultants, particularly if that advice ran counter to the expressed interests of constituents in the precincts and wards. In large part, medical men had their own internal professional squabbles to blame for their exclusion. The degree to which physicians battled among themselves about the causes and treatment of various diseases was equaled only by the arrogance with which they announced their opinions to the public and denounced the findings of their colleagues.

The urban populace had almost no notion of which group of physicians to believe. As one sanitarian lamented: "The public cares little, whether Dr. Sangrado is pitied by Dr. Bolus, or if Dr. Allopathy sneers at Dr. Homeopathy." During the cholera epidemic in Cincinnati in the late 1840s, strife between homeopathic and regular physicians brought about replacement of the board, originally composed entirely of medical men, with one that included a liquor dealer, a lawyer, a newspaper editor, a preacher, and a mechanic. Legislation establishing a board of health in New Orleans in 1848 specified that physicians could not constitute a majority of the membership. In 1860 the Chicago City Council dissolved the board of health and turned its few duties over to the police department. For most of the decade that city had no health board at all. [16]

Self-criticism by physicians mounted during the 1840s. Dr. H. H. Childs warned a beginning class of medical students in 1844 not to be surprised "that intelligent men extend to the profession a hesitating and doubtful confidence, when educated physicians differ so widely among themselves, avowing the most opposite views, both in theory and practice. . . . That 'Doctors disagree,' has passed into a proverb." Some physicians discerned that the public distrusted their profession not only because of its internal squabbles but also because most doctors paid no attention to prevention of disease. About 1845 Edward Jarvis, a prominent Boston physician, charged his fellows with employing themselves "solely with sickness, debility or injury—with diminution of life in some of its forms. But with health, with fullness or unalloyed, unimpaired life, we professionally have nothing to do." [17]

The political nature of the boards and the absence of reliable medical information meant that prior to the 1870s most had little success in enforcing statutes designed to promote the public health. In turn, public health reformers mistrusted both the announcements and the actions of local health boards. When reviewers complained about the illiteracy of health board reports and the glaring lack of facts about sanitary conditions, reformers nodded their heads in agreement. While the evidence of disease and unsanitary practices was visible to any observer, hard information enlivened by sound medical interpretation appeared nonexistent.[18]

A review of medical practice and debates within the profession suggests nineteenth-century medicine hindered as much as it helped the treatment of the unhealthy city.

MEDICINE AND MIASMAS

It is impossible to speak of *the* medical profession in mid-nineteenth-century America. Those professing medical knowledge ranged from outright charlatans to graduates of the best medical schools and contributors to the leading medical journals.

At the top of the profession were individuals who could afford to go to college, to medical school, then on to Europe for advanced training. These physicians, usually living in the largest cities along the eastern seaboard, had the most lucrative practices and customarily held the medical professorships. In the profession's lower ranks were barely literate men who had, perhaps, attended a few medical lectures before proclaiming themselves doctors and entering practice in the hope of supplementing the income from their regular jobs. The bulk of physicians had probably attended a medical school; many had graduated, and others had received licenses from either a medical society approved by the state legislature or a state-appointed medical board. Graduation from a medical college and licensure, however, were no indication of medical ability. A man with a grammar school education could gain admittance to any but the most elite of medical schools, attend one or two sessions of lectures, pay the appropriate fees, and receive a diploma allowing him to practice medicine. State requirements for licensing physicians became so farcical that, by the early 1860s, nearly every state had abandoned the process. Many a graduate, licensee, or self-proclaimed doctor was virtually without medical knowledge or skill.[19]

Among those physicians who were well versed in the state of their art, there was little in the way of therapeutic agreement. The middle third of the century saw some slackening in traditional "heroic" treatments—bloodletting, cathartics to regulate and restore "normal" bodily emissions, emetics to purge the body. In their place came a gradual acceptance of the therapeutics of "natural recovery." Physicians began to talk about the "self-limiting" nature of most ills and the need to aid natural recovery by prescribing rest, a slight change in diet, and small doses of an appropriate drug. Some doctors came to define "appropriate" on the basis of "scientific" clinical experimentation.[20]

Between these two extremes of medical thought lay a world of daily treatments in which most physicians used whatever therapeutic approach appeared to work or whatever one their patients demanded. Such practitioners vigorously debated competing medical theories in public and denounced the methods used by other doctors. New challenges to the practices of regular medicine—such as Thomsonianism, homeopathy, and hydropathy—only heightened disagreements within the profession and further confused a bewildered public. By mid-century, journals like the *Cincinnati Medical Observer* could note: "It has become fashionable to speak of the Medical Profession as a body of jealous, quarrelsome men, whose chief delight is in the annoyance and ridicule of each other." Elisha Bartlett, whose treatise on fevers had earned him national recognition, publicly admitted in 1848 what many of his colleagues privately acknowledged: "The hold which medicine has so long had upon the popular mind is loosened; there is a widespread skepticism as to its power of curing diseases, and men are everywhere to be found who deny its pretentions as a science and reject the benefits and blessings which it proffers them as an art."[21]

Having little scientific knowledge of the causes of disease, physicians emphasized symptomatic treatment. Not until the end of the nineteenth century would a preponderance of American physicians be familiar with and accept a new germ theory of disease causation that would alter their therapeutical practices.[22]

Before the 1870s, medical men, even the most learned, were usually uncertain about whether specific diseases were endemic (indigenous to a particular locale or population) or epidemic (introduced into a locale or population by some foreign agent and affecting many at the same time). Endemic diseases included malaria ("the ague"), dysentery ("the bloody flux"), chronic diarrhea, pulmonary tuberculosis ("consumption"), influenza, pneumonia, and cholera infantum (an intestinal disorder fatal to most children and having nothing to do with cholera). Epidemic diseases, which struck far more terror into the urban populations than those listed above, were cholera, yellow fever, smallpox, typhus, diphtheria, typhoid fever, and scarlet fever. The last three had become such familiar problems by the 1870s that physicians and the public seemed inclined to accept them as endemic disorders about which little could be done.[23]

During the first third of the century, most physicians regarded the bulk of diseases—endemic and epidemic— as stemming from sthenic ("strengthened") conditions of the body, abnormally stimulated states of the vital organs. Swollen limbs, reddened tissue, high fevers, extreme pain: all indicated an overexcited condition, to be countered by heroic measures. By mid-century, however, a growing number of practitioners had begun to describe the symptoms of certain diseases of both types, even some of the fevers, as asthenic ("weakened"). Patients displayed weak pulses, often low temperatures, and a generally enfeebled condition. Physicians debated whether previous diagnoses had been incorrect, or whether a change had taken place in the very nature of the diseases afflicting the American population.[24]

Medical literature of the 1850s and 1860s, in both Britain and the United States, posited a "change-of-type" theory. The version most popular in the United States argued not that the nature of disease had altered, but rather that constitution of the human body had. Some physicians affirmed that both diseases and physical constitutions had changed. As one southern theorist observed: "Constitutions, and habits of life, and modes of living are constantly changing; hence new diseases are making their appearance from time to time, while others have vanished from the world." Physicians and knowledgeable laymen began to concur that present-day Americans were more susceptible than their parents or grandparents had been to diseases of all kinds. But what could have caused such a radical alteration in bodily constitutions?[25]

The most common answer was the physical environment of the city. As the urban population swelled, citizens' ability to avoid disease contracted. All ages and classes fell prey to the debilitating effects of living in an ever more congested city. In 1845 the Massachusetts educator Horace Mann, reasonably well versed in the medical thought of the day, claimed that "the two most grievous misfortunes of a city life are the privations of pure air and of sufficient room and accommodation for bodily exercise." In the city, he complained, "even second-hand air is at a premium, and it is the height of aerial epicurism to get a few whiffs of air that the country people have used and discarded. . . . To walk through the streets of a city, without striking or being struck, is an act for which one needs to be as limber as an eel, a rope-dancer, or a party politician." A little over a decade later, members of the Northern Medical Association of Philadelphia contended that urban growth had caused "a general depression of the vitality of the human organism." Compared with their country cousins, one Philadelphia physician noted, "the inhabitants of a city are on this account, less vigorous in frame, less elastic in constitution, and are less able to bear losses of blood."[26]

These observations, for many physicians, attested to the validity of moral environmentalism. Overcrowded housing; lack of ventilation and access to sunlight; rotting garbage; overflowing privies; the unavailability of clean water and effective sewerage—these and other problems undermined even the possibility of public health. Vaguely defined and little-understood "miasmas" were thought to literally poison the urban atmosphere, causing disease and affecting the constitutions of city dwellers.

Statistics cited at the 1849 meeting of the infant American Medical Association indicated that mortality figures were on the rise in most cities, despite the boosterism of physicians' reports on their hometowns. The principal killers were tuberculosis, stomach and intestinal ailments, pneumonia, diphtheria, scarlet fever, typhoid fever, smallpox, yellow fever, cholera, and, most common of all, malaria. Few doubted that the debilitating conditions of city life were responsible.[27]

THE ASCENDANCY OF ANTICONTAGIONISM

In light of the growing consensus, it is hardly surprising that an environmental theory of disease causation gained strong support among both physicians and lay people involved in the public health movement. The new theory became known as "anticontagionism."

Contagionism, or "contagium animatum," was already a time-honored theory at the beginning of the nineteenth century. It held that disease occurred because of the transference from a sick person to another individual of some chemical or physical influence. This happened either through direct contact or, occasionally and mysteriously, by the passage of the "influence," over relatively short distances, through the air. Without knowledge of germs, physicians were at a loss to explain precisely under what circumstances endemic and epidemic disease transmittal occurred, but most found contagionism the most reasonable theory. Between the turn of the century and the 1840s, however, heated attacks against contagionism split the medical profession in both Europe and the United States. While the common folk might believe that all diseases were contagious, thoughtful medical men speculated that some illnesses, especially those labeled epidemic, did not fit the contagion-contact model. The case of cholera provoked the hottest debates.[28]

When the "oriental scourge" made its first appearance in seaboard cities in 1832, a handful of physicians claimed that it might, under certain circumstances, be communicable, a stance known as "contingent contagionism." Most, however, stated that it was brought about by a change in normal atmospheric conditions: hence its sudden and scattered outbreak and its tendency to strike only certain sections of a city and certain segments of the population. Added to this argument was the notion of "predisposing causes": those who succumbed to the "epidemic influence" had predisposed themselves through intemperate habits, improper diets, sexual excesses, or other factors. In such weakened states, they fell victim to the latent cholera poison in the air.[29]

The argument against contagionism rallied social activists, both physicians and lay people, who were becoming increasingly dissatisfied with what they denounced as the passivity of city fathers in the face of epidemic disease. The customary response to the outbreak of an epidemic had been quarantine of a section of the community or of the entire city through sealing off the port. The notion of isolating portions of the population from each other or of barricading the city against external poisons seemed logical enough to contagionists, and since city councils did not include learned medical men, and since no American city prior to 1866 had a permanent board of health staffed by physicians, quarantine remained standard practice down through the 1860s. But from the 1830s on, it came under fire from several sources.

These sources included urban tradesmen and merchants, who objected that quarantine harmed their profits by delaying and restricting the movement of goods, and political leaders and local boosters, who complained that quarantine was not uniformly applied (what was legal in Boston was not in Charleston) and hurt the image of the hometown. Even reform-minded men and women attacked the quarantine system as too little and too late a response to the problems of public health.[30]

It was the last group, composed of both lay people and physicians, that formed the core of the anticontagionists. Mingling bits of "modern" medical science with a passionate desire to promote the health of individuals and cities alike, the anticontagionists posited a new theory of disease causation that was both medical and social in its implications. They replaced the "antiquated" concepts of contagion and quarantine with attention to living conditions within the cities.

"Foetid vapors" arising from garbage, feces, and the rotting carcasses of dead animals in the streets seared the lungs of unsuspecting urbanites. "Foul miasmas of the air" emanating from industrial activities and other sources hovered in badly ventilated streets and rooms. The lack of clean water forced many in the city to live in filth. The absence of sewage facilities ensured that most city dwellers would continue to live in dirty and disease-ridden communities. Populations packed together in the rising tenement districts, especially the foreign poor who knew nothing about good personal hygiene and who appeared to provide most of the cities' drunken and criminal classes, could hardly expect to escape the ravages of disease.[31]

The rejection of contagionism and the adoption of the "filth theory" dovetailed very neatly with the "change-of-type" analysis of disease causation that emerged in mid-century. Whether grounded in solid medical and scientific evidence or in a commonsense desire to clean up the environment, anticontagionism proved enormously attractive to several generations of public health reformers between the 1840s and the 1880s. That many reformers dismissed, at least on the level of popular action, the forerunner of the germ theory of disease was understandable. The anticontagionists did not want to sit idle while their cities grew more crowded, filthy, and unhealthy.

The crusade against cholera as a contagious disease served the anticontagionist cause quite well. By mid-century, most medical men had not only discarded the contagion theory, but had come to question atmospheric "epidemic influence" as well. Alexander Stevens, president of the New York State Medical Association, said of that notion: "It is improperly called an explanation. It is only a confession of ignorance; and just as strong proof might be adduced that diseases were induced by witchcraft, or the influence of comets and fiery dragons in the heavens; . . . it should be discarded from science; it belongs in the middle ages." It was clear to mid-century physicians, as the historian Charles Rosenberg puts it, that "local filth and lack of ventilation and pure water were the obvious reasons for the concentration of cholera cases . . . in circumscribed slum areas." These new ideas about cholera were extended to other diseases. Anticontagionist theory held sway and lent powerful support to the efforts of public health reformers.[32]

Like the other intellectual winds that occasionally sweep the mental landscape of a generation, anticontagionism blew away much that was useful. Yet it fostered some new practices that proved their worth. One band of anticontagionists created a new profession that grew in numbers and influence from the 1840s on— that of the sanitarian. They played a vital role in improving the quality of life in American cities over the last half of the nineteenth century. The coupling of medical theory and social activism produced a corps of men and women who knew that the quickest way to promote the public health and engage in useful preventive medicine was to clean up, reconstruct, and begin to plan the physical environment of cities. Their first step was to compile accurate information about health and ill health in the cities.

6

SANITIZING THE CITY

D ESPITE MOUNTING ATTACKS on the city as a center of physical and moral decay, the adherents of moral environmentalism had faith that control of pollution and disease lay in human hands. Expertise, education, and technology could reshape the physical environment, thereby renovating the moral environment of urban Americans as well.

The availability of new techniques and technologies, of course, did not always ensure their application. Favorable public, professional, and political opinion was necessary if technology was to work its magic on morbidity and mortality.[1] Mid-century sanitarians focused public attention on the health problems of the urban populace. Through extensive surveys, they documented the conditions that appeared to generate physical and moral disease. Those surveys, and the "facts" they uncovered, led sanitarians to advocate new planning practices aimed at sanitizing the city.

PUBLIC HEALTH AND PUBLIC MORALS

The word "sanitary" first gained common usage in England and the United States during the 1840s. A young English statistician named Edwin Chadwick, who was serving as secretary of the Poor Law Board, authored a report for the Poor Law Commissioners. His disclosures in *Sanitary Conditions of the Labouring Classes of Great Britain* (1842) proved so shocking that an aroused public successfully pushed for appointment of a Sanitary Commission to investigate the health of the entire nation. Chadwick's initial and subsequent reports (published and debated on both sides of the Atlantic) sparked an environmental reform movement that expanded in scope and accomplishments over the remainder of the century.[2]

129

Similar surveys of U.S. cities were undertaken at the same time, apparently building as much upon previous indigenous investigations as upon the British example. These early surveys gave momentum to sanitation campaigns and were one source of the nineteenth-century city planning movement.[3]

Rarely did the phrase "the public health" appear in print without the word "morals" closely following. The early definition of "sanitary" was "tending to promote health." The phrase was deceptively plain. "Health" in daily parlance connoted far more than simple soundness of body or a strong constitution. A Massachusetts scientific association, for instance, called upon the legislature in 1841 to establish an efficient system of registering deaths, births, and marriages "with a view to the interests of science, as well as of humanity, and the public health and morals." The author of an 1845 survey of New York City informed officials that if they improved "the sanitary arrangements of the city," they would see "the increased health of the populace, a much better state of public morals, and, by consequence, a more easily governed and respectable community."[4]

Like fellow reformers pursuing other goals, sanitarians usually viewed the city as shrouded in moral shadows. An 1865 survey of the sanitary condition of New York City, for example, invoked "the gross filthiness of the streets, courts, and alleys, the putrefying masses of animals and vegetable matter, together with dead animals, obstructed sewerage and drainage, and poisonous exhalations from manufactories of various kinds, [which] combine to pollute the atmosphere of the entire city." The consequences, noted the authors, were "of vital importance as relating to economical, social, and moral questions that should receive the earnest attention of every citizen." How, wondered many a nineteenth-century critic, could morals fail to suffer when citizens were packed into this stultifying container? Yet the course of nineteenth-century society invariably pointed cityward. "However unfavorable to public health and personal morals this circumstance may be regarded," observed that 1865 survey, "it is manifestly a fact which we must accept, and duly estimate in all our plans for the physical and the social welfare of society; for it is an inevitable tendency of an advancing civilization, with its institutions of science and art, and with its ever augmenting commercial and social necessities, thus to centralize vast populations in cities."[5]

Time and again, over more than half a century, the sanitarians would link the physical environment of the city to the social and moral behavior of city dwellers. Still, again like many other urban reformers, they displayed ambivalences. Sanitarians thus tempered their distaste for urban conditions with genuine optimism. City fathers could promote public health by initiating programs of preventive medicine, establishing public agencies of sanitary police, and building and rebuilding the city along guidelines laid down by the sanitarians. Precisely because they connected the physical environment, public health, and public morals, the sanitarians could proclaim that improvements in the city as a physical container would invariably produce healthier citizens, who, in turn, would be morally responsible members of the community. Although factions within the sanitation movement disagreed about strategies and about who among them should lead the cause, they rarely departed from this assumption.

SURVEYING THE SANITARIANS

During the formative years between the 1840s and the 1880s, the local and national leaders of the sanitation movement were a curious hodgepodge. Their ranks included physicians, people with some medical knowledge but little formal training, men and women trained in some field of science, civil engineers, and a substantial number of persons without scientific backgrounds but fired with enthusiasm for social betterment. Few were widely known in their own time or in ours. They have not made their way into the general texts of American history.

The exceptions were Lemuel Shattuck, John H. Griscom, and George E. Waring, Jr., whose reform activities revealed the varied goals that bound the sanitationists in common cause and the varied strategies that the sanitationists employed. Each in his own way illustrated the diverse career paths taken by the larger group of men and women who involved themselves in the sanitary campaigns.

Raised in rural New Hampshire in a struggling farm family, Lemuel Shattuck (1793–1859) pursued a variety of careers before finding his calling. He began as a teacher in Troy and Albany, New York, later moving to Detroit, where, in addition to his teaching duties, he established the first Sunday school in Michigan. In 1823 he migrated back to New England and entered the business world as a merchant in partnership with his brother in Concord, Massachusetts. There, with the publication of A *History of the Town of Concord* (1835), he built a reputation as a skilled genealogist. His work in reorganizing the local schools and introducing the first annual school reports in the state added to his luster as an educator.

In 1835 Shattuck moved to Boston to attempt a career as a book publisher. No longer an obscure scholar, he gained election to the Boston City Council in 1837 and to the state legislature the following year. His early work in genealogy and the collection of school records had convinced him of the social importance of accurate vital statistics and led him to the profession for which he became most famous—statistician. In 1839 he helped found the American Statistical Association; in 1842 he persuaded the legislature to enact a law requiring the registration of births, deaths, and marriages; in 1845, at the request of the Boston City Council, he prepared the first comprehensive urban census of the century.

Finally, in 1849, as a member of the legislature and the most renowned statistician of the day, Shattuck undertook compilation of the first major sanitary survey of any state in the union. Publication of the *Report of the Sanitary Commission of Massachusetts* (1850) established him as a national leader in the embryonic public health movement and sparked similar surveys in other states. Although certainly a social reformer in the broadest sense of the term, Shattuck derided other reformers as "governed by theories founded on uncertain and partial data, or vague conjecture." He proclaimed himself "a statist—a dealer in facts." He sought to demonstrate the relationship between the physical environment and the ways in which people lived. "We wish to ascertain the laws of human life," he wrote, "developed by the natural constitution of our bodies, as they actually exist under the influences that surround them, and to learn how far they may be modified or improved. This can only be done by an accurate knowledge of the facts that are daily occurring among us."[6]

John H. Griscom (1804–1874) was a child of the city, a lifetime New Yorker who came to his profession—he was a physician—by following in his father's footsteps. The senior Griscom was a leading philanthropist and, for over thirty years, the best-known teacher of chemistry in New York City. After training at the University of Pennsylvania, the son entered the fragmented medical circles of Manhattan as both a private practitioner and an associate of a number of institutions, including the New York Dispensary, the New York Hospital, and the College of Pharmacy. Having joined with others during the early 1840s to form the New York Academy of Medicine, he broadened his range of activities beyond the medical profession by working with private and public agencies involved with poor relief, prison reform, and immigration administration. Again emulating his father, who had introduced Americans to the latest European scientific thought and discoveries through his carefully crafted translations, the younger Griscom kept up an extensive correspondence with European social reformers and scientists and published their and his own ideas in such fields as the control of infectious diseases, physiology, and ventilation.

By the early 1840s Griscom enjoyed both a local and a national reputation as a physician and popularizer of scientific thought. His appointment in 1842 as city inspector marked his emergence as a champion of public health. Unlike the reports of his predecessors, Griscom's 1842 "Annual Report" presented in detail not only the city's mortality statistics, but also a commentary on general sanitary conditions, especially those of the poor. Citing the efforts of Chadwick in England and Shattuck in Boston, Griscom proposed preventive action as the chief goal of public health. Unhappy with his depiction of conditions and his calls for reform, the Board of Aldermen canceled the doctor's reappointment.

Undaunted, and urged on by a few prominent citizens, Griscom expanded his report and published in 1845 *The Sanitary Condition of the Laboring Population of New York*, a landmark study in the public health field in the United States. For the rest of his life, he worked unstintingly for a systematic public health program. Griscom played an important role in securing passage of a series of health and sanitary codes, which, if seriously enforced, would have given New York City the finest public health program in urban America.[7]

George E. Waring, Jr. (1833–1898), like Shattuck a farmer's son, built his reputation as an expert on scientific agriculture. Trained in agricultural chemistry, Waring, a lifelong self-promoter, first made valuable social connections by managing Horace Greeley's farm at Chappaqua, New York, between 1855 and 1857. Encouraged by Greeley's patronage, Waring in 1857 joined the staff of the landscape architects Frederick Law Olmsted and Calvert Vaux as an agricultural and drainage engineer, working on New York City's

Central Park project. During the Civil War he served with some distinction as a cavalry officer in the Union Army. Following the war he returned to his first love and in a series of technical publications enhanced his stature as an agricultural consultant. He also wrote popular accounts of his European travels for magazines like *Scribner's* and *Atlantic Monthly* during the early 1870s, and authored several well-received horse stories. At the same time, he began to develop an interest in sanitation engineering, spurred by his desire to profit from his financial investment in a British-designed earth closet (an indoor toilet then in competition with the sewer-connected water closet). When the American urban public showed a preference for the water closet, Waring quickly reengineered his thoughts.

By the mid-1870s Waring had become the nation's foremost promoter of the water closet and had begun to establish himself as the best-known crusader for better plumbing and sewerage. *The Sanitary Drainage of Houses and Towns* (1876) proved to be the most influential of his many publications. Between 1878 and 1880 Waring supervised construction of a sewer system in yellow fever-devastated Memphis, Tennessee. The project secured his reputation, as well as lining his pockets, for he owned the American patent on the type of system he installed. In 1879 he accepted a post as special agent for the Tenth Census of the United States to compile urban social statistics for the first time. His two-volume report appeared in 1886 and established a benchmark for the gathering of such information.

For the remainder of his life, Waring was in constant demand as a consulting engineer for water and sewer projects throughout the United States and Europe. Always controversial because of his engineering schemes (many American engineers discounted his technical abilities) and his fervent self-promotion, he nonetheless maintained a reputation as the nation's foremost urban expert in sanitation matters. The press hailed him as the country's leading warrior in the fight against yellow fever, despite his relative lack of medical knowledge. In 1898, as chairman of a commission appointed by the Army, Waring went to Cuba to clean up Havana and end the scourge of yellow fever that was decimating not only that city's population but also the occupying forces of the United States. Having completed a well-publicized survey of sanitary conditions there, Waring triumphantly returned to America, where, five days later, he died of yellow fever.[8]

Thousands of others participated in the public health movement. Ellen Swallow Richards, for example, is well known to students of women's history and the field of home economics. The first
woman to graduate from the Massachusetts Institute of Technology
with a degree in chemistry (1873), she built upon her studies in food
chemistry to elaborate what she called the science of "euthenics"—
the science of improving the development of races and breeds
through the creation of a controlled environment. The chemist and
engineer Leonard P. Kinnicutt is familiar to students of chemical
engineering as an international authority on air, gas, and water.
Kinnicutt co-authored *Sewage Disposal* (1910), which remains an
often-consulted source.[9] Yet the names of other members of the
sanitary movement—John McLeod Keating, Memphis newspaper
editor; Joseph Jones, New Orleans physician; Cady Staley, Cleveland civil engineer; David Boswell Reid, Madison chemist—remind
us only of how little we know about the men and women who spent
part or all of their lives struggling to improve the health of their
fellow citizens.[10]

Survey of these individuals reveals diverse backgrounds and oc-
cupations as well as wide geographic distribution. Not surprisingly,
the two professions best represented were civil engineers and physicians. Nineteenth-century Americans, like their twentieth-century
descendants, sought technological and scientific solutions to their
physical and social problems. Many sanitarians, however, were neither engineers nor physicians. Nonetheless, because they had tried
to occupy the province of public health as their particular domain,
they looked to medical science for inspiration and guidance. It was
no accident that a physician authored the first important urban sanitary survey.[11]

SURVEYS AND SANITATION

Later surveys would prove more "scientific" in facts and factual
analysis than John Griscom's *Sanitary Conditions of the Laboring
Population of New York*, but none deviate from its identification of
the cities' problems or its indignation at their persistence. Griscom
set the tone for subsequent reports on the health and ill-health of
the cities.[12]

Both the contents of the report and its title displayed Griscom's
knowledge of an indebtedness to the work of Edwin Chadwick in
England. Griscom's survey, however, was a home-grown product,

and its author trod a path well worn by his own countrymen. Probably the earliest sanitary survey of an American city had appeared in 1806; in it a select citizens' committee reviewed conditions in New York City and recommended a number of improvements, including an ample supply of pure water, construction of sewers, drainage of marshlands, and "proper" interment of the dead within the city. During the 1820s and 1830s, private citizens and voluntary associations in Boston, Philadelphia, New York, Baltimore, and elsewhere systematically gathered information on the living conditions of the poor.[13]

The Griscom report reflected the growing popularity of the anticontagionist view and the general acceptance of the symbiotic relationship between physical and moral health. The investigation had four goals: (1) to gather, and present, as accurately as possible, facts about the "immense amount of sickness, physical disability, and premature mortality among the poorer classes"; (2) to prove that these problems were "in a great degree the results of causes which are removable"; (3) to show that "these physical evils are productive of moral evils of great magnitude and number" (and hence that the city government, if only to save money, should undertake preventive action); and (4) to suggest practical measures that would alleviate the evils and prevent their recurrence.[14]

Griscom graphically described the tenements, slums, and workplaces of the poor, adding mortality figures and statistics on the hospital and dispensary treatment of the sick poor wherever possible. From the annual reports of the city inspector (including his own 1842 report) he gleaned the information that nearly one-half of the city's deaths from consumption and more than one-third of total deaths happened among the foreign population. He did not find this surprising, since foreigners and their children made up most of the cellar and court dwellers in the city: "the domiciliary condition of these poor beings, the confined spaces in which they dwell, the unwholesome air they breathe, and their filth and degradation, are prolific sources of an immense amount of distress and sickness."

These observations were consistent with anticontagion theory:

The evils thus resulting are occasionally exhibited in an endemic form, i.e., some disease of a marked character will break out and attack a considerable number of persons in the same neighborhood, the extent of its prevalence depending upon the extent of the cause, or the facilities for its propagation. Thus a fever may commence in a certain place inhabited mostly by the destitute and filthy:—if adjoining tenements are occupied by the same class of persons, and kept in the same dirty and ill-ventilated condition, the tenants of the latter will be very liable to attacks of the same disorder. The disease will often be observed to pass by houses in a better condition, and re-appear at a distance, where similar causes prevail.

Physicians who ventured into the "haunts of wretchedness" to treat the sick were well aware of "a silent agency continually at work, destroying annually the health and lives of hundreds of our fellow citizens, and entirely within the power of the city government to control or subdue." The components of the "silent agency" lay in the conditions of the physical environment, not in the physical constitutions of tenement occupants. [15]

Some citizens found scapegoats in the growing numbers of native and foreign-born poor. Unlike many of his contemporaries, Griscom did not lapse into a reflexive nativist hostility toward immigrants. His investigations led him to an environmental, not a "racial," interpretation, and he rejected the presumption that foreigners journeyed to the United States with "bad intentions" of living like cattle in pens, swallowing poison with every breath. Griscom's friend, Lemuel Shattuck, could not have disagreed more. Although he described himself as a statistician concerned only with facts, Shattuck breathed the social atmosphere of Brahmin Boston. That city's elite distrusted the immigrant classes, declaring them the cause of most urban problems. Shattuck held English and Irish immigrants directly responsible for injecting the native stock with poverty and disease and warned that "the healthy, social and moral character we once enjoyed is liable to be forever lost." [16]

Relatively few public health leaders shared Shattuck's extreme nativism. Consider, for example, the conclusions of J. G. Pinkham, a physician who prepared a sanitary survey of Lynn, Massachusetts, in 1877. Having discovered great variations in mortality rates among the streets and districts of the city, he laid the blame on filth, neglect of sanitary laws, and contamination of the water, soil, and air. "If foreigners suffer more than natives," Pinkham explained, "it is not because of any predisposition to disease, or any constitutional weakness of the races, or difficulty in becoming acclimatized, but because they are more exposed to the operation of the causes mentioned." [17]

The sanitarians were hardly free of the biases that characterized nineteenth-century American society. Yet their commitment to the environmental causation of disease overrode all other considerations. They clutched to their bosoms the anticontagionist theory and generally refused to let go, even when confronted with scientific evidence to the contrary.

Over the last three decades of the century, reports of experiments performed in European laboratories that lent strong weight to a germ theory of disease began to generate interest and debate in American medical circles. The German physician Robert Koch isolated both a tubercle bacillus and a cholera bacillus. In France, Louis Pasteur was engaged in similar bacteriological experiments. Other Europeans soon followed suit. Their intellectual curiosity, coupled with technological innovations—immersion lens microscopes and aniline dyes for staining bacteria—produced a new science of microbiology and a bacteriological revolution that eventually reshaped both theories of disease causation and therapeutic practices. To some contemporaries, however, the germ theory marked a return to contagionism.[18] As a result, many American physicians and sanitarians initially proved reluctant to accept it, worried that it might weaken public support for sanitary measures, causing several decades of public health legislation and enforcement to go by the boards. If the medical profession and the public at large firmly came to believe that living germs alone propagated infectious diseases, their resolve to spend tax dollars on purely sanitary measures might dissolve. The most dogmatic sanitarians dismissed the germ theory as nonsense.[19]

The more reasonable ones, firm in their convictions, tried to turn the situation to their own advantage. The respected educator and sanitarian Frederick A. P. Barnard, in a widely quoted speech before the American Public Health Association, admitted the differences in logic and motivation between the contagion and anticontagion stances, but predicted that whichever one prevailed, health legislation was likely to be substantially the same. All sanitarians championed pure air, pure water, thorough drainage, wholesome food, prevention of overcrowded housing, disinfection "of every spot where pestilence may lift its head," enforced cleanliness, severe exclusion of industries that contaminated the air "with noxious gases or offensive effluvia," and the establishment of a well-organized and diligent sanitary police force in every town and city. "These are the objects," Barnard affirmed, "which the guardians of the public health must labor to secure, to whatever school of etiology they may happen to belong." All the people involved in public health efforts, he claimed (with more optimism than realism), "however freely they may splinter lances in the arena of controversy, are always found, in the field of actual warfare and in the face of the common enemy, marching harmoniously side by side."[20]

In the United States the discoveries of medical science moved from laboratories to city streets at a turtle's pace. They were as often resisted as embraced by practicing physicians, sanitarians, politicians, and the public at large. In the late 1880s, however, a newly-appointed public health official in Providence, Rhode Island, named Charles Chapin, founded the nation's first municipal bacteriological laboratory. In 1892 Dr. Hermann Biggs created the New York City Health Department Laboratory and initiated bacteriological testing of thousands of New Yorkers for diphtheria. Identification and treatment of carriers of the disease with a new antitoxin proved a remarkable success. Philadelphia (1895), Newark (1895), Baltimore (1896), Boston (1898), and other cities established their own municipal laboratories and sought to apply bacteriological discoveries to public health practices. By the early years of the twentieth century, urban public health officers across the nation were exploiting the new medical discoveries.[21]

Still prior to the 1880s, sanitarians remained committed to an environmental interpretation of disease causation. They disagreed among themselves about the role played by the urban lower classes in the transmission of disease. Most concurred, as we have seen, that the poor and the foreign-born were not solely responsible for their plight. But if they were not to blame for the unhealthy conditions of the cities, who was?

THE POLITICS OF SANITATION

There were three answers to this question. First, like Griscom, the sanitarians pointed to politics and city government, chastizing officials for not employing even the laws that were on the books. In his report, Griscom complained of the government's "strange neglect"; in an earlier letter to his friend Lemuel Shattuck, Griscom had reflected ruefully on his efforts while city inspector of New York: "but hungry politicians care but little for those things, and I am prepared to walk out."[22]

Repeatedly, sanitarians criticized the timidity and self-interest of politicians. John Bell of Philadelphia, in an 1859 discussion of urban sanitation, ripped into elected officials who "withheld or violated by force or selfishness" the burden of sanitary legislation "in such a way that the people in mass find it difficult to obtain justice." Dorman B. Eaton, author of an article on "The Sphere and Method of Sanitary Administration in Cities" (1873) in one of the first issues of the influential journal *The Sanitarian*, summarized the opinions of his co-workers: "A Board of Health has nothing to do with politics or ward politicians. It should be above and beyond the machinations and changes of party politics. The causes which have to do with the public health have nothing to do with party lines, and all political claims should be disregarded, whether they be city, county, or State." In fact, this article was a statement of principle and a declaration of hope for the future more than a description of present practice.[23]

There were sanitarians who disliked political timidity yet also recognized that politicians alone were not held responsible for these problems. John S. Billings, a nationally known physician, explained in his 1880 presidential address before the American Public Health Association (APHA) that enforcement of hygiene measures always involved a genuine conflict of interests. Whenever a city or state attempted really effective means of preventing disease, Billings noted, opposition could be expected from affected parties. To gauge popular opinion and public support for given legislation was proverbially difficult, "as most politicians know to their cost." When times were prosperous, a community and its leaders could be counted upon to "say to the sanitarian who is warning them: 'Hush! wait a little; don't make a fuss; you will injure the reputation of the city; you will drive away commerce; we are no worse than our neighbors, nor than we have been before; we will attend to these matters bye-and-bye, for you are probably right in your advice; but wait until after the election; we must not propose additional taxation *now* or we shall be defeated,' etc."

Billings warned his listeners that it was not only useless, but injurious to the cause of public hygiene to urge legislation faster than the masses of the people and the business interests of the community demanded it. Having presented a partial excuse for the reluctance of politicians to legislate in the public's behalf, Billings nonetheless commented sarcastically that "We know by experience that when the sanitary fat does get into the political fire, there is a terrible sizzling, and the result is often disastrous."[24]

City government, then, however inept or even corrupt, was not the singular villain. This conclusion logically led to the second and third answers given to the question posed above.

Some participants in the sanitary campaigns gladly accepted the "sewer socialists" label bestowed by their late nineteenth- and early twentieth-century critics. These men and women advocated municipal ownership of water systems, sewers, public transit facilities, and other urban services. None were ideologically committed socialists, but their writings and speeches displayed an implicit or explicit critique of unfettered capitalism. The second group whom sanitarians held responsible for the increasing poor health of cities consisted of private entrepreneurs.[25]

Griscom lambasted the system of tenantage, whose only justification was profit. The authors of an 1849 report on cholera charged that the miserable conditions prevalent in certain districts of Boston were "mainly owing to the fact of their having been originally laid out by private speculators, whose only object was to make a profitable investment for themselves, and who paid but very slight attention to the health or comfort of those who have to reside upon them." A select committee in New York City in 1865 denounced the "criminal selfishness and indifference" of proprietors of "tenant-houses," stating that the construction and management of such dwellings had been left "to the caprice and inordinate selfishness of men whose sole object has been to make small investments and a borrowed capital pay enormous advances, without regard to the poor tenants' welfare, or the public safety." The committee suggested that the legislature intervene to protect the occupants and the city at large. And so it went. During a half-century in which public spokesmen from all walks of life consecrated the virtues of laissez faire capitalism, sanitarians and their allies limned the necessity of municipal corporate intervention in the practices of private enterprise.[26]

Having accused politicians and entrepreneurs of social irresponsibility, the sanitarians proceeded to indict society itself, an analysis common to most American social reform movements. "The community is guilty," charged Griscom. Referring particularly to the foreign-born and native poor, he sermonized:

We are parties to their degradation, inasmuch as we permit the inhabitation of places, from which it is not possible improvement in condition or habits can come. . . . We *suffer* the sub-landlord to stow them, like cattle, in pens. . . . They are *allowed*, may it not be said *required* to live in dirt, when the reverse, rather, should be enforced.

Even as clinical and statistical a survey as Lemuel Shattuck's famous 1850 report imputed blame to the community as a whole, affirming that what was lacking was not a social way, but a social will to challenge the environmental sources of disease.[27]

Survey after survey, sanitarian after sanitarian, repeated and reinforced this notion. Long years after Griscom and Shattuck broached it, as the century wore to a close, Hermann M. Biggs, a leader in local and state health administration, showed the durability of the idea of social guilt. "Disease is a largely removable evil. It continues to afflict humanity," he intoned, "not only because of incomplete knowledge of its causes, and lack of individual and public hygiene, but also because it is fostered extensively by harsh economic and industrial conditions and by wretched housing in congested communities. These conditions can be removed by better social organization."[28]

Politicians, profiteers, the public. The circle of blame was complete.

SANITATION AND CITY PLANNING

The problems, then, were evident. So, believed the sanitarians, were the solutions. Street-cleaning campaigns and quarantines of infected neighborhoods were necessary, but not sufficient, responses. More radical measures must be undertaken. Perceptions of widespread ill health, the increasing dirtiness and dishevelment of cities, and prevailing theories of disease propelled the sanitarians into advocacy of new city planning practices.

An early indication of this line of thought came from the medical community. The fledgling American Medical Association, founded in 1847, formed a hygiene committee the next year to encourage cities to undertake sanitary surveys. Its agenda required data on population, prevalence of disease, drainage, street cleaning, ventilation, sanitation in schools, conditions in hospitals and dispensaries, the source of the water supply, and municipal regulations dealing with these matters so that the AMA might recommend more effective planning procedures. At the 1849 annual meeting, representatives from Boston, Philadelphia, Baltimore, Charleston, New Orleans, Louisville, Cincinnati, Concord, New Hampshire, and Portland, Maine, presented reports whose chief complaint concerned the filthiness of city streets. Doctor L. P. Yandell of Louisville, for instance, noted that "one of the first things that strikes the eye of the stranger is the neglected condition of our streets. He wonders how Louisville can be healthy, with such masses of putrescent matter in its midst." Isaac Parrish of Philadelphia denounced the "numerous piggeries within the limits of the city," while Edward H. Barton of New Orleans emphasized the role of climate in disease.[29]

More direct calls for sanitarians to involve themselves in city planning and rehabilitation soon came from other quarters. One was Lemuel Shattuck's report. Among their numerous suggestions, the sanitary commissioners stated: "We recommend *that, in laying out new towns and villages, and in extending those already laid out, ample provision be made for a supply, in purity and abundance, of light, air, and water; for drainage and sewerage, for paving, and for cleanliness.*" Agreement came from elsewhere in the nation. The Chicago physician N. S. Davis, who in 1865 would become chairman of a city council-appointed committee to investigate the sanitary conditions of the city, presented in 1853 his definition of "modern medicine." A comprehensive medical view, he stated, understood the relations of man to the air he breathed, the earth upon which he trod, and all the other elements "around us." Plans and projects that improved housing construction, preserved pure air and good water, reserved land for ample parks and wide streets, and promoted efficient sewers in all large cities have "not only prevented disease and lengthened the average duration of human life, but they have vastly enlarged the field of human happiness."[30]

Horace Bushnell, a Connecticut minister and educator whose speeches and writings reached a wide audience, concurred. In a speech on "City Plans," in which he listed the requisites of a good plan, Bushnell incorporated the sanitarians' concerns:

No city over which the pale angels of sickness are always hovering becomes ornamental or attractive. Heavy bills of mortality keep down the

tonic energy of art. Not even the best commercial advantages brace the
feeling up to improvement. . . . Even the stone of architecture looks weak
in its lines, and statuary droops in expression, where a funeral miasma
loads the atmosphere. The mere repute of unhealthiness is a heavy bar of
disadvantage, as regards any kind of progress or culture. . . . Still a great
deal can be done for the healthiness of almost any location, if only the
city plan is rightly adjusted and the true sanitary conditions are duly
attended to afterwards.

Some sanitarians might have disagreed with one part of this planning scenario: they wanted "true sanitary conditions" attended to as
part of any adjustment of the city plan.[31]
    The attempt to organize a permanent national public health as-
sociation revealed the sanitarians' long-term goal of involving themselves and the general public in city planning efforts. In 1856 Dr.
Wilson Jewell, health officer of Philadelphia, successfully impor-
tuned the Philadelphia Board of Health to hold a national convention the following year. Delegates came from the principal Atlantic
and Gulf port cities and included both physicians and elected public
officials, many of whom were members of local health boards.
Nominally, the delegates were there to review present maritime
quarantine laws with an eye toward adoption of a uniform national
system. In reality, the 1857 convention and the three that followed
(1858–1860) became arenas in which most of those in attendance
attacked quarantine as a useless disease-prevention method. In its
stead, the leading sanitarians promoted city planning based on anticontagionist principles.[32]
    Significantly, the 1859 convention elected as its president John
H. Griscom. Griscom had at last found a national forum. He used
it to good advantage. At the opening session the former New York
city inspector paraded statistics on morbidity and mortality that, in
his judgment, exposed the uselessness of "external" methods like
quarantine and proved the necessity of "internal" planning measures. Listing deaths from various diseases over the previous twenty-
five years, Griscom argued that "these are diseases which are
generated within the city, . . . against which the city is defenseless."
Along with others at the convention, he urged the erection of a new
superstructure of urban law and underscored the importance of educating the public in hygiene and enlisting their support for sanitary
planning measures: "The masses being those who alone are inter-

ested in public health, it is they who must be first moved to demand reform." That statement was both an acknowledgement of the need to bring public pressure to bear upon recalcitrant politicians and an implicit admission of the limited success that health crusaders had enjoyed in alerting and arousing the public to the dangers of disease in an unplanned and unregulated urban environment.[33]

That convention hummed with debate and dissension between defenders of the old methods like quarantine and the champions of the new planning measures. After hours of acrimonious argument, a majority of members passed a resolution against the use of quarantine in cases of yellow fever; the Committee on the Internal Hygiene of Cities (formed during the 1858 meetings) presented a lengthy series of reports on urban sanitary conditions; and the convention accepted and published a model "Sanitary Code for Cities."

The proposed code was the composition of Dr. Henry Clark, city physician of Boston. A comprehensive summary of suggestions and demands that some sanitarians had promulgated for many years, it called for creation of a state board of health and local boards in every city that would possess genuine powers of planning and enforcement, public provision of water supplies and sewage disposal, control of epidemic diseases, vaccination, regulation of markets, slaughterhouses, drinking shops and lodginghouses, street cleaning, and a host of other proposals. Although some delegates opposed such radical interference with the rights of private citizens, others enthusiastically endorsed the code. By so doing, they demonstrated that a corps of sanitarians had realized that modern cities, bursting at the seams with commercial expansion and a large, heterogeneous population, shared common environmental problems that required similar comprehensive planning solutions.[34]

A new day of planning policy had dawned. With it came a renewed conviction of the possibility of placing control of disease and death in human hands. That conviction perhaps received its clearest statement at the last of the national conventions in 1860—the last because of the advent of the Civil War. Previous conventions and the "Sanitary Code" had been well received by the public, noted Dr. Jacob Bigelow, a consulting physician for the city of Boston. Heralding the proposed regulations as one of the greatest reforms ever undertaken by the nation, he prophesied: "The day is rapidly approaching when clinical doctors will scarcely be needed, and when sanitarians will take their places, and when we shall not so much attend to the health of the human body as to the condition of the body politic." A decade was to pass before the first state—Massachusetts—adopted the code's proposal and established a state health board with teeth. Several decades trundled by before Bigelow's vision of a sanitary science that would effectively treat the "condition of the body politic" gained general public support.[35]

Helping to transform the vision into reality over the last three decades of the century was the growing professionalization and bureaucratization of the sanitation movement. In 1872 a permanent, voluntary, national organization formed. Although from the outset the American Public Health Association included nonmedical members, at core it was a meeting ground for such leading urban physicians and sanitarians as Stephen Smith and Elisha Harris of New York City, E. M. Snow of Providence, John H. Rauch of Chicago, and Joseph Toner and John S. Billings of Washington, D.C. Its meetings and published reports, as well as its house organ, *The Sanitarian*, disseminated the medical views of the sanitationists and vigorously promoted city planning ideas, practices, and legislation. Later in the century the association served as a clearinghouse for information and action in public health affairs.[36]

Hoping to gain wider public recognition of their profession as well as government support for their public health schemes, APHA members lobbied vigorously during the mid-1870s for a National Board of Health. An 1879 act of Congress created that board. For the next five years its membership included the leading sanitarians of the day. Yet from the sanitarians' point of view, the board did not fulfill its promise. It fell afoul of political infighting among congressmen and medical officers of the Army, the Navy, and the Marine Hospital Services and died a controversial death in 1883.[37]

During the late 1870s and early 1880s, sanitarians worked toward acquiring professional autonomy in a new field called sanitary engineering. Joining with civil engineers, plumbing contractors, and plumbers, sanitarians launched a new journal in 1877: the *Plumber and Sanitary Engineer*. In 1880, to advertise their freshly minted profession, the editors changed the name to the *Sanitary Engineer*. That same year a skeptic captured the mood of a field in flux by noting that "there is no lack of wisdom in the sanitary world now, for a host of 'sanitary engineers' have sprung up . . . at a moment's notice. It is true they have been following other professions all their life; but a 'fresh door is open here,' and 'right about face!' is the order of the day, which they gladly obey, and turn in to 'fresh fields and pastures new.' " In 1887 the creation of the Lawrence Experiment Station (for research into problems of water and sewage treatment) by the Massachusetts State Board of Health moved the new field one step closer to definition as a scientific discipline. Participants founded their own professional organization in 1906, the American Society of Sanitary Engineers. In 1911 Harvard University appointed George C. Whipple as its first professor of sanitary engineering. Whipple claimed that his field was "fast coming to be regarded as one of the learned professions," noting with satisfaction that it represented "the application of a new science to a new product of civilization. The new science is bacteriology; the new product of civilization is 'The Modern City.' "[38]

Other educational institutions helping to provide a corps of professionally trained experts in the rising discipline of sanitary science included the Massachusetts Institute of Technology, which, in conjunction with Harvard, established a joint school of public health under the leadership of William T. Sedgwick, a biologist. Sedgwick believed that a sanitarian did not need a medical degree to pursue a career in public health, and following an internal struggle over whether to require one for admission to the program, his forces carried the day. Thus, many of the school's graduates earned diplomas in various scientific or engineering programs. Not until 1918, with the opening of the Johns Hopkins School of Hygiene under the direction of William H. Welch, a physician, was graduate training in medicine genuinely joined to the instruction of sanitarians.[39]

Accompanying and aiding the growing sense of professionalism were changes in American law. In most states a clearly demarcated field of public health bolstered by a body of law gradually emerged. Beginning with Louisiana in 1855 and spurred by the example of Massachusetts in 1869, state legislatures created boards of health. By 1883 twenty-seven states had health departments that nominally functioned on a statewide basis ("nominally" because in some places, notably Louisiana, the "state" board paid attention only to matters in the principal city, while in others—for example, Virginia—the board had appointed officials but no allocated operating funds). By 1900, however, nearly every state and every large city contained a health department staffed primarily by professionals— physicians, bacteriologists, chemists, and engineers. By the early years of the twentieth century, the sanitation crusade that began in the 1840s had reached its goal of legitimacy in the eyes of the public.[40]

While the personnel and tactics changed over the years, one consistent theme threaded its way through the decades of the sanitary campaigns. Holding the mental image of the technologically perfected city as depicted by the urbtopian novelists, the sanitarians repeatedly emphasized the moral nature of their quest. From the 1840s on, the presumptions that we have called moral environmentalism informed generations of urban sanitary reformers. The principal evil of an unhealthy physical environment was the damage it inflicted on moral health. Griscom put it most directly: "This depressed physical condition, and bad moral and social habits and propensities, to my mind, have an intimate relation to each other— they stand clearly in the attitudes of cause and effect." Shattuck sprinkled the pages of his report with dire warnings about the depreciation of "the physical and moral power of living" brought on by the impoverishment and diseases of the urban populace. For most sanitarians, "cleanliness is next to godliness" carried great weight. Reviewing Shattuck's work in the distinguished *North American Review,* one writer commented that the "sanitary movement does not merely relate to the lives and health of the community; it is also a means of moral reform. . . . The ultimate connection between filth and vice has been noted by all writers upon this subject. Outward impurity goes hand in hand with inward pollution, and the removal of one leads to the extirpation of the other. Cleansing the body is not more a symbol, than it is a means and condition of inward purity."[41]

The generation of sanitarians that rose to prominence after the general acceptance of the germ theory of disease in the United States were technically trained, unlike their amateur predecessors of the mid-nineteenth century. Some disavowed the intimate connections between filth and disease assumed by earlier sanitarians. Charles V. Chapin of Providence, Rhode Island, was the nation's leading urban health officer during the opening years of the twentieth century. He devoted nearly 200 pages of his classic 1901 text *Municipal Sanitation in the Untied States* to "Nuisances and Nuisance Abatement" and "Refuse Disposal." Yet Chapin was convinced that the best reason for urban housekeeping was aesthetic. In his 1912 *Sources and Modes of Infection,* he presented the conventional wisdom of his day: "Except for a few diseases, or except for very indirect effects, the cleansing of streets, alleys, and back yards, of dwellings and stables, the regulation of offensive trades, and the prevention of nuisances generally, have, so far as we can see, no effect on the general health, nor any value in the prevention of specific diseases."[42]

Still, while most of his generation no longer equated a filthy physical environment with high rates of morbidity and mortality, many reaffirmed the long-held faith that physical and moral health went hand-in-hand. President Charles Eliot of Harvard University, for example, addressed the 1911 meeting of the American Society of Landscape Architects on the topic "Welfare and Happiness." Supporting views articulated earlier by his son Charles, Jr., a noted sanitarian and landscape architect who had met an untimely death in 1897, the senior Eliot urged his listeners to use their talents "to deal with the evils of diseases, physical and moral, which are caused by congestion of population." The linkage of the physical and moral health of the urban populace, so fervently welded by the first generation of sanitarians, would hold solid for decades to come.[43]

Over the long years, the sanitarians evolved from a small group of men and women devoted to somehow improving the public health of city dwellers into a large community of skilled professionals. Along the way, they had advertised a new theory of disease causation, new techniques of preventive medicine, and new ways of planning cities as humane environments. Since many of the sanitarians' proposals involved the construction and administration of new public works, they early discovered as their most natural allies two other rising groups of nineteenth-century professionals—landscape architects and municipal engineers.

PART FOUR

ENGINEERING THE CITY

Which of you, intending to build a tower,
sitteth not down first, and counteth the cost,
whether he have sufficient to finish it?

St. Luke 14:28

7

PROMOTING PUBLIC WORKS

A BALTIMORE ENGINEER, pushing for public construction and ownership of the city's first comprehensive sanitary system, in 1905 equated the efficiency of sewers and the quality of civilization. Paris, he asserted, "completely sewered, with a low death rate," was "the center of all that is best in art, literature, science and architecture and is both clean and beautiful. In the evolution of this ideal attainment, its sewers took at least a leading part, for we have only to look at conditions existing prior to their construction to see that such a realization would have been impossible before their existence." His sentiments reflected a widespread enthusiasm for public works. [1]

An increasing number of urban Americans had, as we have seen, come to believe that the solution to environmental problems lay in physical and technological innovations. From the mid-nineteenth century on, sanitarians, landscape architects, and civil engineers erected a structure of planning thought and practice that gradually came to dominate the city-making landscape of America. They articulated a new concept of "public works," thereby giving physical expression to the changing social vocabulary of the century's emerging urban culture. That conception urged that the public itself, through its tax dollars and its political support for public works projects, take charge of its own destiny in building a safer, saner, and more sanitary urban environment. While publicizing such projects, the new professionals—particularly landscape architects and municipal engineers—became aware that the implementation and administration of fresh technologies would require alteration in the reach and scope of municipal government.

Those projects—city parks and playgrounds, water and sewer systems, paved streets, among others—promised to halt the physical

153

decay, the spread of disease, and the onrush of moral degradation
that many nineteenth-century Americans associated with the
growth of cities. The new techniques and technologies of public
works advocates formed the foundations both of modern American
city making and of municipal administration.

Our Baltimore engineer, then, did not raise a solitary cry in the
urban wilderness. He merely added his voice to a swelling chorus
that demanded vital public services. Like his nineteenth-century
predecessors, he was certain that physical improvements in the city
would lead inevitably to social and moral improvements in the human condition. Metaphorically, he was not far off the mark: sewers
(symbolic of all public works) were important after all.

THE GREENING OF THE CITIES

On a chilly winter's day in January 1899, ten men and one woman
gathered in Manhattan to establish the American Society of Landscape Architects. The association was new; the profession it represented had originated in the 1840s and 1850s. Over the rest of the
century that profession permanently altered the physical geography
of American cities and constructed new vistas on the moral geography of urban dwellers. Its practitioners prepared plans for beautifying city centers east and west, designed new, leafy towns on the
urban periphery, and laid out rural parks within the confines of
great cities. Above all, the landscape architects educated their countrymen to the physical and moral advantages of taming nature
within the unnatural environment of the growing metropolis. They
brought about the greening of the cities.[2]

Most of those who dabbled in or dedicated their lives to the
greening of the cities were little known by the general public of their
own times. Yet along with the sanitarians and the municipal engineers, such individuals as Andrew Jackson Downing, Frederick Law
Olmsted, Calvert Vaux, Robert Morris Copeland, Jacob Weiden-
mann, Horace William Shaler Cleveland, Charles Eliot, Jr., and
John Nolen touched the lives of countless thousands of urban
Americans.[3]

The landscape architects followed an intellectual blueprint familiar to their contemporaries. Many a literate nineteenth-century
American romantically enshrined nature (or Nature) as the temple
of the national soul. Poets, essayists, and artists fastened upon por-

trayals of nature as a way of establishing a national cultural identity and a code of national morality. Nature, if properly understood as the repository of a divine spirit, could reform lives; art, if centered on nature, could educate and uplift.[4] By mid-century the scenery album was a publishing phenomenon. Appearing by the score, the albums combined literary effort, art, and nationalistic fervor to glorify rivers, lakes, cliffs, mountains, meadows, forests—any natural features that could be labeled "scenic." There was no doubt about nature's message for Americans—at least not in these publications. As one album forthrightly put it: "In viewing magnificent scenes, the soul, expanded and sublimed, is imbued with a spirit of divinity, and appears, as it were, associated with the Deity himself. . . . Grand natural scenery tends permanently to affect the character of those cradled in its bosom, is the nursery of patriotism the most firm and eloquence the most thrilling." Another popular new art form was the urban lithograph. Produced in the hundreds over the later years of the century by a coterie of artists specializing in the genre, many of the pictures highlighted the natural setting of the city, often with little regard for reality.[5]

By emphasizing the improvement of human nature through the incorporation of rural scenery into an urban environment, then, the landscape architects appealed to the temper of their times. Their major contributions to public works and urban planning came with the rise of a public parks movement. First in the great cities—New York, Boston, Chicago—then in St. Louis, Detroit, Milwaukee, Buffalo, Louisville, Minneapolis, Kansas City, and elsewhere, the landscape architects directly influenced nineteenth-century city planning through the design and construction of urban parks.

Although parks varied in size and layout, between the 1850s and the early twentieth century landscape architects developed by consensus a vernacular of park purpose, function, and design. First, they agreed that the city was an artificial, unnatural environment, segregating people from the tranquility and sense of harmony gained by living with and within nature. The construction of great rural parks within the city could restore at least some semblance of the natural world to those who had lost touch with the repose of nature. Second, unlike the formal pleasure gardens of Europe, American urban parks featured woods, open spaces, bodies of water, clusters of shrubbery, clumps of trees, meandering paths, and craggy rock formations. The goal was to elicit in the visitor a sense of natural beauty and serenity nonetheless ordered and harmonized by human effort. Third, in laying out paths for walking, horses, and carriages, the landscape architect rejected the gridiron street patterns of the city in favor of curvilinear patterns more in keeping with the irregular rhythms of nature. Parks were to be integrated into the urban fabric, yet stand in stark contrast to the customary city environment. Fourth, although they disagreed among themselves about the amount of park acreage to devote to recreation grounds, all included recreation areas of some sort in their designs. The result was the creation of a pastoral middle landscape between the man-made environment of the city and the disorderly wilderness of nature itself (see Figures 16, 17).[6]

At the center of the park campaigns stood the gospel of moral environmentalism. Calling for public parks and the rural beautification of cities, the landscape architects evidenced their faith in the morally uplifting, healing qualities of nature. An early Chicago park planner, John Rauch, writing in 1869, fancifully asserted that "man however much he may boast of the superiority of mind over matter is as sensitive to external changes as the barometer is to those of the atmosphere. A pleasing landscape or a bright sunshine exhilarates his spirits, while a dreary waste, or a leaden sky produces depression." Rauch was certain that "we associate these ideas of external nature with our present sources of happiness or misery and carry them into our conceptions of a future fate."[7]

Frederick Law Olmsted was the most widely known and influential landscape architect of his time. Born in 1822, his life spanned the rest of the century and enough careers to occupy a regiment of lesser men. With his partner, Calvert Vaux, Olmsted designed and guided construction of the nation's first major urban park, Central Park in New York City, the first of scores of urban parks he helped shape. During the Civil War he served as executive secretary of the United States Sanitary Commission, an agency that was a training ground for many prominent sanitarians. For many years he shared and swapped schemes with his close friend George Waring, the best-known municipal engineer of the late nineteenth century. Beginning in 1871—the year in which he designed Riverside, a community just outside Chicago—Olmsted championed a suburban planning movement that captivated the imaginations of upper-class urbanites and real-estate developers over the remainder of the century. He shared with Daniel Burnham responsibility for the creation

and construction of the "Great White City" at the World's Columbian Exposition in Chicago in 1893, a testament to the virtues of an
ordered and orderly physical environment that heightened public
enthusiasm for city planning efforts.[8]

Olmsted, then, was one of the nineteenth century's earliest and
most significant urban planners. Or, perhaps more correctly, he was
one of the earliest antiurban planners, a leader of those who denounced the trend of cities' becoming too big, too crowded, too
dirty, too polluted, too filled with strange foreigners, too rife with
class hostilities, too unlike the smaller and presumably safer and
saner communities of the residents' fathers and grandfathers. Olmsted, like other landscape architects, sanitarians, engineers, and
moral reformers of the century, relied upon a time-honored pre-
scription for treating the ills of the evil city—return to the countryside. Forced by the commercial and industrial developments of their
times to recognize the impracticality, if not the impossibility, of re-
versing urban growth, they sought the next best solution—bring the
countryside into the city.

Olmsted claimed time and again over his career that the reason
to build rural parks in the great cities or lay out new communities
on the urban periphery was to democratize and humanize urban
living. Large cities destroyed the human sense of and need for community. City dwellers, he argued, every day of their lives "have seen
thousands of their fellowmen, have met them face to face, and yet
have no experience of anything in common with them." Olmsted
deplored this lack of "communicativeness," as he called it. Parks
would mitigate the physical ills of urban congestion and provide
"lungs for the city" through which fresh air could sweep away the
miasmic vapors that caused disease. But, of even greater importance, parks would bring together all social classes of the city.
There, people could gather "with a common purpose, not at all
intellectual, competitive with none, disposing to jealousy and spiritual or intellectual pride toward none, each individual adding by his
mere presence to the pleasure of all others, all helping to the
greater happiness of each." These noble sentiments were those of a
nineteenth-century liberal and democrat.[9]

Yet the democratic park designer and believer in moral environmentalism shared the disdain of many members of the urban elite
toward the working classes and immigrant poor. The tenement
house, he stated, was evil because of the "demoralization which it

works on the more incapable class of working people." A beautiful and healthful pleasure ground could alleviate the damaging impact of the physical environment: "No one who has closely observed the conduct of the people who visit the Park," he noted of Central Park in 1870, "can doubt that it exercises a distinctly harmonizing and refining influence upon the most unfortunate and most lawless classes of the city—an influence favorable to courtesy, self-control, and temperance."[10]

Lest we think, however, that Olmsted's principal aim was to paternally reform the poor, we must remind ourselves that he pushed for park planning in the interests of the upper classes. He repeatedly stated that men of wealth and refinement offered the true measure of a city's greatness. In his abortive plan for a San Francisco park, for example, he urged that "to offer inducements to men of wealth to remain, . . . [and regard] San Francisco as their home for life, . . . must be a primary purpose of all true municipal economy, and no pleasure ground can be adequate to the requirements of the city, the design of which is not, to a considerable degree, controlled by this purpose." His greatest achievement, Central Park, demonstrated his conviction that parks should, first and foremost, be pleasure grounds for the well-to-do and offer recreation and relaxation to middle-class citizens who had the time to take advantage of them.[11]

Olmsted's class biases were even more evident in his thoughts on and plans for suburban development. By the late 1860s he approvingly noted "a counter-tide of migration, especially affecting the more intelligent and more fortunate classes" out of the congested hearts of large cities. His plans for Riverside, Illinois, for New York's newly annexed twenty-third and twenty-fourth wards, which would later form a major portion of the Bronx, and for subsequent suburban tracts were informed by the same attitudes. Writing about those who lived or would come to live in suburbs around New York, he observed that "such men, living under favorable circumstances and with capital and energies economically directed to matters of general interest, are the most valuable constituents of a city; and it is by their numbers, wealth and influence, more than anything else, that a city takes its rank in the world as a metropolis."[12]

Whatever Olmsted's biases—which he shared with other important landscape architects of the period—there is no doubt about their contributions. More than simply designing parks or elite suburbs, they conceived comprehensive and ideal forms of the well-planned city long before the term "comprehensive" became a daily part of planners' vocabularies in the early twentieth century. Two examples will suffice.

Horace William Shaler Cleveland was a somewhat older contemporary and occasional collaborator of Olmsted's. Cleveland's most important contributions were in the Middle West, where he designed parks for Chicago and Minneapolis-St. Paul. He moved from Boston to Chicago in 1869 to become architect for a new South Park development recently authorized by the Illinois legislature. That same year he published *Public Grounds in Chicago: How to Give Them Character and Expression*, which would be widely read by others in his young profession during the rest of the century. Its vision of the social role of urban parks was similar to Olmsted's. Of greater significance, both in his own day and for our purposes, was his small 1873 publication, *Landscape Architecture as Applied to the Wants of the West*. This was apparently the first book to use that name for the new profession. Not content with planning parks in existing communities, Cleveland urged the planning of entire towns.

He divided proposed cities into specialized residential and commercial-industrial sectors. Encircling each sector and lacing through the various portions of the city were open spaces for parks, pleasure grounds, and greenswards. A series of parkways and broad boulevards radiated outward to connect with suburban districts. The greenery in the central city not only enhanced the beauty of a livable urban environment but also literally erected barriers against pollution and disease by containing business and industrial activities. For those working-class people who had to live within the central city, especially for the urban youth, the green open spaces provided a natural, countrylike atmosphere and exerted a strong moral influence. The closer one lived to "scenes of simple natural beauty," the further one was from the artificial conditions of urban life. "The elements of beauty should be everywhere present," he stated, "pervading all portions of the city as an essential ingredient."[13]

Cleveland thus imagined the ideal city as a total environment with nature as its bindings. The creation of new physical arrangements would in turn create a new set of values and moral awareness among urban Americans. Although he never had a chance to test his ideas, they attested to the scope of vision shared by some of the landscape architects. That conception of the integrated totality of the physical environment was even more explicit in the work of Robert Morris Copeland.

In the early 1870s, an almost two-decade-old landfill planning project was in full gear in Boston's Back Bay area. In the midst of the project, Copeland, an enterprising landscape architect, seized the opportunity to advance a comprehensive plan for remaking all of Boston. Copeland and Cleveland had formed a partnership many years earlier (1855). In 1856 the two had published a small pamphlet entitled "A Few Words on the Central Park" to present their views on the proposed New York project. Even at that early date, they had pleaded for long-range and thorough planning, noting that "it is foolish to say that we should plan only what we can immediately execute." By 1872 Copeland had transformed the call for comprehensive park planning into a summons for comprehensive city planning. [14]

Copeland denied that urban land-use patterns had to unfold according to the whims of individuals and the vagaries of the marketplace: "We have supposed that, for some unnamed reason, planning or a city's growth and progress could only be done as it grows; . . . this is a fallacious belief." Confronting the tradition of unfettered individualism in American cities, he argued that the best way to protect private property rights was to plan carefully for the future. Boston's physical, economic, and social wants could be "digested for its future progress" by dividing the city into parts and by measuring the relationship of each of the parts to the whole. "The city whose area is carefully studied, which shows by plans where wharves may be built, where new avenues are to be laid out, and where factories may congregate; where parks, gardens, and palaces, if desired, may be made, will grow," Copeland predicted, "in a sure, orderly, and progressive way."

Long-range planning and thoughtful engineering would satisfy all the city's present and future needs: "merchandise can be easily transported, business done, water and gas supplied, amusements furnished, fires limited, and sewage provided for." Accompanying his presentation were maps and plans for street patterns, public parks, suburban transportation corridors, commercial and industrial districts, public buildings, and the like.

Although the primary purpose of his plan was to guarantee the rational conduct of business, as crucial to a community's strength, Copeland stressed the importance of physical and scenic beauty, as crucial to public health and public morals. Trees, gardens, a series of small parks, and "fine avenues" connecting the various districts of the city would ensure a vital harmony between the man-made and the natural environment. Nor did he confine his plans to the city proper. He foresaw a day when the rural attractiveness of Boston's suburbs would diminish before the onrush of population growth and building density unless careful planning prevented it. In sum, Copeland understood the city as an organism whose needs were more than purely economic. "A city or town," he affirmed, "is to be considered as a whole, and in relation to all of its wants, as well as its necessities."[15]

Boston did not adopt Copeland's plan. It was too sweeping and too potentially expensive to appeal to cost-conscious city fathers. Still, he contributed significantly to the continuing public discussion about comprehensive planning for the urban future, demonstrating the growing conviction among planning enthusiasts that the city as a whole was greater than the sum of its parts.

The landscape architects did not ignore the individual physical problems of cities while awaiting opportunities to implement their larger schemes. Through designing and overseeing construction of scores of parks and suburban developments, they made a measurable impact on the urban physical environment of their times. Conceiving of their parks as central to broader public works campaigns, they cooperated with other physical planners to meet the challenges of booming American cities.

Among the many problems confronting nineteenth- and early twentieth-century city dwellers, three stood out—providing adequate water supplies, building efficient sewerage systems, and paving the streets. Each, in its own way, was part and parcel of the urban environmental crisis. Each seemed to contemporaries to call for technological innovation. Innovations, in turn, when partly or wholly successful, bulwarked both the deepening faith in technology as the best solution for society's ills and the growing conviction that long-range planning was possible and desirable. The first of the three to capture the attention of sanitarians, landscape architects, and engineers was water.

WATERING THE CITIES

Over the first half of the nineteenth century, most American cities used local sources for their water supply. Public wells and pumps drew local groundwater. Private citizens dug backyard wells, collected rainwater in barrels, or hauled water from streams, lakes, and nearby ponds. Those who could afford it purchased from a private entrepreneur's water wagon as it rolled through their neighborhoods. As towns and cities became more congested, the quantity and quality of local water sources suffered. A small number of physicians warned that impure water was responsible for a host of stomach disorders. But few medical men possessed either knowledge or evidence to support that contention.[16]

Most physicians judged as pure any water that was tasteless, odorless, and clear. Not until the 1850s and 1860s did substantial scientific evidence begin to document a relationship between polluted water and epidemic diseases. The investigations of Dr. John Snow of London established that public water supplies, contaminated by infected feces, spread cholera. In 1856–57 his fellow countryman Dr. William Budd identified water-borne sources of infection as responsible for typhoid fever epidemics. That discovery excited little interest in the United States prior to an 1873 report by an American doctor, Austin Flint, on the "Relations of Water to the Propagation of Fever," and only in the 1880s did irrefutable evidence convince a majority of medical experts that impure water was the principal transmitter of typhoid. Nonetheless, and for a variety of reasons only partly related to medical opinion, many cities had begun a search for new and purer water supplies years earlier.[17]

City officials had long understood the importance of *adequate* water supplies. As early as 1801 Philadelphia opened the first sizable public waterworks system in the United States, principally to flush the streets in the city's core. By the late 1830s, New York City, Richmond, St. Louis, and Pittsburgh had followed suit. City boosters recognized the difficulties of attracting new citizens and businesses to a community lacking sufficient water. That recognition surfaced earliest in cities undergoing rapid industrialization. In addition, fears of epidemics and fires, the pollution of public and private wells by seepage from graves and privies, and the destruction of streams by sewage or land-filled forced city officials to tap new sources and often to bring in water from outside municipal boundaries.[18]

As in all nineteenth-century public works projects, the question quickly arose: who should construct and administer the new systems, the private sector or the government? In a handful of communities the early response was "government." Spurred by cholera epidemics and a spate of costly fires, in 1835 the New York City Committee on Fire and Water strongly supported public ownership of a new water supply system, declaring that "in the hands of any other power than the Common Council, this free use [of water] would be restrained, and the experience of all other Cities (and our own included) teaches us the sad lesson that the trust of this power would be abused." City voters agreed, overwhelmingly approval a bond issue for a municipal waterworks that same year. Construction began in 1837, when engineers dammed a portion of the Croton River far to the north of the city and laid more than forty miles of masonry aqueduct to the city limits. The Croton Aqueduct was ready to service the city by the fall of 1842. Baltimore and Boston also soon developed upland water sources.[19]

Until well into the 1850s, however, most cities relied upon private aqueduct firms. Rarely was that reliance rewarded. The initial outlay and subsequent maintenance expenditures for wooden or masonry conduits were so large, and the resultant profits so minimal, that most private systems failed to serve the entire public, leaving the poorer and more remote districts without water supplies. As these areas expanded and became ever more congested, health problems mounted accordingly. To maximize profits, private firms stalled construction of fire hydrants and tried to avoid giving cities water to flush drains and storm sewers. For the same reason, they often refused to abandon expensively constructed sources—wells, for example—that had become polluted.

Nor were the companies eager to anticipate the future needs of cities. Unlike some municipal governments, private firms could not undertake legal condemnation proceedings under nuisance law or the police power should they want to service new areas of the city with water and gain a predictable source of profit over ensuing years. Moreover, as a water-minded sanitarian aptly named Thomas M. Drowne pointed out in 1893, when arguing for a city-owned waterworks in the spa of Newport, Rhode Island: "A private corporation, actuated with the best of intentions toward its fellow-citizens, cannot treat a question of large expenditure solely on the side of the good of the community. Only the city itself should deal with questions involving the public health."[20]

The companies' reluctance to extend water systems—coupled with an increasing demand for water for private, business, industrial, and civic needs—pressured officials to sponsor public waterworks. Across urban America, municipal ownership and administration gradually took hold between the 1850s and the 1890s. In 1860 each of the nation's sixteen largest cities had waterworks, with all but four—in New Orleans, San Francisco, Buffalo, and Providence—municipally owned. By the turn of the century, only nine of the fifty largest cities still had privately owned water supplies. By 1910, more than 70 percent of cities with over 30,000 inhabitants owned their waterworks.[21]

The building of public waterworks did not always solve the problem of water supply. Chicago's demand for water went unmet, for example, despite the creation in 1851 of the Chicago City Hydraulic Company and passage in 1852 of a $400,000 bond issue. By 1860 most Chicagoans still depended upon backyard wells and pumps for water increasingly polluted by drainage from privy vaults. During the 1860s and early 1870s, the new Chicago Board of Public Works commissioned tunnels built several miles out into Lake Michigan to improve the city's water supply. Not until 1898 was the city able to integrate its facilities into an adequate system.[22]

Other communities experienced similar difficulties. These were partly due to increased demand: as is always true of new technologies, an improvement in material comfort heightens expectations and requires further innovations.

Initially, urban leaders sought water for *civic* uses. They wanted hydrants and hoses for fire fighting, aqueducts for washing away the filth on city streets (in accordance with anticontagionist principles), fountains in public parks, connections to serve businesses and industries, and pipes to supply the public bathhouses in which the majority of citizens cleansed themselves, when they bathed at all. There was no notion of running water as a *household* necessity before mid-century.

With the new waterworks technology, all that changed. By mid-century, upper-class households commonly had running water. Soon middle-class families expected to have it as well. The hand-pump in the kitchen sink and the movable washbasin and bathtub began to give way to permanent fixtures. Detroit, which had built a waterworks in 1841, contained nearly 7,000 connected homes by 1859. Within five years after opening the Cochituate Aqueduct in 1848, Boston had 31,750 water fixtures in use; a decade later the number had reached almost 87,000. Around the nation, water use soared. Detroit went from 55 gallons of daily per capita consumption in 1856 to 149 in twenty-five years. Cleveland increased its usage sixfold between 1857 and 1872. Chicago's daily consumption was 33 gallons per person in 1856 and over 144 gallons per person by 1882. In 1848 Bostonians opposed to the Cochituate Aqueduct had ridiculed the notion that the city could ever use 7.5 million gallons of water a day. In 1860 that city's Water Board warned that demand would soon outstrip supply and moaned that the average daily use of 97 gallons of water for each inhabitant was "without parallel in the civilized world." Everywhere, more and more Americans were finding new uses for running water. Some were even drinking it, a novel experiment in a nation that one historian has labeled the "alcoholic republic."[23]

The increased water supply made possible another new piece of technology. The water closet, or flush toilet, had received a patent in England at the close of the eighteenth century, and one in the United States in 1833. Expense and lack of sufficient water limited use of the new "convenience" until mid-century. At first, only the wealthy could afford the luxury of an indoor toilet. In 1856 New York, the nation's richest city, had only 10,384 water closets for a population of over 630,000. Even when water became more plentiful and plumbing cheaper, many middle-class urbanites resisted the innovation, apparently fearing the sanitary implications of bringing the disposal of human wastes indoors. Others, disdainful or jealous of the well-to-do, identified indoor plumbing with aristocratic pretensions. When President Millard Fillmore ordered the first permanent bath and water closet installed in the White House in 1851, partisan critics denounced his action as "both unsanitary and undemocratic."[24]

After mid-century, however, a new room—the bathroom—began to appear in American homes. Lifestyles, expectations, and concepts of the "good life" would never again be the same. A family's ability to devote an entire room solely to bodily functions became a measure of social success. Installation of indoor plumbing increased fairly rapidly during the 1860s and 1870s. Buffalo, for instance, by the mid-1870s had nearly 5,200 dwellings connected to the city water system; over 3,300 contained water closets. By 1880 roughly one-fourth of all urban households held water closets.[25]

Efforts to provide adequate water for the cities did not end environmental pollution. They increased it. New technologies often produce unexpected results. Cities now had to dispose of vast quantities of water brought in by the new aqueducts. Existing surface drainage in most communities was inadequate. As more dwellings and businesses became connected to the expanded water systems and as the installation of water closets increased, so did disposal problems. At first cities tried to remove excess water by dumping it into street gutters, stormwater sewers, or cesspools. But the new water supplies overran existing systems of disposal. Water closets overflowed the old privy waste-disposal systems, soaked the urban water tables, and converted large portions of city lands, cellar dwellings, and streets into a stinking morass. Shortly after the introduction of a new water system, a report of the Pawtucket, Rhode Island, City Council lamented that "water was here and had become a nuisance." Everywhere, as water flowed in abundance, the tide of complaints rose.[26]

Throughout urban America the pattern of events was the same. Soon after the construction of new waterworks, legislators found themselves inundated by petitions for relief from angry citizens. Not all came from their own residents. Upset about health problems presented by installation of the new water closets in urban homes, an 1869 editorial in *Scientific American* charged that "the present water closet system, with all its boasted advantages is the worst that can be generally adopted, briefly because it is a most extravagant method of converting a moll-hill into a mountain." The water closet, the writer explained, "merely removes the bulk of our excreta from our houses, to choke our rivers with foul deposits and rot at our neighbors' door." One city's "satisfactory" removal became another community's problem. A Cincinnati sanitarian noted in 1879 that the Ohio River, the principal water source for dozens of towns and cities, was "a gigantic sewer which conveys into the Gulf the excrementitious matters of the vast populations now residing on its banks."[27]

Political prattling, a customary response of elected officials, could neither divert nor dispose of citizens' cries for relief. City leaders had to find a way to deal with problems presented by the new technology. The solutions proposed for these new problems were once again physical and technical. Sanitarians, city officials, and municipal engineers urged and engaged in two massive and related public works projects—building sewers and paving streets. Both lengthened the reach of city governments into the lives of private citizens. Both strengthened the premises and promises of long-range city planning.

SEWERING THE CITIES

Even before the large-scale introduction of the new water systems, many sanitarians and civil engineers had argued that a good sewer system was an investment in the present and future health of the citizenry. John Griscom observed in 1845 that sewers were "not only the most economical, but the *only* mode, in which the immense amounts of filth daily generated in this large city, can be effectively removed." Others concurred. John Bell, a Philadelphia physician reporting in 1859 for the national Committee on the Internal Hygiene of Cities, argued that "paving ought to precede the erection of houses, and drainage follow habitation at a very early period. A neglect of these two preliminary conditions for public health has been productive, in all ages, of a fearful waste of life."[28]

In the late 1870s George Waring vividly conveyed the relationship between sewers and health. Writing about the piecemeal construction of sewers in Boston and New York, Waring charged that they were "huge gasometers, manufacturing day and night a deadly aeriform poison, ever seeking to invade the houses along their course; reservoirs of liquid filth, ever oozing through the defective joints, and polluting the very earth upon which the city stands."[29]

Warnings about a "deadly aeriform poison" stemmed from a sewer gas theory of disease. That theory—known in the glory days of Athens and Rome—reemerged in France and Germany during the 1820s and 1830s, and in Britain soon afterward. American reformers became familiar with it through the writings of the English sanitarians Edwin Chadwick and Charles Murchison. Bell's 1859 report devoted several pages to the subject. So fearful did the consequences appear that the Chicago sanitary engineer George Preston Brown said in 1881 of sewer gas: "I believe that it has, and will, conquer cities. So sure as there is a future, this city is doomed to perish at the breath of this relentless enemy, sewer-malaria."[30]

Physicians first described sewer gas as a single, specific entity derived from decomposing organic matter in sewers. It took two forms, one foul-smelling, the other odorless. The latter was allegedly the more deadly, since its presence was difficult to detect. By the 1870s researchers recognized varieties of vitiated air and suggested using the phrases "sewer gases" or "sewer air." In the 1880s other investigators claimed that sewer gases emanated from sewage wherever found, not only in sewers, but in leakage from cesspools and privies as well.[31]

Elaborate experiments and chemical analyses were conducted to underscore the alleged dangers. The spurious theory gained substantial support from many involved in the public health movement, especially engineers. Engineering periodicals generally supported the theory: one editorialized that "sewer gas, according to all the works on medical sanitary science, is one of the most destructive poisons and fruitful causes of disease in large cities, producing diptheria, typhus, brain and bilious fevers, malaria and many other forms of disease." Among the "other forms," physicians specified pneumonia, cholera, dysentery, scarlet fever, and cerebrospinal meningitis. Common effects included weakness, drowsiness, loss of appetite, vomiting, and sore throats. Some writers affirmed that sewer gas was a major cause of insanity.[32]

By the 1880s, under the influence of the germ theory, researchers expanded the dangers of sewer gas to include harboring undetectable pathogenic bacteria that could cause a host of specific diseases. Debates over whether gases or germs were the chief cause of disease heated up over the last fifteen years of the century. More often than not, however, proponents of the sewer gas theory accepted many of the tenets of the germ theory without abandoning the anticontagionist position. Although Waring was the most prominent promoter of the sewer gas theory (holding his own patent on a system designed to combat the problem), scores of engineers offered technical schemes for preventing the escape of the gas through sounder construction of sewers.[33]

The beauty of the theory was that it could be neither proved nor disproved decisively, particularly in regard to the odorless version of the gas. The lack of final proof, however, did not allay the fears of physicians, engineers, and citizens; it probably heightened them.

Some turned to their own advantage the widely advertised threats to health. Physicians earned substantial incomes from treating alleged victims, especially after the personal physician to President James A. Garfield published in *Popular Science Monthly* a scary piece calling upon citizens to return to bedside basins and outhouses. Plumbers found work repairing or replacing supposedly faulty connections of water closet pipes to sewer drains. Public outcry against plumbers' abuses resulted in the last two decades of the century in city and state licensing and regulation. The National Association of Master Plumbers was formed to encourage self-regulation and promote the public image of its members. By the early 1890s, public health officers could note that plumbing was no longer a "mere trade"; its importance to health, and "its requirements regarding scientific knowledge, have elevated it to a profession."[34]

Some city dwellers found more immediately practical uses for the sewer gas theory than did physicians and plumbers. One journal in the early 1880s reported the following incident in a girls' school: "An examination was coming on, several of the young ladies were not prepared for it, and accordingly they put their heads together to devise a scheme for preventing its holding. One suggested that a sewer gas scare would be about the thing, and accordingly the fellow conspirators scattered limburger plentifully throughout the desks. The odors which resulted convinced the principal that there was something fatally wrong about the sanitary arrangements of the building, and the examination was indefinitely postponed."[35]

The sewer gas theory, of course, could not have captured public attention in the absence of sewers. To appreciate the sense of urgency compelling construction of new sewer systems from mid-century on, we must briefly review earlier conditions.

At the outset of the century, only the largest cities—New York, Boston, and Philadelphia—had any kind of underground drains, and these wooden or brick sewers were used only to drain stormwater. Although it sometimes occurred, the depositing of human wastes in the sewers was against the law. Elsewhere, for much of the century, surface gutters running along the edges of streets or down the middle provided the sole source of drainage. As population densities and water supplies increased, so did the inadequacies of traditional methods of human waste and wastewater disposal.

Cities like New York that saw the introduction of water closets during the 1840s had ordinances forbidding connection of the new devices to sewers intended for stormwater. When Manhattan and several other cities allowed connection of water closets to existing sewers (beginning in the mid-forties), results were disastrous. The stormwater drains did not permit a rapid enough flow of water to dilute human wastes and effectively remove them, wherever the final outflow might occur. Clogged drains, both underground and surface, spilled their noxious contents into the cities' subsurface water tables, polluting the water supply, or into the streets. In a handful of the largest urban centers, wealthy citizens paid for private construction of short-run sewer lines in their neighborhoods. At mid-century no American city had anything approaching an integrated system of underground sewers for disposal of human wastes.[36]

The notion of a water-carriage system to flush away human excrement emerged first in England during the 1840s. Over the next decade English sanitarians proposed a network of brick sewers to eliminate both stormwater and household wastes. As the historian Joel Tarr notes, this new technology stood in vivid contrast to the cesspool-privy vault system: it was capital-intensive and demanded construction of large public works; it employed batch rather than individual collection, ending the need for workers to clean private homes and businesses and haul away the wastes through city streets; and it elevated municipal responsibility over private initiative.[37]

The new system of pipe sewers, with interceptors to free shorelines and urban lands of piles of filth, promised to rid cities of both household and street wastes and to replace privies with indoor plumbing. Initially, in cities like Boston and New York, city councils empowered the piecemeal construction of new sewerlines, a few miles here, a few there. Without an integrated system, these only made matters worse. Some districts of a city, usually the downtown business section and a small number of wealthy neighborhoods, experienced a distinct improvement; other areas often stood awash in the outflow of the sewer lines and the overflow of the old privy waste-disposal system.[38]

Ravaged by epidemics during the late 1840s and early 1850s, Chicago had the highest average death rate of any city in the United States. Construction of the first comprehensive sewer system in the nation began there in the 1850s. In 1855 the Illinois legislature authorized the city to create a Board of Sewerage Commissioners charged with building a system to drain surface water and industrial and household wastes. As chief engineer, the board appointed Ellis

S. Chesbrough, Boston's first city engineer and commissioner of the Boston Water Works. In his initial report, Chesbrough labeled privy vaults "abominations that should be swept away as speedily as possible," for "to construct the vaults as they should be, and maintain them even in a comparatively inoffensive condition, would be more expensive than to construct an entire system of sewerage for no other purpose, if the past experience of London and other large cities was any guide for the future of Chicago."[39]

Chesbrough's plan, accepted and implemented by the board, called for a combined system to carry off sewage from both streets and buildings. It was to be an intercepting system of brick sewers, three to six feet in diameter, with main lines and lateral connectors. The chief question was where to drain the outflow. The engineer offered four alternatives. First, drain sewage into the Chicago River, which bisected the city, then, in its diluted form, into Lake Michigan (see Map 1). Second, dump it directly into Lake Michigan, although that might affect the city's water supply and present maintenance difficulties during the winter months. Third, drain sewerage into reservoirs from which it could be pumped and sold to farmers. Chesbrough worried about health hazards from foul odors, though, as well as the uncertainty of future demands for fertilizer. Finally, he proposed construction of a "steamboat canal" from the lake to the Des Plaines River a number of miles to the southwest. That river flowed into the Illinois River some 50 miles to the south, which in turn emptied into the Mississippi about 250 miles away. Although this fourth alternative was later (1892) adopted, Chesbrough regarded it as impractical, because too expensive, in the mid-fifties.[40]

From the standpoint of health and cost, the first alternative appeared the most reasonable. All the west division's sewage, all the north division's except for the lakefront areas, and about one-half the south division's would flow into the Chicago River and eventually pass into Lake Michigan. The board agreed with Chesbrough and told him to get to work.

Another problem immediately presented itself. Chicago's unusually flat terrain militated against construction of underground sewers that depended upon gravity for drainage. Chesbrough's solution was simple: raise the grade level of the city while building the sewer system. As construction moved away from the river, workmen raised streets above the sewer lines, then covered them with packed earth, which became the foundation for newly laid and graded streets. Vacant lots were no problem; land-fill raised them to the new level. Stone and brick buildings were another matter. Chesbrough had workmen dig around their foundations, install hydraulic jacks at strategic points, and then, on signal, lift the structure from the mud and fill in hard-packed dirt beneath.[41]

By modern standards, the land-raising and sewer construction project was impressive. By mid-nineteenth-century standards, it was nothing short of monumental. Completion of the task took nearly ten years. The city spent in excess of $10 million to construct almost fifty-four miles of sewers and to raise the grade level of the streets by as much as twelve feet in the emerging central business district. Yet Chesbrough's hope that river and lake water would dilute sewage sufficiently proved vain. The Chicago River, especially the South Branch, turned into an open sewer, and Lake Michigan's shore waters became polluted. Since the lake was Chicago's principal source of drinking water, citizens soon began to complain about its taste and smell. Several other large-scale engineering projects were required during the 1860s and early 1870s to provide better sources of water and more efficient drainage.[42]

Although building the new integrated sewer system did not accomplish everything promised, it measurably alleviated Chicago's soil- and water-pollution problems. Chicago's successes certified the claims of sanitarians and engineers that construction of a comprehensive network of sewers was technologically possible, economically feasible, and hygienically desirable. The Board of Sewerage Commissioners had originally charged Chesbrough to construct a system whose main purpose was to "improve and preserve" the citizens' health. The first project, together with its successors, contributed to a significant decline in the city's mean annual death rates (see Table 1). At the end of Chesbrough's service as city engineer (1879), he could take great pride in having improved the health of the city and pioneered a host of new techniques emulated by other engineers across urban America.[43]

By 1880 Chicago had extended its sewer system to a total of 337 miles of main and lateral pipes. The relationship between the public's health and the availability of sewerage appeared certain. No less a personage than John H. Rauch confirmed this. The first commissioner of Chicago's new board of health (1867), Rauch helped to found the APHA in 1872 and became its president in 1876. The

TABLE 1
Mean Annual Death Rates (per 1,000) in Chicago, All Diseases, 1843–1877

Years	Death Rate
1843–1856	37.91
1856–1870	23.97
1870–1877	22.13

Source: John H. Rauch, *The Sanitary Problems of Chicago, Past and Present* (Chicago, 1879), pp. 1–15.

following year he accepted the challenge of heading up the newly created Illinois State Board of Health. As a nationally renowned leader of the public health movement, his views carried great weight. His 1879 survey of Chicago's sanitary conditions gained wide readership. Comparing death rates for various wards during the summer months, when malaria and typhoid fever were particularly virulent, Rauch found impressive differences. The critical factor, he explained, was the extent of sewer lines: the more sewer lines, the lower the mortality rates.[44]

Despite considerable public debate, the English water-carriage system of sewerage caught on quickly in the United States during the last three decades of the century. Opponents, including a number of private waste-removal companies, decried the costs of building a public system and pointed to pollution hazards such as sewer gas. In a number of cities, the debates delayed construction of sewer systems for many years. Still, public demand carried the day. Scores of reports by city engineers sent abroad to investigate European practices advertised the virtues of these systems. The discovery during the 1880s that many diseases, including the killer typhoid, were water-borne accelerated campaigns for pure water, sewer construction, and filtration of both water and sewage. Sanitarians and engineers might debate whether the best reason for sewer construction was sympathy for the sick or financial savings to the city through the improved health of the citizenry. But all agreed, on the basis of their own experience and available statistical evidence, that sewering the city impressively reduced pollution and improved public health (see Table 2). The largest cities generally constructed combined systems (with stormwater and human wastes in the same pipe), while smaller communities opted more often for sanitary sewers alone. In 1890 only twenty-six cities with populations over

10,000 had no sewers at all. By 1907 nearly every city had them. Experiments during the 1890s created a new technology of filtration and demonstrated its efficacy. Filtration of water and sewage brought a dramatic drop in typhoid mortality rates, a drop that averaged 65 percent in selected major cities.[45]

The lessons were clear. Water and sewer systems were a city's lifelines. As such, they were too vital to be left to the piecemeal approach of either private enterprise or municipal construction. The recommendation of the Massachusetts Drainage Commission of 1884–85 was typical of developing attitudes: that "the supervision of matters pertaining to water supply, sewerage, and the pollution of waters generally, be assigned to some board . . . to enable it to introduce system and method in these important departments of the common welfare." Comprehensive systems, built and administered by experts and funded by local government, had to replace the unsystematic methods of the past.[46]

TABLE 2

Mortality rates (per 1,000), all diseases, by Race and Miles of Sewers in Cities, 1890–1900

	All Citizens		Colored		Sewers (miles)	
	1890	1900	1890	1900	1890	1900
All Cities (28 largest)	23.3	18.6	n.a.	n.a.	176.1	366.5
Newark	29.0	19.8	44.9	29.7	87.0	186.9
New York*	27.1	20.4	36.2	28.4	844.0	1467.0
Baltimore	24.8	21.0	36.4	31.2	28.0	43.8
Boston	24.8	20.1	33.3	25.5	291.0	581.9
Philadelphia	22.7	21.2	32.4	31.1	376.0	951.1
Chicago	21.1	16.2	23.3	21.6	525.0	1529.0
St. Louis	19.1	17.9	34.6	32.2	328.0	522.2
Mean	24.09	19.51	34.44	28.53	354.1	754.6

*New York City figures for 1890 include death rates and miles of sewers for Brooklyn, then an independent city, but by 1900 a borough of New York City.

Sources: U.S. Bureau of the Census, *Eleventh Census, 1890*, vol. 4, part 2, *Vital Statistics* (Washington, D.C.) pp. 2–4, 21–22, 75–99; and *Social Statistics of Cities* (Washington, D.C.), "Table 67," pp. 78–87; *Twelfth Census, 1900* (Washington, D.C.), in *Abstract*, "Table 95," pp. 186–96; sewer figures cited for 1900 are from 1902, *Bulletin 20*, "Table 12," pp. 126–31.

Between 1870 and 1910, municipal construction and control of unified systems gained widespread public acceptance. By 1901 the standard text on urban public health, Charles V. Chapin's *Municipal Sanitation in the United States*, testified: "Even the need for sewers has scarcely to be urged by health officers. The public so well appreciates their advantages that they are usually demanded when needed, even if they must be entirely paid for by the abutters." A cost-conscious citizenry had become as well a health-conscious citizenry. Nor should we forget the convenience factor. Which home owner, businessman, industrialist, or politician could fail to appreciate the aesthetic improvement of no longer having to pass over streets piled with filth, no longer having to walk to the backyard privy in rain or snow? Planning enthusiasts had capitalized on both facts and fears to persuade their fellow citizens to sewer the cities.[47]

During the years of the sewer campaigns, the sanitarians, landscape architects, and municipal engineers also labored to inform and convince the public of the importance of improving the streets themselves. The new water and sewer systems, to work effectively, required improvement in the quality of the streets beneath which ran the urban lifelines. The response was to pave the cities.

PAVING THE CITIES

As late as 1890, approximately half the street mileage of the nation's largest cities remained unpaved, more often because of lack of finances than lack of concern or effort. Between the 1870s and the turn of the century, city governments across the country undertook expensive paving programs to improve drainage and to cover wastewater-saturated soil. These measures were in part, as we have seen, a response to the new abundance of water.[48]

They also aimed to improve the clean-up and disposal of the refuse that clogged even the main thoroughfares of large cities. For most of the nineteenth century, littering was acceptable social behavior. Household garbage, rubbish, ashes and cinders, scrap metal, industrial wastes, animal manure—all were piled in and along city streets. From mid-century on, as urban populations boomed, human and animal traffic moved more slowly or stalled in the streets. Passersby found it increasingly difficult to make their way along the sidewalks (which first came into common use in American cities during the 1850s). In the last three decades of the century, sporadic complaints gave way to a growing movement of private groups and public officials determined to deal with the situation.[49]

Among those groups were women's clubs. Both sexes then found it natural for women to take the lead in "municipal house-keeping." One of the earliest organizations to shoulder this burden was the Ladies' Health Protective Association, formed in 1884 in New York City. "It is the climax of aggravation to the painstaking house-keeper," the women told the major, "to look out of her windows and see ash barrels standing forgotten on the sidewalk from hour to hour and often from day to day; to have those barrels toppled over by sportive boys or raked over by grimy ragpickers, and the contents left in hillocks in the street from one month's end to another; and sup-posing even that she personally . . . carefully sweeps and washes her own area flags and space of sidewalk, to have these covered within two hours by the sticks, loose papers and powdered manure that blow upon them from all quarters alike." Proper waste disposal was necessary, the women urged, for both sanitary and aesthetic reasons. All city dwellers ought to enjoy "the outside neatness, cleanliness and freshness, which are the natural complement and completion of inside order and daintiness and which are to the fem-inine taste and perception, simply indispensable, not only to com-fort but to self-respect." To the accomplishment of those ends, the LHPA, joined by similar women's groups in other cities, worked dil-igently into the early twentieth century.[50]

Sanitary engineers and public health officers, no less than the women's organizations, demanded new techniques of street cleaning and new technologies of refuse disposal. Among the new technolo-gies were "cremators" and "incinerators," adapted from British de-signs, and a reduction process that extracted oils from garbage. But another piece of technology garnered the greatest support. George Waring, for instance, as street-cleaning commissioner of New York City in the 1890s, estimated that asphalt paving would reduce street-cleaning expenditures by half a million dollars a year. Waring's voice was only one among many. Underlying the arguments for and against paving improvements were changing uses and perceptions of streets.[51]

For much of the nineteenth century, urban Americans, like their counterparts in England and France, considered streets an extension of their own property. To be sure, public streets served public purposes. They were thoroughfares for the free movement of people and goods, communication devices if you will. They also functioned as architectural baselines, the organizing devices of both public and private uses of space. Most important, as far as most city dwellers were concerned, streets met social needs. They were gathering places for a variety of activities: shopping in open-air markets or at peddlers' carts; promenading on a Sunday afternoon; dancing on festive occasions; drinking and playing cards with friends and neighbors; overseeing the games of children frolicking in the street as playground. Until about mid-century, most private homes directly fronted the streets, which introduced fresh air and light into the interior of houses; and since few houses had entry halls, people leaving their homes stepped directly into the streets. Americans treated streets as if they were front yards, and most municipalities, which legally could have acted otherwise, acquiesced in this practice. [52]

If streets had any form of pavement, for instance, it was because neighborhood property owners wanted it. As the principal users of most streets, abuttors (the legal term for those owning frontage property) had to pay for any street improvements. They would hold a neighborhood or block meeting, and if a majority voted for paving, they would choose the type of pavement and petition elected officials to secure for them a paving contract. It was only at this point that the city entered the street improvement business to hire a contractor, guarantee him payment, and enforce a special assessment against all abuttors, including those who had voted against paving. Depending upon one's viewpoint, this was *private* planning at its best or worst in a democratic society. [53]

For over two-thirds of the century, the most commonly used paving materials were cobblestone, gravel, and macadam (a form of crushed stone). The census of 1880, the first that gathered such figures, revealed that 26.1 percent of paved streets in large cities used cobblestones, while over half of the total paved street mileage consisted of either gravel or macadam. The latter, named after the Scottish engineer who developed it, came into use in the United States in the 1820s, although not until the 1860s, with the invention of the steamroller and the mechanical stone crusher, were engineers able to lay "proper" (that is, tightly enough packed) macadam pavements. Although all three were satisfactory for residential streets with light traffic, none proved useful for heavily traveled urban streets. Drainage was inadequate, especially once water became more abundant; maintenance costs were high and soared as heavy commercial traffic increased. Most cities were unable or unwilling to provide necessary maintenance. Street filth, garbage, and horse droppings wedged into the crevices of even newly laid pavements.[54]

The disadvantages of these pavement types led to exhaustive efforts from mid-century on to find the perfect urban pavement. Cities experimented with granite blocks, bricks, concrete, and even iron wheelways. Between the late 1850s and the 1870s, however, the most popular new paving technique employed wooden blocks, even in east coast cities where wood was much more expensive than in the booming cities of the Midwest. Among the varieties of wooden pavement, the favorite was the system patented by Samuel Nicholson shortly before the Civil War. Engineers nailed uniformly square blocks of wood to a plank foundation, with spacer boards between the blocks coming to within two inches of the surface to provide a toehold for horses. To prevent disintegration, the blocks were coated and grouted with tar.[55]

The early success of this type of pavement in Chicago, along with vigorous promotion, led to wide adoption, but its success was short-lived. Poorly treated and poorly laid in most cities, Nicholson pavement usually began to decay within two or three years. Laid too loosely, entire streets floated away in a heavy rainfall. Packed too tightly, the blocks contracted in cold, dry weather and expanded in hot, humid weather: in several cases the built-up pressures exploded whole rows of blocks five to ten feet into the air or caused entire streets to bow and break the curbstones. In the absence of such dramatic instances of failure, wooden blocks still posed aesthetic and sanitary problems. Over much of the year heavy traffic would grind horse manure into the blocks, while urine and diluted garbage would seep into the pores of the wood. In the heat of summer, Nicholson pavements would disengorge their contents.[56]

American cities next turned to asphalt, already used by European cities, with indifferent results, for several decades. The material was introduced in Newark, New Jersey, in 1871, but it was its successful use in Washington, D.C., several years later that persuaded other cities to adopt the new technology.[57]

Asphaltic oil is a bitumen (a class of solid or semisolid hydrocarbons intermixed with impurities) that occurs naturally or as a residue of petroleum-refining processes. Once purified and combined with sand or stone dust as a binder, the oil becomes a flexible mass that can protect foundations from erosion and perform the weight-bearing functions of a pavement. Although relatively expensive, asphalt recommended itself in several ways. It had greater durability. The oil's elasticity allowed pavement to expand and contract with less breakage. It was inexpensive to patch and maintain. Its flexibility afforded less wear-and-tear on horses' hooves and wagon wheels. The smooth surface was easy to clean, which made it attractive for both aesthetic and sanitary reasons. In tandem with the new use of Portland cement as a foundation, asphalt paving became the dominant type of smooth pavement in American cities between the mid-1880s and the turn of the century.[58]

Given all the aesthetic, environmental, and sanitary reasons for paving, we might question why massive paving programs did not occur until the later years of the nineteenth century. The timing of technological knowledge and innovation provides only part of the answer. Americans knew about earlier European successes and failures with various types of street pavement long before they undertook similar experiments themselves. As early as 1841, for example, Henry Halleck, a prominent American engineer, had praised the potential of asphalt pavement for urban streets. The rest of the answer to our question lay in significant changes in the uses of streets in post–Civil War urban America.[59]

The rapid expansion of the urban core and the rise of central business districts in postwar cities altered the functions of many city streets. They now became the lifelines of new public services. Water mains and sewer lines, as well as pipes holding gas for lighting, ran beneath them. Telegraph and telephone wires, and by the 1880s electric power lines, stretched above them. The horse-car, then the cable car, the electric trolley, and, in some cities, the elevated train transformed many streets into new corridors of travel. All these public facilities demanded properly laid, graded, and paved streets.

A number of central-city residents resisted municipal attempts to pave more and more miles of streets, fearing loss of personal autonomy, shocked by mismanagement and corruption in city government, or simply unwilling to incur the costs. Still others wanted to preserve the older uses of streets as the extensions of private property. An 1896 petition from a Brooklyn neighborhood attested to the staying power of tradition. Asphalting a particular street, these residents protested,

will make——a thoroughfare from——to——for carts and vehicles of all
kinds, including bicycles . . . , and the resulting noise will be so
intolerable that it will make the street undesirable for private residences.
The lives of our children would be in constant danger from reckless riders
and drivers, if this private street is to be made a thoroughfare. We would
prefer the privacy of the street as a residential street, and for the safety of
our children who would not be menaced by the additional travel of
bicycles and other vehicles.[60]

It was not only the needs of central cities that hastened, or in some instances impeded, street paving programs. The greatest growth of postwar cities occurred on the urban fringe. New suburban subdivisions and annexations led to reevaluations of policies on public works expenditures, including streets. Municipal reformers stressed the necessity of centralizing control of the streets; engineers repeatedly claimed that efficiency and savings would result from long-range planning for public works in both the core city and the new subdivisions. It seemed to make little sense, for example, to widen and pave streets in the central city without providing for their ultimate extension into the suburbs. Over the last three decades of the century, urban property owners, suburban developers, streetcar company executives, politicians, and municipal engineers fought a series of running battles over control of the streets. The outcome of those skirmishes, as we shall see, bolstered the concept and practices of professional city planning.[61]

American civic leaders viewed cities as, first and foremost, containers for business activity, and the single most important reason for paving city streets was to ease the movement of goods, services, and human traffic. The Philadelphia engineer Lewis Haupt was only one among many who believed that "it may safely be assumed that facility of communication is one of the most potent elements of human progression and development, hence any obstacle to mobility, however small, becomes a bar to progress and ought to be removed." The well-known engineer Francis Greene claimed in 1890 that "the streets of the city are built for the same purpose as railroads between cities—viz. to provide for the transportation of freight and passengers." Still, many a city leader gave nearly equal weight to public health considerations. Certainly the engineers who shepherded the projects emphasized their sanitary benefits almost as much as their traffic-bearing value.[62]

Street paving, new water and sewer systems, park planning— these and other technical feats would solve both the crisis of the physical environment and the crisis of the social and moral order in booming American cities. Or so their advocates hoped and claimed. An increasing number of urban Americans had become aware of an environmental crisis of major proportions overtaking their communities. Groups of new professionals had emerged, eager to inform fellow citizens about the rising tide of problems and enthusiastic about technological cures for the diseases of the body or the human spirit—or both, for many involved in planning efforts equated the physical environment of the cities and the moral environment of the citizens. More often than not, the sanitarians, landscape architects, and municipal engineers in the forefront of public works campaigns had linked concerns about the quality of human life to the kinds of technological responses they proposed.

All were important contributors to the construction of the new urban culture. The landscape architects and sanitarians clearly had an impact on the physical environment of the cities and helped to change formulation of public policies and the administrative reach and authority of municipal governments. The latter changes in many ways proved to have the most far-reaching significance for modern urban America. Among the planners, the vanguard of public policy innovators were municipal engineers. Both administratively and as a partially planned container for the conduct of human life, the modern American city emerged as an engineered metropolis.

8

THE ENGINEERED
METROPOLIS

A T THE HEART of the engineered metropolis stood a new and expanding profession of municipal engineers. During the post–Civil War years, they were the principal promoters of technological solutions to urban ills. Virtually the only problems successfully attacked by nineteenth-century urban leaders were those susceptible to engineering expertise. As we have seen, for example, many cities dramatically lowered their disease and mortality rates with the construction of paved streets and efficient water-supply and sewage systems.

Municipal engineers solidified their growing reputation as problem-solvers in three ways. First, they made themselves indispensable to officials eager to boost their city's expansion. Second, they proclaimed (and apparently persuaded the public) that they were neutral experts who stood above partisan politics. Third, within their own ranks, they created a professional bureaucracy that outsiders came to admire as a model of efficiency. As an often-cited early twentieth-century text on sanitation and planning observed about the construction and administration of all types of public works, "details have been wisely left to the engineers."[1]

That affirmation was partly wishful thinking, partly admonition. On numerous occasions, urban partisan politics and short-sighted efforts to cut corners and save money had interfered with public works construction. Still, if city officials had not left everything to the engineers, they had often entrusted the details of planning and construction and most of the details of administration to them.

By doing so, officials recognized and supported the growth of a new profession in the United States—municipal engineering—and set in motion processes that would ultimately help restructure municipal government. For local governments and the public at large had come to accept the concept of city planning, if not always the actual practice. From citywide water and sewer systems to plans for every feature of the urban physical environment was but a short step of the imagination. A major engineering journal developed this logic in 1877: "If the grading, drainage, paving, cleansing, and policing of towns are worthy of careful and systematic control, so are also the general shaping of the towns, the preservation or destruction of the natural features of their sites, and the distribution of their population and residences. Just what are the proper limits of public interference in such matters is a political question upon which we cannot venture; but public neglect has shown itself to be both costly and pernicious."[2]

Engineers shepherded remarkable innovations in technology, helped shape the directions of city planning thought and practice, and laid the groundwork of modern municipal administration. Scrutiny of the emerging profession and its part in reshaping the urban physical environment underscores the importance of engineers in the developing urban culture of the United States.

ENGINEERING A BUREAUCRACY

The functions of modern municipal administration were inherent in water and wastewater technologies. Sewerage and water supplies required permanent construction and thus necessitated some kind of long-range planning. If engineers did not plan systems to accommodate future growth, the city would have to lay new aqueducts and trunk sewers each time the population increased even slightly or began to move into new subdivisions. A system that met present needs and anticipated future growth might be expensive in the short run but economical over time. City officials quickly learned these facts and also that disastrous health and financial consequences ensued if they ignored the advice of experts.

Consider several examples. During the early 1870s Alexander Shepard, boss of the District of Columbia, wasted a $5 million bond issue when contractors hired for political reasons built lateral sewers that had to run uphill to empty into the main sewers. In the absence of effective pumping mechanisms (most systems at the time depended upon gravity flow rather than steam pumps), Shepard's system was worse than useless. Partly because of this fiasco, the District lost home rule and became subject to a federally appointed commission that had to include at least one officer of the Army Corps of Engineers. St. Louis had to reconstruct its water-supply system and Cincinnati its sewer system within ten years after completion; both city administrations had rejected engineers' proposals in favor of politically popular decisions to cut costs. Partisan politics and graft counted more than engineering considerations in the construction of Detroit's sewer system, as the city's reform mayor, Hazen Pingree, complained when its concrete pipes began to crumble into dust during his regime in the 1890s. And so the story went from city to city.[3]

Water and sewer systems required centralized construction and administration. There were economies of scale in building only one reservoir and one main aqueduct. An integrated sewer system with a receiving sewer at the lowest grade level and an outfall at a site that minimized pollution also considerably reduced costs over the long haul. The new technologies thus demanded a permanent bureaucracy to acquire land, oversee construction, administer on a day-to-day basis, and plan for long-term needs. Technological and managerial experts who could survey topography, choose appropriate construction materials, and draw readily upon the experiences of their counterparts in other cities gradually gained recognition as the most efficient builders of public works.

Such experts usually had to cope with problems extending beyond the core city. Topography ignored municipal boundaries. An efficient sewer system that followed natural gradients to achieve a gravity flow often had to stretch beyond a city's political limits. The dumping of one community's sewage might and often did pollute the water supply of a neighboring community. Newark, for instance, drew its water supply from the Passaic River at a point below the sewer outflows of Paterson and Passaic. Mill towns in the Merrimac Valley of New Hampshire and Massachusetts were notorious for fouling one another's water supplies. To combat pollution in such locales, the engineering press began urging regional cooperation in water and sewer services during the early 1870s.

Although there were earlier isolated examples of such metropolitan "authorities"—usually public health boards and park planning commissions—permanent administrative bodies arose in the late 1880s and early 1890s in response to pollution. City officials gained state legislative approval to create metropolitan water and sewer districts such as Boston's Metropolitan Sewage Commission (1889) and similar districts in Chicago, the Passaic Valley, and elsewhere. These were the forerunners of such twentieth-century metropolitan authorities as the Port Authority of New York. In most cases, municipal governments vested control of extra municipal projects in their city engineer's office. By the early 1890s, moreover, engineers in a few cities had obtained the power to approve plats in areas beyond city limits to ensure that subdividers' street plans would facilitate travel and accommodate the installation of subsurface utilities. In some cities engineers could abate nuisances beyond city limits, thus gaining authority to protect watersheds and to engage in an early form of zoning regulation as well.[4]

In exercising their increasing responsibilities, municipal engineers raised a banner around which urban reformers could rally. Their own offices were a model of hierarchical, bureaucratic organization that promised greater efficiency in the management of urban problems. They propagated division of responsibility, offered standardized systems for monitoring costs, and suggested new methods of formulating fiscal policies. Well before organizations like the National Conference for Good City Government and the National Municipal League (both founded in 1894) began to publish data on tax and budgetary policies, the engineering press had identified most of the major issues and had shaped the framework for discussion.[5]

Engineers and their projects served to centralize metropolitan administration of public works vital to the health and safety of city dwellers. A substantial minority of engineers active late in the century (almost 28 percent of those born before 1820) had had some legal training, and engineers often advised other city officials on broadly defined administrative and legal questions. In Boston during the 1870s, for example, engineers instigated, drafted, and oversaw enforcement of public welfare laws. Thanks to their successes in public works construction and management, engineers often found city councils receptive to their requests for additional responsibilities. In late nineteenth-century Chicago, the Public Works Department added garbage collection and street cleaning to its specified duties. Gradually, the offices of city engineers and public works boards acquired the reputation of being wise managers who could streamline government operations.[6]

Engineers were apparently the first officials of the emerging administrative bureaucracies to attain anything resembling job security. Ellis Chesbrough, chief engineer of the Chicago Board of Sewerage (1856–61), served as that community's first city engineer from 1861 to 1879, an amazing longevity at a time when most municipal jobs changed hands with every election. Others had equally long terms. E. P. North, director of the Croton Water Works for New York City; Robert Moore, municipal engineer of St. Louis; George Benzenberg, city engineer of Milwaukee—all had at least twenty years of continuous service in the same city before 1900. Retention of an engineer familiar with the local system saved money, and in some jurisdictions courts reinforced the tendency toward long tenure by ruling that engineers held title to whatever plans they had drawn. A city that fired its engineer might lose the blueprints to its sewer system.[7]

Still, longevity in office is attributable to factors other than simple cost considerations. Civil service reformers repeatedly praised engineers as models of efficient bureaucrats and the District of Columbia, largely administered by the Army Corps of Engineers from the mid-1870s on, as an example of good city government. European cities with autonomous engineer-administrators, often military officers like Baron Georges E. Haussmann in Paris, also garnered plaudits from American reformers. Engineers, therefore, were among the earliest municipal employees to receive civil service protection under the new laws of the 1880s in a recognition of their role in managing the physical needs of cities. Their political caution, growing stature as problem-solvers, and reputations for fairness all worked to the engineers' advantage.[8]

They bolstered their claim to be neutral experts by institutionalizing the role of consultant. Operating in a cosmopolitan context, engineers were as responsive to their professional peers as to local pressures. George Waring and Rudolph Hering, the two most prominent sanitary engineers of the period, worked almost exclusively as consultants, moving from one city to another. Chesbrough, Benzenberg, Moses Lane of Milwaukee, Joseph P. Davis of Boston, and Colonel Julius W. Adams of Brooklyn were home-based but traveled widely to consult on major projects in other cities. The consultant role reflected both the status of engineers and their aloofness from the pendulum swings of partisan politics. Nineteenth-century city leaders generally viewed their communities as competing with others for economic growth and new population. A reputation for excellence in public works and healthfulness served local boosters well in the wars of urban imperialism. Yet city engineers were so valued as in-house experts that local politicians could not deny them the opportunity to advise rivals.[9]

Engineers secured job tenure through professionalization. At a time when few if any clearinghouses for the exchange of ideas and practices benefited cities nationwide, the engineers built up a remarkable communications network among themselves. Their common training, whether in engineering schools or apprenticeships (usually on the major railroads), bound them together. The practice of review by outside consultants reinforced these connections. Engineers belonged to local and regional professional clubs that corresponded with one another, publishing and exchanging reports about conditions in their respective cities. Numerous professional journals provided forums for discussion and debate.

During the late 1870s and again in the late 1880s, the most prestigious of these journals, the *Engineering News*, printed a lengthy series comparing cities around the country. Reports described water supply, sewerage, streets, parks, housing design, transportation terminals, and other elements of municipal planning. They dealt also with administrative and legal questions. The engineering press also covered European developments, paying particular attention to the important research trips abroad of Chesbrough and Hering. Finally, engineers belonged to the same national organizations. The majority held membership in the American Society of Civil Engineers, which frequently published papers on municipal engineering projects with appended comments from experts throughout the nation. In 1894 professionals involved principally with urban problems formed their own specialized national organization, the American Society for Municipal Improvements.[10]

Engineers were not bashful about asserting their importance to municipal administration. They advertised themselves, one engineer observed, as having "a high reputation for fairness and a capacity to render wise and just decisions." They strongly and repeatedly criticized proposals by citizens' associations for needed public works, stating that such matters were best left to professionals. They even claimed a steward's right to oversee the acts of elected public officials, asserting that the city engineer was "to a certain extent responsible for holding the successive political officials to a consistent, progressive policy. . . . To him, even more than to the successive mayors, falls the duty of serving as the intelligence and brains of the municipal government in all physical matters." Gustavus Karwiese, consulting engineer to the District of Columbia in the late 1870s, capped the claims for his profession when he told Congress that "it is the civil engineer . . . who is, by the silent command of the great Architect, the trustee of human happiness."[11]

That city engineers trumpeted their own importance is not surprising. The core of professionalism is the assertion of knowledge and skills available only to group members. Modern skeptics might doubt the engineers' claims of political neutrality. In some cities, as one scholar has noted, "engineers owed at least their early careers to machine politicians who, in an effort to promote growth and curry voter support, proposed, funded, and completed hundreds of sewer, water, horsecar, railroad, and bridge projects." Engineers' growing importance as managers of the physical city involved them intimately with elected officials and raised the potential for abuses of power. Yet there is in fact little or no evidence of city engineers' being "on the take," embroiled in the numerous political scandals, large and small, that amused, bemused, or outraged post-Civil War city dwellers. Although they served the immediate interests of local boosters and elected officials, the engineers could claim that over the long run their work benefited all citizens.[12]

The administrative techniques of engineers, along with their reputations as problem-solvers, carried great prestige. Within their specialized functions, engineers had developed centralized agencies capable of long-range, comprehensive planning and staffed by cosmopolitan experts. They had also advocated, with considerable success, the extension of their brand of organization to municipal administration as a whole. Albert F. Noyes, one of the leading city engineers of the period, echoed conventional sentiments in 1894 when he claimed that "the office of the municipal engineer is of the greatest importance to the community. . . . In fact, the city government of today is in a large measure a matter of municipal engineering, and the character of the city engineer's department is a safe index to the intelligence shown in the development of a municipality."[13]

The engineers offered city governments a corps of individuals skilled in the technology and management of large-scale enterprises, experts who could solve the physical problems of the cities. Decades before early twentieth-century political reformers depicted their ideal bureaucrat, municipal engineers embodied all of his characteristics: efficiency, expertise, and professionalism. They had emerged, in Suzanne Keller's telling phrase, as a "strategic elite" in American society. [14]

ENGINEERING AND CITY PLANNING

Over the last half of the nineteenth century, engineers repeatedly demonstrated the value of long-range planning to municipal administration. Not only did the profession offer solutions to such physical problems as water and sewer supply; it also contributed comprehensive planning schemes that illustrated the interaction of technology with the social, economic, and political structure of cities. Planning ideas that evolved from the paving of streets and the construction of water and sewer systems foreshadowed the later city plans of John Nolen, Daniel Burnham, George B. Ford, and others. Some proposals surveyed the urban physical container more thoroughly than did many plans of the early twentieth century. Frequently working with landscape architects and sanitarians, many engineers showed great sensitivity to and a deep understanding of the health needs of the populace.

The engineering press consistently advertised both the practical and the utopian ideas of the sanitarians. *Van Nostrand's Engineering Magazine,* for instance, reprinted in 1876 the utopian scheme of the British sanitarian B. W. Richardson. "Hygeia—A City of Health" outlined the elements of climate, site selection, water supply, sewerage, street layout, park construction, and housing design that could reduce mortality rates and transform the city into an ideal environment. George Waring presented "New York, A.D., 1997—A Prophecy," combining practical technology and social reform goals. The city of the future, he predicted, would be built upon the solid foundations of well-designed transportation, adequate water and sewer systems, the use of electrical power, streets rid of the filth of horses and other domestic animals, universal public education, and efficient government freed of bossism and political corruption. The Chicago sanitarian J. M. Gregory told the Chicago Medical Society, in a speech promptly reprinted by *Engineering News,* that "a great city is a vast laboratory, in which the energies imported in the food supplies and stored in the atmosphere are transmitted into human life, or rather, into thousands of human lives, but which are momentarily and perpetually exposed to that further transmutation which crumbles organized being back to its chemical elements."[15]

The sanitarians' image of the city as an organic being stirred sympathetic response in the engineers. Such metaphors were common in the engineering press. Sewerage works, one engineer rejoiced, had created "an entire urinary and intestinal tract, and . . . an artificial anus" for the city. Using the same imagery, a writer observed in 1894 that "the city engineer is to the city very much what the family physician is to the family. He is constantly called upon to advise and direct in all matters pertaining to his profession. . . . He does know the character, constitution, particular needs and idiosyncracies of the city, as the family physician knows the constitutions of the family." Engineers, accustomed to thinking about unified systems, joined with sanitarians in viewing the city as a vast, integrated unit within which the efficient functioning of one part depended upon the efficient functioning of all the parts.[16]

Belief in their "physician" role led some engineers to advance comprehensive planning schemes focusing on all the interconnected parts of the urban system. During the post-Civil War years, a number of plans of this type appeared. Most remained soldiers in a paper brigade. Three plans that enjoyed varying degrees of success illustrate the scope of the planners' vision.

In the late 1850s, Boston undertook a massive landfill operation and development project for its Back Bay area. Other historians have recounted the full story of this two-decade-long operation, but for present purposes several elements need emphasis. The city enforced restrictive covenants in deeds for lots in the newly filled land. These covenants limited nonresidential use of land, imposed building height restrictions, and dictated the distance that houses must be set back from the street. In other words, they constituted an early effort at what in the twentieth century would be called zoning legislation. The entire area pivoted around a principal traffic artery, Commonwealth Avenue. On the model of European boulevards, the paved road included a strip of park down the middle. Land-use restrictions and the boulevard enhanced the attractiveness of the new residential area. They also presumably diminished the quantities of sewer gas and other miasmic materials in the air and thus, in the contemporary view, ensured the inhabitants' health. Boston also began a major reconstruction of its sewer system so that wastes drained into the

South Bay rather than the more stagnant waters of the Back Bay. The city forced railroad lines to relocate from the Back Bay to a freight yard on newly filled land in the South Bay, thereby turning that district into an attractive site for industrial activities.[17]

In the late 1870s, when engineers had finished most of the Back Bay development, the city sought to complete the project with yet another engineering scheme. To further reduce pollution and provide recreational and health amenities, the city hired Frederick Law Olmsted to design and oversee construction of a park system (the Back Bay Fens) along the Muddy River, which drained into the bay (see Figure 18). Working with William Jackson, Boston's city engineer, Olmsted produced a plan that the city accepted and implemented quickly. Descriptions of the project underscore contemporary attitudes about the city as an ecosystem. "The leading and only justifying purpose of the Back Bay improvement, under the present design," observed Olmsted, "is the abatement of a complicated nuisance, threatening soon to be a deadly peril to the whole city as a propagating and breeding-ground of pestilential epidemics." This carefully engineered project sparked enthusiasm for similar planning efforts in other cities.[18]

Our second example takes us to New York City. Between 1865 and 1877, Olmsted and John J. R. Croes, a civil engineer, surveyed and prepared a thorough plan for a portion of the Bronx recently annexed to New York City. Initially charged with planning a street system and a rapid-transit steam railroad to connect the annexed wards to Manhattan, Olmsted and Croes instead proposed comprehensive development of the area as a suburb *before* potential residents could purchase property. Their design implicitly argued for thorough planning of all the undeveloped areas that one day would make up greater New York City.

The Croes-Olmsted plans, presented in three reports, called for the development of a business district bordered by a residential section on the high ground around the center of the area, with suburban homes on the northern and western edges. They offered street patterns that would provide gravity drainage, thereby lessening the costs of subsurface water and sewer facilities. They urged construction of wide north-south avenues along valleys and the tops of the ridges that dominated the topography. These avenues would cover water and sewer lines and also accommodate elevated railroads built up the middle to minimize disturbance to the surrounding environment. Linear parks would protect creeks and the Bronx River from pollution, and parkways would facilitate travel to the downtown area. The two wanted to preserve the most scenic lands in the area for recreational and health purposes. They suggested granting extramunicipal powers to city engineers to abate nuisances along the Westchester County headwaters of Bronx streams and thus prevent industries from locating along the small, slowly flowing waterways.

Throughout their reports the planners minimized private development decisions and elevated the comprehensive planning role of the public authority, in this case the Board of Commissioners of Public Parks. Those suggestions proved to be the plan's undoing. The desire of board members and real-estate speculators to populate the area quickly by the traditional means of unrestricted private development won the day. Nuisance abatements, restrictive covenants as land-use and housing controls, and comprehensive planning and construction before settlement were too radical: Croes and Olmsted lost their battle, as did yet-unborn residents of the area. The new sections of the Bronx grew in the helter-skelter fashion that typically resulted from private land-use decisions.[19]

Bits and pieces of the Back Bay scheme and the Bronx plan soon appeared in other cities. Between the mid-1880s and the turn of the century, Chicago, Kansas City, Boston, and Buffalo, among others, had built or had under way multipurpose park systems that went far beyond the provision of recreational land usage. Each of these plans protected rivers and streams from inordinate industrial pollution. Each provided new transportation networks that eased travel in and about the city. Each promised a solution to public health problems. Each projected improved housing facilities for large numbers of city residents.[20]

Yet another example of the comprehensive approach was a sort of anthology of public works proposals prepared by the Engineers' Club of Philadelphia during the early 1880s. Lewis Haupt, professor of engineering at the University of Pennsylvania, presented a number of papers on street layout and the need for rapid transit. He even tried to devise an accurate method of forecasting population growth. In form and recommendations, his proposals resembled but antedated the model Progressive-era transit and traffic surveys prepared by Bion Arnold, an engineer, and the consulting firm of Kelker, De Leuw. Rudolph Hering, then a resident of Philadelphia, contributed a paper on the city's future sewerage requirements in which Philadelphia is conceived of as a sprawling but integrated unit. Other papers dealt with housing regulation, water supply, and bridge and harbor improvements. All the papers emphasized the necessity of comprehensive physical planning. Throughout the 1880s and the following decade, other local engineering clubs in St. Louis, Chicago, Cleveland, Kansas City, and elsewhere prepared similar reports.[21]

Each of our three examples produced at least a kernel of accomplishment for the comprehensive planning viewpoint and presaged its greater success and greater popular acceptance in the twentieth century. Perhaps the most telling way to evaluate success, however, is to examine the costs of failure. The experience of Baltimore during the 1890s and early 1900s encapsulated all that had gone before.

THE CITY AS SEWER

Among major American cities, Baltimore alone put off construction of the kinds of public works projects that sanitarians, landscape architects, and engineers had called for since the 1840s. In 1859, 1881, and again in 1893, commissions appointed by the mayor and led principally by engineers had urged planning and construction to remedy the city's problems. On each occasion the public's reluctance to spend tax dollars, along with partisan politics, had sunk the proposals. Baltimore alone had ignored mounting evidence of the ties between the cleanliness or filth of the environment and rates of disease and mortality among city dwellers. Its citizens paid dearly for the delay. Although the census of 1890 judged Newark, New Jersey, the nation's unhealthiest city, the Chesapeake Bay community did not lag far behind—and Baltimore was two-and-a-half times as populous as Newark, with vastly larger financial resources.[22]

In 1890 Baltimore was one of only seven cities in the United States with a population of 400,000 or more. During the eighties it more than doubled its physical size through annexation, a tool used by every large American city in this period. Annexation, coupled with immigration, boosted Baltimore's population during the eighties by more than 102,000 people. This sudden spurt, paralleled in every other metropolis in the United States, placed stress on Baltimore's ability to provide adequate urban services. Unlike the other large American cities, it would not respond to the problems of development until the close of the first decade of the twentieth century. Between 1890 and roughly 1910, Baltimore remained one of the nation's prime examples of the city as sewer.[23]

Baltimore lines the banks of the Patapsco River, an arm of Chesapeake Bay, with a peninsula splitting the river into a Middle and a Northwest Branch. Along the latter branch as it stretched northward into the city stood factories, grain elevators, warehouses, and the wharves of the nation's third-largest port. Beyond these stood the central business district. Bisecting the city from the north and ending at a harbor formed by the Northwest Branch ran a ravine threaded by a foul stream called Jones Falls. Industrial wastes fed into the stream and poured into the harbor. On one side of Jones Falls lay East Baltimore, housing most of the city's working-class population. Slum tenements huddled in rows along the harbor and the lower sections of the falls. To the north of East Baltimore was most of the land annexed during the 1880s, containing some of the wealthiest sections of the city as well as rapidly growing middle-class suburbs. Immediately west of the core of the city, on the other side of Jones Falls, was the principal black ghetto (next to Washington, Baltimore had the largest Negro population of any American city in 1890). North of the ghetto was a district called Bolton Hill, where lived many of the city's professional and business families. Frequent rainfall, the rolling topography of the city, and the geographic separation of different sections had long hindered provision of an adequate water supply and an effective sewage-disposal system.[24]

During the first half of the nineteenth century, the private Baltimore Water Company supplied the community with water from a number of small reservoirs along Jones Falls. In 1854 the city purchased the water company and expanded service while still depending on Jones Falls for its supply. As population grew and indoor plumbing became popular, that source became inadequate. Between 1875 and 1881, city engineers constructed a new reservoir that tapped a different water source. Although expanded, however, the water supply system, which depended largely on gravity flow, was far from perfected. The houses built during the eighties on hillsides surrounding the Jones Falls valley stood above the reach of existing reservoirs. Baltimore met the problem by building new reservoirs in various districts of the city and installing pumping mechanisms to fill them with water. The pumps often broke down, resulting in water shortages. That was not unusual; other cities at the time faced the same difficulties with the new technology. Nor was it unusual that the new supplies of water were hardly pure. In many large cities thorough filtration and purification of water did not become standard practice until the early 1920s.[25]

Thus, with regard to water supplies, Baltimore's experience was typical—in provision of a municipal water system and in the timing of construction, Baltimore was on track with the rest of urban America. That decidedly was not the case for the city's handling of sewage disposal.

For most of the nineteenth century, Baltimore relied upon "natural" disposal. Rainwater soaked the soil of backyards and the largely unpaved streets, eventually running off through streams. Householders customarily dropped kitchen refuse and domestic wastewater into surface street gutters. Cesspools drained the excrement from privies; in the rainy seasons seepage turned backyards into putrid marshes. As the century wore on, the problems of sewage pollution increased. In some of the wealthier sections, private citizens contracted for the construction of storm drains. There was little or no coordination of these scattered efforts, which served only a small proportion of the city's citizens and polluted nearby streams. Some 15,000 homes owned by the city's elite had privately built sewer lines that funneled raw household wastes into Jones Falls.[26]

Most Baltimoreans periodically had their cesspools cleaned by private companies, notably the inaptly named Odorless Excavating Apparatus Company. The streams, the surface gutters, the private lines, and cesspool seepages all finally dumped their burdens into the harbor, with the predictable result that in spring and summer that body of water was afloat with rotted garbage and the flotsam and jetsam of urban wastes, smelling like "a billion polecats." When prevailing winds shifted, citizens in all parts of the city sensed that they were in for another Baltimore summer. Since most of those who lived on the harbor's fringes were slum dwellers, however, the better classes of Baltimoreans turned up their noses at the problem.[27]

For those who resided in the oldest, most congested parts of the city, the lack of an adequate sewage system was especially acute. Many lived in cellar apartments or in buildings that had earth-packed basement floors. For several months of the year, even under the best of conditions, the "floors" softened into muddy wading-pools of filth. During heavy rainfalls, flooded basements awash with liquid wastes were not uncommon. City inspectors responded to complaints with the helpful suggestion that building owners or residents pave over the dirt. Matters only worsened for the slum dwellers, and to a lesser extent for all Baltimoreans, with the expansion of the city's water supply and the growth of the city's industries.[28]

Wastewater disposal, from all sources, had become a problem of epic dimensions by 1890. "Natural" sewerage had proved an abject failure. The commissioner of health, possessing limited powers to act, could only report of the privies, for example, that "many of them overflow, and the liquid contents flow into yards and gutters, emitting most offensive odors. . . . " These were, he asserted, "a fruitful source of disease, operating indirectly in its production, and directly in lowering the vital stamina of the unfortunates compelled to breathe a polluted atmosphere." The "unfortunates" included most citizens. The privies, he concluded, "are the most dangerous enemies of our lives and happiness." Although his etiology was outmoded, his comments on the prevalence of disease were, as we have seen, pertinent.[29]

In 1890 the death rate from all physical ailments of residents of the nation's twenty-eight largest cities averaged 23.3 persons per thousand. Newark, with a population of 182,000, had a mortality rate of 29 per thousand, highest among American cities with populations of 100,000 or more. Among major cities—those with 400,000 or more citizens—only New York had a higher death rate than Baltimore. By 1900 matters had improved little. Newark's death rate had fallen to 19.8, while Baltimore's had declined to 21 per thousand. Philadelphia, with a rate of 21.2, barely edged the Chesapeake Bay community in the death race, or Baltimore would have stood alone at the top of the heap. Baltimore did capture top honors, however, in 1890 and finished a close second in 1900, for mortality among its colored population (see Table 2).

By the turn of the century, conditions had become so wretched that even well-to-do Baltimoreans could tolerate them no longer. Engineers and sanitarians were no longer alone in calling for the construction of a citywide integrated sewer system. Organizations of prominent, reform-minded citizens, such as the Municipal Art Society and the Reform League, demanded action. Mendes Cohen, a director of the Municipal Art Society and a civil engineer, became chairman in 1893 of a citywide commission to remedy sanitation problems. Aided by two consulting engineers, his commission researched the sewerage systems of the United States and Europe. Its report eventually served as the basis for a city plan prepared by the Olmsted Brothers and privately underwritten by the Municipal Art Society. Businessmen, particularly those whose companies stood in low-lying areas, joined the fray in the late nineties, led by the president of the Merchants' and Manufacturers' Association.[30]

Finally, in 1905, through a series of intricate political maneuvers, a new mayor appointed a blue-ribbon sewerage commission empowered to oversee the building of a comprehensive system. Construction began in 1906 and concluded in 1915. By then, nearly 500 miles of integrated sanitary sewers served more than 100,000 homes. Once stirred into action, the city moved with efficiency and dispatch. In less than a decade, Baltimore transformed itself into one of the best-sewered cities in the nation.[31]

Demands for a host of other public improvements brought about street widening and paving projects, park planning schemes, new transportation networks, and new schools, police stations, and firehouses during the first decade and a half of the twentieth century. In all cases, new administrative procedures governed implementation of city planning proposals. The city charter adopted in 1898 had provided for a five-person Board of Estimates to conduct Baltimore's financial affairs. One of the five was the city engineer, appointed by the mayor. His task was principally to coordinate the activities of several boards charged with administration of various public works and oversee plans for future public improvements.[32]

By the early years of the new century, the city had joined the rest of urban America, which had long since recognized the importance of engineering expertise in the construction and administration of public works projects and city planning. Baltimore's leaders and citizens alike might regret the years of delay, yet take pride in having finally fallen in step with the nationwide march toward the reforming of cities.

REFORMING THE CITIES

In 1905 Frederic C. Howe, a ten-year veteran of political wars to improve urban government in Cleveland and around the nation, published a self-styled "manual of reform." In *The City: The Hope of Democracy*, he catalogued the concerns of urban reformers of his generation. Like others he denounced immigrant-dominated political machines as economically wasteful and morally indefensible. Boodling politicians, men who cared more about lining their pockets through graft and bribery than serving the public at large, worked hand-in-hand with unscrupulous businessmen in a spoils system that robbed decent citizens of their chances for progress. Or so Howe and other like-minded reformers charged. Wearied by wars against daily greed, Howe outlined a new order of battle, one that presented a practical strategy of technical solutions even as it paraded moral indignation.

For all his diatribes against political bosses and profit-hungry private corporations, Howe identified the "elemental problems" of cities as the building of sewers, streets, transit systems, and public parks. Such public works, he claimed, had become "a necessity to the life, health, comfort, convenience, and industry of the city." They were too important to be left in the hands of private individuals or public officials skilled only at getting themselves elected: these were "executive matters requiring special training or scientific knowledge of the work to be done." University-trained men—political scholars, scientists, and especially engineers—should lead the cities onto the pathways of progress.[33]

To harness new technologies to meet social needs was the aspiration of many so-called progressives, particularly those enthusiastic about city planning. As the landscape architect John Nolen put it in 1909: "Intelligent city planning is one of the means toward a better utilization of our resources, toward an application of the methods of private business to public affairs, toward efficiency, toward a higher individual and collective life." The watchwords of these reformers, as Nolen suggested, were "conservation," "efficiency," and "social engineering." Each goal required the application of technology to human problems; each demanded innovative methods of administration. Many a reformer championed city planning of one type or another, facilitated by municipal ownership of utilities and administered by new governmental institutions.[34]

Some reformers of this era emphasized one particular planning goal—for example, new transit systems—while others advanced what they called comprehensive planning. Howe expressed the latter in his autobiography. Recalling his enthusiasms, he mused: "I had an architectonic vision of what a city might be. I saw it as a picture. . . . It was a unit, a thing with a mind, with a conscious purpose, seeing far in advance of the present and taking precautions for the future. I had this picture of Cleveland long before the advent of city-planning proposals; it was just as instinctive as any mechanical talent."[35]

It was "instinctive," as other passages of the autobiography made clear, precisely because the young Howe grew up with and was educated by the planning attitudes that had evolved as part of the new urban culture of the nineteenth century. When Howe wrote "long before the advent of city-planning proposals," he meant those of the early twentieth century. He was not ignorant of past efforts. The planning efforts—partial and comprehensive—of Howe's predecessors in the public works crusades had helped shape the reform outlook of the early twentieth century. The reformers' embracing of "comprehensive" planning in the progressive era was in some ways simply a restatement of long-standing attitudes, and in other ways a logical culmination of decades of thought and action.

Many urban political reformers of the early twentieth century found themselves in agreement with Howe. In terms of both process and personnel, changes in the structure of municipal government during the progressive era drew heavily on the technological and administrative skills exhibited by engineers over the last half of the nineteenth century. The cumulative impact of the engineers' contributions helped to create two new professions in early twentieth-century America—city planners and city managers. Both were central in reforming the cities. Both substantially altered the administrative functions of municipal government and its reach into citizens' lives. Both confirmed the maturation of the emerging city culture of the nineteenth century.[36]

PLANNING AND MANAGING THE CITIES

In May 1909 a large group of prominent individuals met in the nation's capital to convene the First National Conference on City Planning and the Problems of Congestion. Among them were engineers, landscape architects, public health officials, conservationists, economists, lawyers, social workers, journalists, corporate leaders, and public officials. A sense of urgency pervaded the gathering.

John Nolen denounced present trends in city development as "fatal" and called upon cities to investigate their problems, promote cooperation between public authorities and private individuals, and achieve "prompt and courageous execution of the plan found to be

best for all concerned." Benjamin C. Marsh, the era's leading pro-
ponent of comprehensive city planning, demanded surveys, public-
ity, and new legal weapons "against which corporate interests cannot
contend." Representing some of those corporate interests (presumably the "responsible" ones) was the financier Henry Morgenthau,
who identified congestion as "an evil that breeds physical disease,
moral depravity, discontent, and socialism—and all these must be
cured and eradicated or else our great body politic will be weakened." Frederick Law Olmsted, Jr., reflecting the views of many
other participants, described the glories of town planning in Germany, pointing out that German plans included not only street layouts "and so forth, but the whole code of building regulations,
health ordinances, police rules, and system of taxation in so far as
they have a direct influence upon the physical development of the
city." Some participants sought to encourage purely local responses
to problems, while others called for federal action. But the conference was in full agreement about its final goal—comprehensive
planning in and for urban America. [37]

At that first meeting, the noted landscape architect Robert
Anderson Pope emphasized the pressing need for "a profession
equipped to make city planning the social and economic factor it
ought to be." The National Conference on City Planning continued
to meet once a year, in a different city each time, advertising principles of comprehensive planning to countless thousands of urban
Americans. Gathering together a broad cross-section of people concerned about city problems, the conference served both as an information center for the exchange of practices and ideas and as a
public relations outpost for the professionals involved. It also stimulated enthusiasm among some participants for a different forum in
which the several varieties of technocrats could discuss and debate
technical details of planning that might well bore the general public. In short, the conference sparked commitment to the formal creation of the profession Pope had called for. [38]

The role of engineers in the emerging profession was considerable. New York City's chief engineer, Nelson P. Lewis, author of
one of the earliest and most widely consulted texts on city planning,
dedicated his 1916 volume "To the Municipal Engineers of the
United States, the first men on the ground in City Planning as in
City Building." Of the fifty-two charter members of the American
Institute of Planners (first called the American City Planning Insti-

tute) in 1917, thirteen were engineers. Only landscape architecture provided more members (fourteen), and several of them had some engineering training. The newly formed AIP included the individuals who had prepared most of the comprehensive city plans advanced since 1905. In that same year a committee of the American Institute of Architects published a nationwide survey, *City Planning Progress*; its editors noted that "the Committee has laid particular stress on the economic and engineering side of city planning, because it believes that that is fundamental to progress." Mel Scott, historian of the AIP, has calculated that through the 1920s most middle-sized and smaller cities continued to delegate all responsibility for planning to their city engineer's office. With the solitary exception of Delos Wilcox, a political reformer, engineers dominated the most important of the new specialties, transportation planning. [39]

The direct contributions of engineers to municipal administration during the early years of the twentieth century were even more impressive than their role in the growth of the city planning profession. However much political reformers disagreed about the details of structural change, they agreed that the professionalization and bureaucratization of government were steps in the right direction. Members of the National Municipal League left no room for doubt on this point.

In 1899 a subcommittee of the league composed "The Municipal Program," a document promoting theories about the "right organization" of municipal government. The bucket of nineteenth-century Jacksonian democracy—the notion that any common man could govern his fellows—had sprung too many leaks. Cities had to throw it away. Reporting to the tenth annual meeting in 1904, Delos Wilcox declared that one of the core principles of the "Program" was that city officials had to know their business: "It is gradually dawning upon the American mind that special knowledge is required to run the machinery of city government, if we are to avoid a wreck. . . . The complex machinery of a city can be run only by those who know how to do that particular thing. . . . The whole body of municipal officials need special knowledge and long experience to give the city the benefit of good service." Characteristic of progressive-era structural reform was an emphasis on efficiency, specialized training, and administrative accountability. No single political change better reflected those values than the managerial revolution in urban government.[40]

In brief, the progressives wanted to replace ward bosses and corrupt machine politicians with trained, nonpartisan professionals who could carry out the day-by-day administration of government without regard for the vicissitudes of the political arena. An elected commission or council—having gained office through an at-large, citywide election rather than through the traditional ward-by-ward process—should establish public policies and appoint a skilled professional to handle executive functions. Such a centralized administration would manage municipal services with businesslike efficiency Reformers repeatedly charged that machine politicians cared not about efficiency but about staying in office to loot the public treasury. Machine leaders controlled elections by garnering the votes of ignorant immigrant dwellers living in the urban core. A favor given here, a job secured there—these were the coins of the realm for exploiting the immigrants for their votes. Meanwhile, the machines failed to represent the interests of the "better sort" of citizens, the middle- and upper-class people who had left the city for the suburbs in an effort to escape the corruption of the core. Or, so the reformers asserted. A city-manager form of government would reduce the voting power wielded by the lower-class central wards while elevating the influence of the business and professional elites living on the urban periphery and in the suburbs. To critics who warned about the dangers to democracy inherent in the scheme, supporters retorted that "democracy need fear no setback through the introduction of this new form of administration; and efficiency . . . can come into her own at last."[41]

The new city-manager form of government first surfaced in Staunton, Virginia, in 1908. The city council appointed Charles E. Ashburner, charging him with improving the community's streets while also holding the line on public expenditures. Within three years, Ashburner had placed the city on a sound financial basis, improved the water and sewage systems, directed installation of effective street lighting, and accelerated the street-paving process tenfold, lifting the community, as one contemporary put it, from "mud to asphalt." Other cities, including communities in both Carolinas, Oregon, and Michigan, soon followed suit. For the most part, these were small cities, and their problems therefore appeared easier to treat than those of larger, more industrialized communities. A more dramatic example was needed.[42]

One came in Dayton, Ohio, in 1913. That city of some 110,000 citizens had governmental problems akin to those of the largest cities. A devastating flood in March focused national attention on Dayton while also revealing the inability of local machine politicians to respond efficiently. Led by John H. Patterson, the wealthy head of the National Cash Register Company, a group of Dayton professionals and businessmen succeeded in gaining election to office, whereupon they drafted a city-manager charter that they sold to the electorate. Early in 1914 the new council appointed Henry M. Waite to the post of city-manager. He not only solved the immediate problems of rebuilding municipal services, but also engaged in social engineering, providing free legal aid, a milk-inspection program in the city's schools, and free medical examinations for children. The "Dayton Plan," as contemporaries called it, spread rapidly throughout the nation over the next few years.[43]

The new city-manager form of government, as attested by the National Municipal League in 1913, promised administrative unity, clear lines of responsibility, expertise at the top of the administration, and discipline and harmony within the ranks of government servants. By 1919 the league had incorporated the position of city manager into its model charter for urban governmental reform. The new professionals brought administrative expertise, a taste for bureaucracy, and the battle cry of "efficiency" to the management of scores of small and middle-sized cities over the first few decades of the twentieth century.[44]

It is not my purpose here to describe in detail the impact of the managerial revolution. Rather, I want to sketch a profile of these new technocrats and look at how their efforts reflected growing public acceptance of the necessity of expertise in planning and managing cities.

A profile of the new profession reveals common backgrounds. The first city managers of Staunton and Dayton, for example, were both practicing civil engineers. Ashburner had worked for railroad and electrical companies and for the Public Roads Administration of the federal government. Waite came to his Dayton post directly from a highly successful career as city engineer of Cincinnati. The 1919 *Yearbook* of the new City Managers' Association showed that 48 percent of the total membership were engineers. In 1920 a survey of California city managers stated that of the twenty-one listing their backgrounds, thirteen were engineers. Surveys taken during the 1920s and 1930s demonstrated that of those managers with bachelor's degrees, 75 percent had trained as engineers. By the time the "typical" manager assumed his job, he had engaged in practical engineering work and had held one or more posts in government, usually as a department head. As late as 1940, a major nationwide survey related that more than 63 percent of city managers over the previous quarter-century had trained as engineers.[45]

Many contemporaries saw the establishment of the new profession of city manager as the high-water mark of progressive reform in municipal administration. The managers themselves were recruited primarily from another profession that had long since proved its central importance to the orderly functioning of cities. Over the half-century preceding the progressive era, the job of municipal engineer had developed into a profession that had helped reshape the physical landscape of urban America. Of equal significance, it had provided a corps of experienced experts and a model of administrative skill that latter-day progressives would use as a basis for the structural reform of urban government.

In both the technological and the political arenas, municipal engineers played an increasingly important part. Over the last half of the nineteenth century, they stamped their long-range visions of metropolitan planning on the public consciousness. Their demands for political autonomy in solving the physical problems of cities contributed to an ultimate insistence on efficient government run by experts. At the center of physical and political changes in the administration of American cities—indeed, at the very core of city planning by the first decade of the twentieth century—stood the work of municipal engineers.

CONCLUSION

THE AFFAIR OF THE FAIR

O N 1 MAY 1893 a marvel of engineering and artistic skill greeted the first of over 21 million visitors. The Chicago World's Fair (known officially as the World's Columbian Exposition in honor of the alleged discovery of America 400 years earlier by Columbus) was a triumph of architectural symmetry and order. It clustered monumental neo-classical buildings, coated with white plaster, whose grand facades, glistening in the sunshine and gleaming at night in the light of the new wonder, electricity, justified the name "The White City" (see Figure 19). It stood in stark contrast to the dingy gray city of industrial Chicago some seven miles to the north and west. Located in undeveloped Jackson Park, on a scrub-brush stretch of sandbars and swamps hugging the shores of Lake Michigan, the Fair was the product of coordination and cooperation among the nation's leading architects and artists under the guidance of the Chicago architect Daniel H. Burnham and Frederick Law Olmsted. The world's largest building, the Manufactures and Liberal Arts Building, covered thirty acres and reached as high as a nineteen-story skyscraper: this and other exhibit halls contained the latest miracles of modern technology. Other structures represented various states and foreign nations; art galleries displayed the works of the world's leading artists; statuary lined broad avenues; and the Midway Plaisance, with the world's largest Ferris Wheel, miniature Irish villages, Algerian theaters, English concert halls, Moorish mosques, Turkish coffee houses, and Chinese tea houses attracted visitors by the thousands each day. "The fair! The fair! Never had the name such significance before," gushed a reporter. "Fairest of all the World's present sights it is. A city of palaces set in spaces of emerald, reflected in shining lengths of water which stretch in

undulating lines under flat arches of marble bridges and along banks
planted with consummate skill."[1]

For most visitors, the Fair was a family excursion, a day of ex-
citement and adventure. For its designers it was a once-in-a-lifetime
opportunity to work cooperatively with one's peers, or, as one of
them put it, "the greatest meeting of artists since the fifteenth century!" But to a smaller number of shrewd observers, the Exposition
symbolically towered above its tallest and most monumental structures. The architect Louis Sullivan, whose Transportation Building
was the only major building to depart from the classical style, be-
moaned the long-range impact of the Fair on American architectural innovation. "The damage wrought by the World's Fair," he
claimed, "will last for half a century from its date, if not longer. It
has penetrated deep into the constitution of the American mind,
effecting there lesions significant of dementia." Critical of many
parts of the Exposition, the historian and philosopher Henry Adams
nonetheless marveled at the totality and saw in it enormous significance for the future. "Chicago asked in 1893 for the first time,"
Adams mused, "the question whether the American people knew
where they were driving. . . . Chicago was the first expression of
American thought as a unity; one must start there."[2]

"One must start there" was a refrain echoed by other contemporaries and by historians of American city planning. For our purposes, the Fair was important for two reasons.

First, the building of the White City physically expressed in one
locale all those earlier features of city planning thought and practice
that we have examined. The charge given Daniel Burnham as chief
of construction was to "control all forces needed to prepare the
grounds and erect the buildings for the Exposition." Those forces
included "surveys and grades, landscape works, architecture, sculp-
ture, decorations, general superintendence, sewers, water and fire
protection, steam plant and other machinery, electrical plant, transportation of persons and goods, guard and secret service, fire department, medical department, construction accounts, purchasing,
attorneys." Urban law, sanitation facilities, landscape art and architecture, efficiently engineered and professionally administered public works—all found expression in the planning and construction of
the White City.[3]

Second, the Fair was significant as a metaphor—to contemporaries and later historians it stood as a prophecy of the future

metropolis. The Exposition closed its gates in October 1893. All the buildings, save one, fell to fire and the wrecker's ball. Yet despite its brief life as a fanciful stage set, the Fair inspired the imaginations of many enthusiasts of urban planning. Bidding farewell to the White City in language that might have come directly from an urbtopian novel, the *Chicago Tribune* lamented the passing of "a little ideal world, a realization of Utopia, in which every night was beautiful and every day a festival, in which for the time all thoughts of the great world of toil, of injustice, of cruelty, and of oppression outside its gates disappeared, and in which this splendid fantasy of the artist and architect seemed to foreshadow some far-away time when all the earth should be as pure, as beautiful, and as joyous as the White City itself." More prosaically and many years later, John W. Reps, the dean of American planning historians, asserted that "the Chicago Fair of 1893 changed the architectural taste of the nation and led to a new direction in American city planning."[4]

Events during the next two decades appeared to confirm that judgment. As prosperity returned after the depression years of the early 1890s, planners hastened to offer schemes to redo the face of urban America. In a number of major cities, municipal art societies led drives to clean streets and beautify public places. An 1899 national conference of those organizations stressed the necessity of city planning and labeled "the object of this municipal art movement, 'The City Beautiful.' " In 1901 the United States Senate resolved to physically renew Washington, D.C. Three veterans of the Columbian Exposition staff, led by Daniel H. Burnham and joined by Frederick Law Olmsted, Jr., offered the following year a plan that reiterated and expanded the 1791 L'Enfant plan. Subsequently, New York City, Philadelphia, Baltimore, Hartford, New Haven, Cleveland, San Francisco, and other communities ordered preparation of similar monumental plans. In 1904 St. Louis staged the Louisiana Purchase Exposition, which spurred the movement forward. With the Burnham-prepared *Plan of Chicago* in 1909, the City Beautiful movement reached full stride. That same year the first National Conference on City Planning met, sparking the creation a few years later of the American Institute of Planners.[5]

Much of the City Beautiful planning activity seemed curiously to ignore the lessons taught by earlier generations of city planning advocates. Unlike their predecessors, City Beautiful promoters tended to value aesthetics over substance. To be sure, the various plans gave attention to improved rapid transit facilities, new parks, the legal possibilities of controlling land use on the urban periphery. The most thorough of the plans, Burnham's, even made reference in passing to housing and sanitation, asserting that "the slum exists today only because of the failure of the city to protect itself against gross evils and known perils, all of which should be corrected by the enforcement of simple principles of sanitation."[6]

But, overwhelmingly, the City Beautiful plans concentrated on reshaping street patterns to provide grand boulevards, grandiose public plazas, and imposing civic centers. At their silliest, the plans stressed the desirability of lining the grand boulevards with ornamental wrought-iron lampposts, scenic gardens, and hanging flower baskets. Campaigns for modern street lighting emphasized how it would increase property values, attract new businesses, reduce crime, and illuminate the City Beautiful decor. One rapturous soul praised the results of City Beautiful planning: "in many blocks not a single post is without its decoration, while there is hardly a block without several lamp post gardens. Thus has Minneapolis the 'Flour City' become Minneapolis the 'City of Flowers and Hanging Gardens.' " It would be difficult to find a significant number of nineteenth-century planning enthusiasts so effusive about cosmetics. Perhaps it was the successes of those earlier stalwarts that permitted early twentieth-century planners to concentrate on aesthetics.[7]

If we accept the view that City Beautiful projects were the first fruits of modern urban planning, then ample evidence apparently exists to identify the Chicago World's Fair as its birthplace. One could argue, in turn, that the City Beautiful movement, which evolved into the so-called City Efficient movement around 1910, was a principal component of the more broadly based activities of a generation of economic, political, social, and moral reformers whose crusades collectively became known as Progressivism. Writing about the City Beautiful movement, Paul Boyer affirmed that "it sprang from the conviction that a more livable and attractive urban environment would call forth an answering surge of civic loyalty from the urban populace, and that this in turn would retard or even reverse the decay of social and moral cohesiveness which seemed so inevitable a concomitant of the rise of cities." Certainly Daniel Burnham, who basked in his growing reputation as the nation's leading urban planner, regarded himself as the leader of the progressives' aesthetic and planning cadre.[8]

But more was at stake in city planning than mere aesthetics, as reformers and political leaders far removed from the actual designing of new city plans attested. The principal goals of the diverse reformers gathered under the umbrella of Progressivism were to restore political, economic, and social order to a chaotic society, to render more efficient the functioning of all human endeavors, and, above all, to reinstate morality as the core of human behavior. The president of the New York City Board of Aldermen concisely expressed the integral role played by city planning on the wider stage of progressive reform: "City planning is the guidance into proper channels of a community's impulses towards a larger and broader life. On the face it has to do with things physical. . . . Its real significance is far deeper; a proper city plan has a powerful influence for good upon the mental and moral development of the people."[9]

That echo of the sentiment that I have called moral environmentalism reveals that the affair of the Fair was *not* the starting point of modern American city planning thought and action. Rather, it was a culmination and crystallization of ideas and activities over the previous seventy-five years.

The best way to underscore that point, if it is not self-evident after all these pages, is to introduce one final player in our cast of characters. We might have considered him earlier, but I have reserved his story for now. His name was Robert Fleming Gourlay.

Gourlay, a Scotsman, paid extended visits to the United States during the 1830s and early 1840s, the period in which the social vocabulary in which Americans discussed their cities began dramatically to alter. Appalled by the chaotic conditions of Boston and New York, Gourlay published in 1844 a set of plans for remaking both cities. His agenda for reform entailed a conception of the city as an integrated environment that Daniel Burnham and other progressive-era planners might well have envied. Writing about Boston, he observed that "the peninsula is already crowded, and here want of forethought has caused confusion past remedy." Having despaired, he provided the remedy.[10]

In his plan for the Hub City, Gourlay urged new public works and sanitation facilities; designed an entire transportation network for a regional metropolitan area (although with the typical planner's disdain for topography); called for the creation of a series of "New Towns"—suburbs in our parlance—connected to the city by commuter railroads; envisioned the city laced with a series of parks and

connecting grand boulevards sweeping through scenic panoramas of
natural splendor and decorated with arches and other ornamental
embellishments that would have made a later City Beautiful planner
proud; and integrated monumental architecture and street layout to
eliminate congestion in a manner that anticipated the 1909 *Plan of
Chicago* in nearly every detail. In justification of his grandiose
schemes, Gourlay appealed to the citizens of Boston "to consider
that physical order and beauty may be made accessory to mental
refinement, enlargement, and perfection," for "moral and physical
improvement naturally aid each other, and should go, hand in
hand."[11]

At the time Boston's leaders and citizens paid scant attention to
the Scotsman's schemes. Save for a handful of his suggestions about
railroad connections and improvements in the Back Bay area, Gourlay might never have lived. For the dramatic purposes of our larger
story, however, their disregard was unimportant. Robert Fleming
Gourlay was only one of many nineteenth-century city dreamers
and planners who promoted a comprehensive vision of what the
American city could and should become.

At best, then, the Chicago World's Fair acted as a catalyst,
blending the city planning ethos of the entire nineteenth century
with the reform impulses stirring in late-century industrial, urban
America, energizing the era of progressive crusades.

Behind the various reforms of the progressive years lay decades
of responses to the physical, social, and moral difficulties posed by
urban growth. Throughout the nineteenth century, and especially
from the 1830s on, a variety of trends had refashioned citizens' definitions and expectations of the "good life," and where one could
live it. Rapidly changing environmental conditions, new technologies and searches for better ones, as well as new attitudes, had provoked reconsiderations of the quality of urban life, and these
became more urgent with each passing decade. Contemporary literature, the new body of urban law, sanitary reform campaigns, and
public works projects all provide evidence that urban Americans had
gradually constructed a new urban culture. Whether urbanites
feared or welcomed urban growth, damned or praised the city as the
locus of nineteenth-century American civilization, they did not perceive the urban environment as their predecessors had.

Their changing perceptions in turn slowly led them to recon-
sider and reconstruct their conceptions of the role of government in

their daily lives. Especially from mid-century on, urban voters of all classes demanded the extension of municipal services and the building of public works throughout the nation. Civic leaders' responses to those demands often generated intense political conflict. In centers like Milwaukee, Chicago, New York, and Philadelphia, taxpayer revolts, usually spearheaded by the wealthier classes, became almost yearly events. Over the remainder of the century, the most volatile issues in local government politics involved services and public works. Businessmen, machine politicians, factory workers, and civil servants had radically different agendas. Still, by the close of the century, American city dwellers enjoyed the highest standards of public services in the world.[12]

To be sure, much remained to be done. The campaigns of Progressivism, building upon the past, accomplished much, if only in piecemeal fashion. Change came slowly and, in the pluralistic political arenas of the era, often painfully. Christine Rosen argues in *The Limits of Power* that "because of physical, economic, political, and technological constraints, city dwellers did *not* have the power they needed to adapt their environment to their multi-faceted, ever changing needs in an effective way." Perhaps. Still, segments of the urban upper, middle, and working classes alike stood firmly on the social and intellectual foundations laid by predecessors who had articulated and championed city planning reform. In the face of the obstacles, their accomplishments by the end of the nineteenth century were exceptional.[13]

Part of the explanation for that remarkable record of achievement lay in the crusades of the moral environmentalists and the growth of the new urban professions: the sanitarians, landscape architects, municipal lawyers, and engineers. Just as the physical and moral problems of expanding cities had called forth fresh groups of technical experts to provide solutions, administrative problems seemed to require a new body of skilled managers. By approximately 1920, as we have seen, the nineteenth-century currents of urban planning thought and practice had merged to form both a nascent corps of city managers and an embryonic profession of city planners.

By then, the decades-long construction of a new urban culture for an emerging urban nation was complete. At the beginning of the nineteenth century, urban Americans numbered about 6 percent of the nation's population. The total number of communities with

25,000 or more citizens stood at seven. Most shrewd observers of
the national scene were at best ambivalent about the growth of large
cities. Few discerned the nation's urban destiny, and those who
even speculated about it warned against certain kinds of city growth.
William Tudor, founder and editor of the *North American Review*,
mused that "the fate of some of our cities seems yet undecided. The
natural course of events will lessen the number that will be great
depots. . . . With the fullest belief, however, of the utility and necessity of manufactures, I am not anxious for the growth of large
manufacturing towns, and the kind of population that exists in them
in Europe." In large manufacturing cities, Tudor stated, "health
and morals are both disregarded, and too frequently destroyed
altogether."[14]

By the 1840s, when changes in the social vocabulary employed
to discuss urban problems signaled the beginning of a shift in attitudes and expectations, urban dwellers accounted for slightly under
11 percent of the nation's total population. Only twelve cities contained populations of 25,000 or more. During the years following
the Civil War, both the number of cities and the urban population
swelled. Each decade from 1870 to 1900 saw an average population
growth of 30 to 40 percent for the nation's giants—New York, Chicago, Philadelphia, and Baltimore, among others—while urban
growth rates of 50 to 60 percent were not uncommon elsewhere in
the country. The federal census of 1920 disclosed that over 51 percent of the nation's people lived in cities. There were 287 cities of
25,000 citizens or more. The United States had become an urban
nation.

The statistics reveal far more than simply a population tilt cityward. They confirm the centrality of the city and the pervasiveness
of urban culture in modern American society. In 1909, for example,
the *American City* began publication, a national magazine dedicated to serving as a clearinghouse for experiments in urban life and
to rebuilding cities "along better lines." In the first issue its editor,
Arthur H. Grant, asserted that the very existence of the magazine
was evidence of Americans' recognition that "it pays to look a bit
ahead of present needs. The American City is outgrowing its irre-
sponsible childishness and is coming of age." A few years later, in
the second edition of his widely read *American Municipal Progress*,
the sociologist Charles Zueblin noted that "the twentieth-century
city is in a class by itself. . . . The meditative rustics at the general

store chew their cud and discuss abstract democracy. The city dwellers collectively put water and sewerage systems under the streets that they are going to pave and they learn concrete democracy. . . . The compulsion of cooperation makes the city the laboratory of applied democracy."[15]

The number of toilers in the urban "laboratory" had increased dramatically over the previous one hundred years. Many were little-known or unknown footsoldiers, enlistees in local campaigns. A smaller group were technicians who promoted public works for the present while planning the urban environments of the future. A handful earned national recognition for their efforts. Long before the formal creation of a profession called city planning in the early years of the twentieth century, long before the great White City arose against the backdrop of a dirty Chicago at the World's Columbian Exposition in 1893, a host of often unheralded individuals had labored to improve the quality of city life. Each and all, through a variety of endeavors, had constructed an urban culture for a modern America.

NOTES AND INDEX

NOTES

PREFACE

1. Horace Bushnell, "City Plans," in his *Work and Play; or, Literary Varieties* (New York, 1871), p. 308. This collection originally appeared in 1864 and consisted of "recent essays." Judging from the order and dating of the other essays, I conjecture that Bushnell composed this one in 1860.

2. For example, see Thomas Adams, *Outline of Town and City Planning* (New York, 1935); Robert A. Walker, *The Planning Function in Urban Government* (Chicago, 1941); John L. Hancock, "Planners in the Changing American City, 1900–1940," *Journal of the American Institute of Planners* 33 (1967), 290–304; and Mel Scott, *American City Planning Since 1890* (Berkeley, 1969).

Quotation from Roy Lubove, *The Progressives and the Slums: Tenement House Reform in New York City* (Pittsburgh, 1962), p. 217. See also John W. Reps, *The Making of Urban America: A History of City Planning in the United States* (Princeton, 1965), pp. 497–525; Thomas S. Hines, *Burnham of Chicago: Architect and Planner* (New York, 1974); David F. Burg, *Chicago's White City of 1893* (Lexington, Ky., 1976); Jon A. Peterson, "The City Beautiful Movement: Forgotten Origins and Lost Meanings," *Journal of Urban History* 2 (1976), 415–34; R. Reid Badger, *The Great American Fair: The World's Columbian Exposition and American Culture* (Chicago, 1979).

CHAPTER 1. DREAMERS OF URBTOPIA

1. Edward Bellamy, *Looking Backward, 2000–1887* (reprint ed., New York, 1960), pp. 43, 206, 213, 209. Among other works on utopian fiction and American ambivalence about cities, see Northrup Frye, "Varieties of Literary Utopias," and Lewis Mumford, "Utopia, the City and the Machine," in Frank E. Manuel (ed.), *Utopias and Utopian Thought* (Boston, 1966), pp. 25–49, 3–24; Eugene Arden, "The Evil City in American Fiction," *New York History* 35 (1954), 259–79; Morton White and Lucia White, *The Intellectual Versus the City* (reprint ed., New York, 1977); George Arthur Dunlap, *The City in the American Novel, 1789–1900* (Philadelphia, 1934); Janis P. Stout, *Sodoms in Eden: The City in American Fiction Before 1860* (Westport, Conn., 1976); James L. Machor, *Pastoral Cities: Urban Ideals and the Symbolic Landscape of America* (Madison, 1987); Vernon Louis Par-

rington, Jr., *American Dreams: A Study of American Utopias* (2d ed., New York, 1964); Robert L. Shurter, *The Utopian Novel in America, 1865–1900* (reprint ed., New York, 1973); Ellene Ransom, *Utopus Discovers America: Critical Realism in American Utopian Fiction, 1798–1900* (Folcroft, Pa., 1970); and Kenneth M. Roemer, *The Obsolete Necessity: America in Utopian Writings, 1888–1900* (Kent, Ohio, 1976), the most provocative of recent works. For a comprehensive bibliography, see Glenn Negley, *Utopian Literature: A Bibliography with a Supplementary Listing of Works Influential in Utopian Thought* (Lawrence, Kans., 1977).

2. Raymond Williams, *The Country and the City* (New York, 1973).

3. Shifting usages may be traced in the *Oxford English Dictionary* and the *Dictionary of Americanisms*. Jacob Bigelow, *Elements of Technology, Taken Chiefly from a Course of Lectures Delivered at Cambridge, on the Application of the Sciences to the Useful Arts* (Boston, 1829), p. 6. Two insightful brief discussions of the subject are Hugo A. Meier, "Technology and Democracy, 1800–1860," *Mississippi Valley Historical Review* 43 (1957), 618–40; and John B. Rae, "The 'Know-How' Tradition: Technology in American History," *Technology and Culture* 1 (1960), 139–50. The most satisfying of recent monographs is John F. Kasson, *Civilizing the Machine: Technology and Republican Values in America, 1776–1900* (New York, 1976).

4. "Effects of Machinery," *North American Review* 34 (January 1832), 229. For a fascinating discussion of workers' responses to the introduction of new machine technology, see David A. Zonderman, "Aspirations and Anxieties: New England Workers and the Mechanized Factory System, 1815–1850" (Ph.D. dissertation, Yale University, 1986).

5. Timothy Walker, "Defense of Mechanical Philosophy," *North American Review* 33 (July 1832), 122–36.

6. Ibid., pp. 135–36.

7. I accept here the definition of technology offered by the anthropologist V. Gordon Childe: "Technology should mean the study of those activities, directed to the satisfaction of human needs, which produce alterations in the material world." Quoted in Charles Singer et al. (eds.), *A History of Technology* (5 vols., Oxford, 1954–58), 1:38.

8. Jacques Ellul, *The Technological Society*, trans. John Wilkinson (New York, 1964), pp. 3, 5, and passim. For an insightful discussion of technological determinism, see Robert L. Heilbroner, "Do Machines Make History?" *Technology and Culture* 8 (1967), 335–45.

9. Edward Everett, *Orations and Speeches on Various Occasions* (2 vols., 6th ed., Boston, 1860), 2:71.

10. Among numerous works on the subject, see especially George H. Daniels, "The Big Questions in the History of American Technology," *Technology and Culture* 2 (1970), 1–35; David S. Landes, *The Unbound Prometheus: Technological Change and Industrial Development in Western Europe from 1750 to the Present* (Cambridge, 1969); Siegfried Giedion, *Mechanization Takes Command* (New York, 1948); and Nathan Rosenberg, *Technology and American Economic Growth* (New York, 1972).

11. Thomas Jefferson to General Thaddeus Kosciusko, 28 June, 1812, in *The Works of Thomas Jefferson*, ed. Paul L. Ford (12 vols., New York, 1904–5), 2:260–

61. For a discussion of industrial inventiveness and urbanization, see H. J. Habakkuk, *American and British Technology in the Nineteenth Century* (New York, 1962); Eric E. Lampard, "The Evolving System of Cities in the United States: Urbanization and Economic Development," in Harvey S. Perloff and Lowden Wingo, Jr. (eds.), *Issues in Urban Economics* (Baltimore, 1968), pp. 81–139; and Allan R. Pred, *The Spatial Dynamics of United States Urban-Industrial Growth, 1800–1914* (Cambridge, Mass., 1966).

12. "History of Lowell," *American Magazine of Useful and Entertaining Knowledge* 2 (November 1835), 98–99. Helpful discussions of early textile towns and bucolic imagery include Thomas Bender, *Toward an Urban Vision: Ideas and Institutions in Nineteenth-Century America* (Lexington, Mass., 1975), pp. 71 –128; Kasson, *Civilizing the Machine*, pp. 53–106; Marvin Fisher, *Workshops in the Wilderness: The European Response to American Industrialization, 1830–1860* (New York, 1967); and Leo Marx, *The Machine in the Garden* (New York, 1964).

13. On cultural images of the city, see Glenn H. Blayney, "City Life in American Drama, 1825–1860," in A. Dayle Wallace and Woodburn O. Ross (eds.), *Studies in Honor of John Wilcox* (Detroit, 1958); and Robert H. Walker, "The Poet and the Rise of the City," *Mississippi Valley Historical Review* 49 (1962), 85–99.

14. Beaumont quoted in Yehoshua Arieli, *Individualism and Nationalism in American Ideology* (Cambridge, Mass., 1964), p. 181. Bryce quoted ibid., p. 319. See also Maren Lockwood, "The Experimental Utopia in America," in Manuel, *Utopias*, pp. 183–200; and Rosabeth Moss Kanter, *Commitment and Community: Communes and Utopias in Sociological Perspective* (Cambridge, Mass., 1972), pp. 1–161.

15. For the estimate of 100,000 see the admirable work by Dolores Hayden, *Seven American Utopias: The Architecture of Communitarian Socialism, 1790–1975* (Cambridge, Mass., 1976), p. 9. See also Arthur Bestor, "Patent-Office Models of the Good Society: Some Relationships Between Social Reform and Westward Expansion," *American Historical Review* 58 (1953), 505–26, and his *Backwoods Utopias: The Sectarian Origins and the Owenite Phase of Communitarian Socialism in America, 1663–1829* (2d ed., Philadelphia, 1970).

16. The most useful and comprehensive guide to the study of utopian communities is Robert S. Fogarty, *Dictionary of American Communal and Utopian History* (Westport, Conn., 1980). The most thorough bibliography on the communitarian experiments remains Bestor, *Backwoods Utopias*, pp. 273–310.

17. Ralph L. Rusk (ed.), *The Letters of Ralph Waldo Emerson* (6 vols., New York, 1939), 2:353.

18. Hayden, *Seven American Utopias*, pp. 8–31, quotation on p. 16.

19. Albert Brisbane, *A Concise Exposition of the Doctrine of Association* (2d ed., New York, 1843), pp. 73–74; Charles Nordhoff, *Communistic Societies of the United States, from Personal Visit and Observation* (New York, 1875), p. 405.

20. Edward Kent, "A Vision of Bangor in the Twentieth Century," and Jane Sophia Appleton, "Sequel to the Vision of Bangor in the Twentieth Century," in *Voices from the Kenduskeag* (1848), pp. 61–73 and 243–65 respectively, both reprinted in Arthur O. Lewis, *American Utopias: Selected Short Fiction* (New York, 1971), with original pagination. Appleton quotations on pp. 255–56, 257.

21. Daniel Drake, *Natural and Statistical View, or Picture of Cincinnati and*

the *Miami Country* (Cincinnati, 1815), p. 226. Scott quotation from J. W. S., "The Great West," *De Bow's Review* 15 (July 1853), 51–52. For useful accounts of western urbanization see Richard C. Wade, *The Urban Frontier* (Cambridge, Mass., 1959); Gunther Barth, *Instant Cities: Urbanization and the Rise of San Francisco and Denver* (New York, 1975); Richard A. Bartlett, *The New Country: A Social History of the American Frontier, 1776–1890* (New York, 1974), pp. 399–440; and Lawrence H. Larsen, *The Urban West at the End of the Frontier* (Lawrence, Kans., 1978). On the imagery associated with western urbanization see Machor, *Pastoral Cities*, pp. 121–44.

22. Discussions of the platting of such communities appears in John W. Reps, *Town Planning in Frontier America* (Princeton, 1968), pp. 344–429.

23. "Commercial Delusions—Speculations," *American Review* 2 (October 1845), 341–57, reprinted in Charles A. Glaab, *The American City: A Documentary History* (Homewood, Ill., 1963), pp. 147, 148, 157.

24. "Architecture in the United States," *American Journal of Science and Arts* 17 (1830), 103; Robert Morris Copeland, *The Most Beautiful City in America: Essay and Plan for the Improvement of the City of Boston* (Boston, 1872), p. 10.

CHAPTER 2. THE CITY THAT NEVER WAS

1. Robert L. Shurter, *The Utopian Novel in America, 1865–1900* (reprint ed., New York, 1973), p. 143.

2. Mark Twain, "The Curious Republic of Gondour," *Atlantic Monthly* (October 1875), reprinted in Arthur O. Lewis, Jr., *American Utopias: Selected Short Fiction* (New York, 1971); William Dean Howells, *A Traveler from Altruria: A Romance* (New York, 1894), and *Through the Eye of the Needle: A Romance* (New York, 1907); Edward Bellamy, *Looking Backward, 2000–1887* (Boston, 1888), and *Equality* (New York, 1897); Mary Griffith, "Three Hundred Years Hence" (1836), reprinted in Lewis, *American Utopias*; Charles W. Caryl, *New Era: Presenting the Plans for the New Era Union to Help Develop and Utilize the Best Resources of This Country* (Denver, 1897); Cosimo Noto, *The Ideal City* (New York, 1903); Warren S. Rehm [Omen Nemo], *The Practical City: A Future City Romance; or, A Study in Environment* (Lancaster, Pa., 1898). For discussion of utopian novels within the larger arena of book publishing, see Alice Payne Hackett, *Seventy Years of Best Sellers, 1895–1965* (New York, 1967); Robert L. Shurter, "The Utopian Novel in America, 1888–1900," *South Atlantic Quarterly* 34 (1935), 137–44; Allyn B. Forbes, "The Literary Quest for Utopia, 1880–1900," *Social Forces* 6 (1927), 179–89; Charles J. Rooney, Jr., "Utopian Literature as a Reflection of Social Forces in America, 1865–1917" (Ph.D. dissertation, George Washington University, 1968); and Vernon Louis Parrington, Jr., "The Charles H. Kerr Company and Utopia," in his *American Dreams: A Study of American Utopias* (2d ed., New York, 1964), pp. 116–28. Because scholarship on Bellamy is abundant, no detailed discussion of his writings appears in these pages. On Bellamy's and other works, see Sylvia Bowman, *The Year 2000: A Critical Biography of Edward Bellamy* (New York, 1958); W. Arthur Boggs, "*Looking Backward* at the Utopian Novel, 1888–1900," *New York Public Library Bulletin* 64 (1960), 329–36; and John L. Thomas, "Utopians for an

Urban Age: Henry George, Henry Demarest Lloyd, Edward Bellamy," *Perspectives in American History* 6 (1972), 135–63.

3. Chauncey Thomas, *The Crystal Button; or: Adventures of Paul Prognosis in the Forty-Ninth Century* (Boston, 1891); King C. Gillette, *The Human Drift* (Boston, 1894). Kenneth M. Roemer's *The Obsolete Necessity: America in Utopian Writings, 1888–1900* (Kent, Ohio, 1976) contains an excellent annotated bibliography of works published between 1888 and 1900.

4. Roemer, *Obsolete Necessity*, pp. 8–12.

5. Edward Everett Hale, *Sybaris and Other Homes* (Boston, 1869), and *How They Lived in Hampton: A Study of Practical Christianity Applied in the Manufacture of Woolens* (Boston, 1888); Howells, *Traveler from Altruria*, p. 190; Milan C. Edson, *Solaris Farm: A Story of the Twentieth Century* (Washington, D.C., 1900). Two other interesting examples of rural romanticism were Henry Olerich, *A Cityless and Countryless World: An Outline of Practical Co-operative Individualism* (Holstein, Iowa, 1893), in which a portion of the population lived on co-op farms; and Titus K. Smith, *Altruria* (New York, 1895), in which people commuted from the city to work on farms. In both cases, however, the principal feature of the world of tomorrow was an urban environment.

6. Reynolds' story may be found most readily (without pagination) in Lewis, *American Utopias*.

7. An interesting essay could be written on the evolution of the phrase "middle landscape." It has appeared frequently in recent works on American urban history, principally in reference to communities set in cultivated natural surroundings as opposed to raw wilderness or the city. That is, the phrase usually signifies either the small, rural town on the eve of industrial growth or the modern suburb. The phrase, or rather the concept, may have originated in the eighteenth century when Hector St. John Crevecoeur in *Letters from an American Farmer* (1782) identified American farmers living in the "middle settlements," halfway between wilderness and seacoast towns, as those who had brought civilization to the frontier. The phrase seems to have gained its current popularity since the publication of Leo Marx's *The Machine in the Garden* (New York, 1964).

One fact is certain: a host of novelists established their perfect communities in a "middle landscape" setting; towns and cities stood surrounded by and interspersed with cultivated nature. Among others see the already-cited Olerich, *A Cityless and Countryless World*; and Rehm, *The Practical City*; as well as Alfred Denton Cridge, *Utopia; or, The History of an Extinct Planet* (Oakland, Calif., 1884); Ismar Thiusen [John Macnie], *The Diothas; or, A Far Look Ahead* (New York, 1883); Zebina Forbush, *The Co-opolitan* (Chicago, 1898); Ignatius Donnelly, *The Golden Bottle; or, The Story of Ephram Benezet of Kansas* (New York, 1892); Bryon A. Brooks, *Earth Revisited* (Boston, 1894); Alexander Craig, *Ionia: Land of Wise Men and Fair Women* (Chicago, 1898); William Stanley Child, *The Legal Revolution of 1902* (Chicago, 1898); Arthur Bird, *Looking Forward: A Dream of the United States of the Americas in 1999* (Utica, 1899); Clark Edmund Persinger, *Letters from New America; or An Attempt at Practical Socialism* (Chicago, 1900); and William Alexander Taylor, *Intermere* (Columbus, Ohio, 1901).

8. Griffith, "Three Hundred Years Hence," pp. 33–34, 38–56, 65–66, 71–78.

9. Calvin Blanchard, *The Art of Real Pleasure: That New Pleasure for Which an Imperial Reward Was Offered* (New York, 1864), pp. 17–18, and passim.

10. Noto, *The Ideal City*, p. 164; David A. Moore, *The Age of Progress; or, A Panorama of Time in Four Visions* (New York, 1856), pp. 19–26, quotation on p. 26. During the nineteenth century the theme of the pastoral city filled the pages of mainstream American literature as well. For an insightful recent discussion see James L. Machor, *Pastoral Cities: Urban Ideals and the Symbolic Landscape of America* (Madison, 1987).

11. Cridge, *Utopia*, p. 6. Two other interesting works describing the incorporation of nature, in addition to works cited in 7, were William H. Bishop, *The Garden of Eden, U.S.A.: A Very Possible Story* (Chicago, 1895), and Thomas Blot [William Simpson], *The Man from Mars: His Morals, Politics and Religion* (San Francisco, 1891).

12. C. W. Wooldridge, *Perfecting the Earth: A Piece of Possible History* (Cleveland, 1902), p. 251. See also Joaquin Miller, *The Building of the City Beautiful* (Cambridge, Mass., 1893), pp. 32–35, 108–13, 130.

13. On the New York City subway, see John Anderson Miller, *Fares Please! A Popular History of Trolleys, Horsecars, Buses, Elevateds, and Subways* (1941; rev. ed., New York, 1960), pp. 88–90.

A novel-by-novel list of engineering innovations would run for several pages. Each of the novels referenced thus far contains discussions of these and other technological wonders. It is striking that discussions of technology in the novels parallel the speculations and the reports of actual developments in the scientific and engineering journals of the last half of the century, including such popular journals as *Van Nostrand's Eclectic Engineering Magazine*, *Popular Mechanics*, and *Scientific American*. The popularity of the utopian novels may well have stemmed in part from public fascination with how things work (even today Americans make "how to" books bestsellers) and in part from the mirror effect of "recognition"—that is, some readers probably delighted in discovering their personal knowledge paraded through the pages of a novel. An abundant literature of cognition psychology attests to the seductiveness of this latter effect.

Surely it is no historical coincidence that at the very time when municipal engineers were taking charge of various aspects of city planning activities (see Chapters 7–8), urbtopian writers were building their dream cities on sound engineering principles. A few authors explicitly identified the new planning professionals as the creators of future cities. In William Simpson's urbtopia, "saniatary and civil engineers" selected sites and oversaw construction; in Clark Edmund Persinger's new world, professional architects planned towns; in Cosimo Noto's engaging projection of a future New Orleans, a commission of engineers, in consultation with physicians and landscape architects, formulated the plans. See Simpson, *Man from Mars*, p. 103; Persinger, *Letters from New America*, pp. 11–15; Noto, *The Ideal City*, p. 165. On the importance of the engineers, see Stanley K. Schultz and Clay McShane, "To Engineer the Metropolis: Sewers, Sanitation, and City Planning in Late-Nineteenth-Century America," *Journal of American History* 65 (1978), 389–411.

14. There is no mention of Thomas in either the *Dictionary of American Biography* or James D. Hart's *The Oxford Companion to American Literature*, both standard sources. Brief biographical information appears in Parrington, Jr., *American Dreams*, pp. 64–68, and in an introductory essay by Ormond Seavey in a reprint edition of *The Crystal Button* (Boston, 1975), pp. v–xiii.

15. See "Author's Preface," pp. v–vi, and "Editor's Preface," pp. vii–xi, in Thomas, *Crystal Button*, ed. George Houghton (Boston, 1891). For a favorable review, see *Catholic World* 52 (1891), 935–36.

16. Thomas, *Crystal Button*, p. 114.

17. Ibid., pp. 121, 191–206, 261–62, 38, and passim.

18. Ibid., pp. 41, 49–57, 58–60, 77–83, 85–86, 93–94: quotation about "fully organized city" on p. 81.

19. On zoning legislation see Commission on Building Districts and Restrictions, *Final Report June 2, 1916* (New York: City of New York, Board of Estimate and Apportionment, Committee on City Plan, 1916); S. J. Makielski, Jr., *The Politics of Zoning: The New York Experience* (New York, 1966). For the "Radiant City" and tower cities plans see Le Corbusier, *The City of Tomorrow and Its Planning* (1924; trans. Frederick Etchells, 1929; reprint ed., Cambridge, Mass., 1971); and Paolo Soleri, *Arcology: The City in the Image of Man* (Cambridge, Mass., 1969).

20. M. Auburré-Hovorrè, *The Milltillionaire (n.p.*, 1895), reprinted in Lewis, *American Utopias*, pp. 5–6, 7–9, 19–20.

21. Bishop, *The Garden of Eden*, pp. 117–21, 144, and passim. An emphasis on model housing, usually massive in scale, characterized the works of other authors besides Thomas, Auburré-Hovorrè, and Bishop. In addition to those discussed in the text below, see Olerich, *A Cityless and Countryless World*, pp. 81, 95, and 115, which envisioned structures similar to Bishop's "Domicile Blocks"; Craig, *Ionia*, pp. 147–50, which described workers' immense, block-long dwellings; and Arthur Brinsmade, *Utopia Achieved; A Novel of the Future* (New York, 1912), pp. 24–25, 26–29, which depicted the better classes of the city as living in three-story, detached cement houses while the working classes dwelled in model skyscraper tenements. For a discussion of an experimental garden city, small in scale, but similar to Bishop's, see Rehm, *The Practical City*, pp. 12–16, 21–29, and the author's drawing of his city plan at the conclusion of the work.

22. Gillette, *Human Drift*, pp. 87–93, quotations on pp. 87 and 90. For other works that paid tribute to the "White City" of the Columbian Exposition, see Child, *Legal Revolution of 1902*, p. 318; and a fascinating story by Henry Demarest Lloyd, "No Mean City." Written sometime during the 1890s, Lloyd's tale described the future growth of Chicago from the World's Fair down through 1971. See Lloyd, *Mazzini and Other Essays* (New York, 1910), pp. 201–32. On the organically planned, cellular city environment, see Victor Gruen, *The Heart of Our Cities: The Urban Crisis—Diagnosis and Cure* (New York, 1964), pp. 266–96; and Paul Goodman and Percival Goodman, *Communitas: Means of Livelihood and Ways of Life* (2d ed., New York, 1960), pp. 119–224.

23. Gillette, *Human Drift*, pp. 91–92, quotations on pp. 108–9, 3. For a diatribe against a carefully planned city, see Anna Bowman Dodd, *The Republic of the Future; or, Socialism a Reality* (New York, 1887), esp. pp. 19–23.

24. Caryl, *New Era*, pp. 99–121, and passim.

25. Ibid., pp. 134–36.

26. Ebenezer Howard, *Garden Cities of Tomorrow* (1902; reprint ed. with additions from the 1898 ed., Cambridge, Mass., 1965); Daniel H. Burnham and Edward H. Bennett, *Plan of Chicago* (Chicago, 1909); Charles Mulford Robinson, *Modern Civic Art: The City Made Beautiful* (New York, 1903). See also Dugald MacFadyen, *Sir Ebenezer Howard and the Town Planning Movement* (Cambridge,

1970); Marsha Peters, "The Natural City: Landscape Architecture and City Planning in Nineteenth Century America" (M.A. thesis, University of Wisconsin—Madison, 1971); David B. Cady, "The Garden City Ideal and Its Influence on American Planning and Housing Reform, 1900–1940" (Ph.D. dissertation, University of Wisconsin—Madison, 1972); and Jon A. Peterson, "The City Beautiful Movement: Forgotten Origins and Lost Meanings," *Journal of Urban History* 2 (1976), 415–34.

27. Wooldridge, *Perfecting the Earth*, pp. 23–26.

28. Ibid., pp. 38–61, 94–108, 138–44. On eighteenth-century Savannah see John W. Reps, *The Making of Urban America: A History of City Planning in the United States* (Princeton, 1965), pp. 185–203. On the "superblock" see Clarence S. Stein, *Toward New Towns for America* (rev. ed., Cambridge, Mass., 1965).

29. Wooldridge, *Perfecting the Earth*, pp. 174–78, 181–83, 188–206; quotation on p. 299.

30. Ibid., pp. 286–318, 174–78, quotation on p. 244.

31. Roy Lubove, *Community Planning in the 1920s: The Contribution of the Regional Planning Association of America* (Pittsburgh, 1963).

CHAPTER 3. THE LEGAL LANDSCAPE

1. *Lindsay v. Comm'rs*, 2 Bay 38, 46, 53 (S.C. 1796), discussed in Arthur Lenhoff, "Development of the Concept of Eminent Domain," *Columbia Law Review* 42 (1942), 598. On constitutional requirements see Charles Grant, "The 'Higher Law' Background of the Law of Eminent Domain," *Wisconsin Law Review* 6 (1931), 67, 70.

2. Walter H. Hamilton, "Property—According to Locke," *Yale Law Journal* 41 (1931–32), 864–80. Quotations from Blackstone appear in the magnificent study by Daniel J. Boorstin, *The Mysterious Science of the Law* (1941; reprint ed., Boston, 1958), pp. 171, 173.

3. For a discussion of the extent of regulation during the colonial period, see Carl Bridenbaugh, *Cities in the Wilderness: Urban Life in America, 1625–1742* (New York, 1938); his *Cities in Revolt: Urban Life in America, 1743–1776* (New York, 1955); and Philip Nichols, *The Law of Eminent Domain* (2d. ed., Boston, 1917), p. 20.

4. See Jon C. Teaford, *The Municipal Revolution in America: Origins of Modern Urban Government, 1650–1825* (Chicago, 1975), pp. 91–110.

5. The quotation is from *Van Horen's Lessee v. Dorrance*, 2 Dall. 310 (Pa. 1795). On "taking" construed only as the physical appropriation of land, see Joseph M. Cormack, "Legal Concepts in Cases of Eminent Domain," *Yale Law Journal*, 41 (1931), 221–61, esp. 221–35.

6. Morton J. Horwitz, *The Transformation of American Law, 1780–1860* (Cambridge, 1977), pp. 63–66.

7. James Kent, *Commentaries on American Law* (4 vols., Boston, 1826–30), 2:275. The Shaw decision came in *Wallington, et al. Petitioners*, 16 Pick. 87, 102–3 (1834).

8. Edward Stanwood, "Topography and Landmarks of the Last Hundred Years," in Justin Winsor (ed.), *The Memorial History of Boston* (4 vols., Boston,

1881), pp. 34–38; *Boston Water-Power Co. v. Boston and Worcester RR.*, 23 Pick. 360, 392, 394.

9. *West River Bridge Co. v. Dix*, 6 How. 520–21 (1848). For informed discussion of the Charles River Bridge and its importance, see Stanley I. Kutler, *Privilege and Creative Destruction: The Charles River Bridge Case* (Philadelphia, 1971). On the significance of Shaw's stance in the 1839 water company case, see Leonard W. Levy, *The Law of the Commonwealth and Chief Justice Shaw* (Cambridge, 1957), pp. 123, 271.

10. On general trends during the period, see Horwitz, *Transformation of American Law*, pp. 64–66, 70–74, and 61–108 passim.

11. Edward W. Constant II, "State Management of Petroleum Resources: Texas, 1910–1940," in George H. Daniels and Mark H. Rose (eds.), *Energy and Transport: Historical Perspectives on Policy Issues* (Beverly Hills, 1982), pp. 157–75, quotation on p. 174.

12. The leading nineteenth-century discussion of nuisance law was H. G. Wood, *A Practical Treatise on the Law of Nuisances in Their Various Forms; Including Remedies Therefor at Law and in Equity* (Albany, 1875). For contemporary views on the relation between nuisance law and the police power doctrine, see Thomas M. Cooley, *A Treatise on Constitutional Limitations* (Boston, 1868); Christopher Tiedemann, *A Treatise on the Limitations of the Police Power* (Saint Louis, 1886); and W. G. Hastings, "The Development of Law as Illustrated by the Decisions Relating to the Police Power of the State," *Proceedings of the American Philosophical Society* 39 (1900), 359–527, esp. 410–17.

13. William Blackstone, *Commentaries on the Laws of England in Four Books*, ed. George Chase (4th ed., New York, 1925), 3:738–39; William Prosser, "Nuisance Without Fault," *Texas Law Review* 20 (1942), 410–20; Wood, *Practical Treatise on the Law of Nuisances*, p. 17.

14. Among other cases, see *Vanderbilt v. Adams*, 7 Cow. 349 (N.Y. 1827); *Lansing v. Smith*, 8 Cow. 146 (N.Y. 1828); *Hart v. Mayor of Albany*, 9 Wend. 571 (N.Y. 1832); *Baker v. Boston*, 12 Pick. 183 (Mass. 1831); *Smith v. Boston*, 7 Cush. 254 (Mass. 1851); and *Radcliff's Executor v. Mayor of Brooklyn*, 4 N.Y. 195 (1850).

15. *Lexington & Ohio Rail Road v. Applegate*, 8 Dana 289 (Ky. 1839). For an interpretation of the case as "atypical," a view that I do not share, see Horwitz, *Transformation of American Law*, pp. 74–75.

16. For discussion of the anticontagionist theory of disease, see Chapter 5 below. Cases cited and quoted in this paragraph, in order, were *Coates et al. v. The Mayor of New York*, 7 Cow. 585, 605 (N.Y. 1827); *Vandine, Petitioner*, 6 Pick. 187 (Mass. 1828); and *Van Worman v. Mayor*, 15 Wend. 262 (N.Y. 1836). Insightful discussion of New York City cemetery cases appears in Hendrick Hartog, *Public Property and Private Power: The Corporation of the City of New York in American Law, 1730–1870* (Chapel Hill, N.C., 1983), pp. 71–81.

17. *Commonwealth v. Tewksbury*, 11 Metc. 55, 57 (Mass. 1846). For discussion of the significance of the case, see Levy, *Law of the Commonwealth*, pp. 246–47. For discussion of the expanding power of municipal corporations to abate nuisances, see Wood, *Practical Treatise on the Law of Nuisances*, ch. 22, "Municipal Corporations."

18. For example, see *Palmer v. Mulligan*, 3 Caines 307 (N.Y. 1805), and *Thurston v. Hancock*, 12 Mass. 220 (1815).

19. *Callender* v. *Marsh*, 1 Pick. 418 (Mass. 1823). For discussion of *Callender* see Horwitz, *Transformation of American Law*, pp. 72–73; and Scott M. Reznick, "Land Use Regulation and the Concept of Takings in Nineteenth Century America," *University of Chicago Law Review* 40 (1973), 856–57.

20. *Lansing* v. *Smith*, 8 Cow. 149 (N.Y. 1828). *Callender* had used a slightly different phrase—"damnum sine injuria"—with the same meaning. On the attractiveness of the philosophy of utilitarianism, see Herbert W. Schneider, A *History of American Philosophy* (2d ed., New York, 1963), pp. 91–111. The originator of the term was John Stuart Mill.

21. *Radcliff's Executor* v. *Mayor of Brooklyn*, 4 N.Y. 195 (1850); *O'Connor* v. *Pittsburgh*, 6 Harris 187 (18 Pa. St., 1851). Discussion of this and similar cases appears in Cormack, "Legal Concepts," pp. 226–31.

22. Edward S. Corwin, "The Doctrine of Due Process of Law Before the Civil War," in *Selected Essays on Constitutional Law* (5 vols., Chicago, 1938), 1:234. In addition to that article and cases cited below, readers interested in untangling this Gordian knot of doctrinal development will profit from the following works, although these differ in emphases and interpretations: Andrew King, "Law and Land Use in Chicago: A Prehistory of Modern Zoning" (Ph.D. dissertation, University of Wisconsin—Madison, 1976), ch. 4; Levy, *Law of the Commonwealth*, ch. 13; Elmer E. Smead, "*Sic Utere Tuo Ut Alienum Non Laedas*: A Basis of the State Police Power," *Cornell Law Quarterly* 21 (1936), 276–92.

23. For discussion of the growing demand for municipally provided services see Charles R. Adrian and Ernest S. Griffith, A *History of American City Government: The Formation of Traditions, 1775–1870* (New York, 1976).

24. For changing definitions see the *Oxford English Dictionary* and the *Dictionary of American English*. I found especially helpful the discussion in William W. Crosskey, *Politics and the Constitution in the History of the United States* (2 vols., Chicago, 1953), 1:148–55; 2:1163–64.

25. *Commonwealth* v. *Alger*, 7 Cush. 85 (1851); *The Slaughter-House Cases*, 83 U.S. (16 Wall.) 36, 62 (1873); Ernst Freund, *The Police Power: Public Policy and Constitutional Rights* (Chicago, 1904), p. 3; John W. Burgess, quoted in Ruth Locke Roettinger, *The Supreme Court and State Police Power: A Study in Federalism* (Washington, D.C., 1957), p. 11.

26. For discussion of the "principle of conditions" as fundamental to the evolution of the police power doctrine, see Scott M. Reznick, "Empiricism and the Principle of Conditions in the Evolution of the Police Power: A Model for Definitional Scrutiny," *Washington University Law Review* (Winter 1978), 1–92.

27. *Republica* v. *Duquet*, 2 Yates 493 (Pa. 1799); *Minutes of the Common Council of the City of New York, 1784–1831* (21 vols., New York, 1917–30), 2:498–99; 3:198; *Corporation of the Brick Presbyterian Church* v. *The Mayor of New York*, 5 Cowen's 538 (1826); *Mayor of New York* v. *Ordrenan*, 12 Johns. Cas. 122 (1815); Blackstone, *Commentaries*, 4:162.

28. See, for example, H. G. Wood, *Practical Treatise on the Law of Nuisances*, pp. 770–73; Cooley, *Constitutional Limitations*, pp. 572–97; Christopher G. Tiedemann, A *Treatise on the Limitations of the Police Power in the United States, Considered from Both a Civil and Criminal Standpoint* (St. Louis, 1886), passim; W. G. Hastings, "The Development of Law as Illustrated by the Decisions

Relating to the Police Power of the State," *Proceedings of the American Philosophical Society* 39 (1900), 410.

29. *Van Worman* v. *Mayor,* 15 Wend. 262 (1836); *Stone* v. *Mayor of New York,* 25 Wend. 157 (1840); *Russell* v. *Mayor of New York,* 2 Denio 461, 484 (1845); F. Dwarris, *A General Treatise on Statutes* (New York, 1871), pp. 444ff.; and, for brief discussion of the concept, Reznick, "Empiricism and the Principle of Conditions," pp. 19–20.

30. *Smith* v. *Boston,* 7 Cush. 254 (1851).

31. Among other sources, see Joseph Angell, *Watercourses* (1st ed., New York, 1824; 2d ed., 1833); T. E. Laurer, "The Common Law Background of the Riparian Doctrine," *Missouri Law Review* 28 (1963), 60–85; Horwitz, *Transformation of American Law,* pp. 34–47. To trace the evolution of this principle see *Palmer* v. *Mulligan,* 3 Cai. R. 307 (N.Y. 1805); *Platt* v. *Johnson,* 15 Johns. 213 (N.Y. 1818); and, for the quotation, *Tyler* v. *Wilkinson,* 24 Fed. Cas. 472 (1827).

32. *Milne* v. *Davidson,* 5 Martin N.S. 412 (1827); *Coates et al.* v. *Mayor of New York,* 7 Cowen 604 (1827).

33. *Vanderbilt* v. *Adams,* 7 Cowen 349, 350, 351–52 (N.Y. 1827).

34. *Baker* v. *Boston,* 12 Pick. 193 (Mass. 1831); *Lumbard* v. *Stearns,* 4 Cush. 60 (Mass. 1849); Levy, *Law of the Commonwealth,* p. 248.

35. *Commonwealth* v. *Alger,* 53, 59, 62–64.

36. Ibid., 84–85, 95–96, 102–4.

37. *State* v. *Paul,* 5 R.I. 191 (R.I., 1858). See also *Thorpe* v. *Rutland & Burlington Railroad,* 27 Vermont 140, 149 (Vt. 1854).

CHAPTER 4. THE LAWFUL CITY

1. On changing conceptions of local autonomy and charters, see Gerald E. Frug, "The City as a Legal Concept," *Harvard Law Review* 93 (1980), 1095–1109.

2. The "bag" phrase appears in Lawrence M. Friedman, *A History of American Law* (New York, 1973), p. 459.

3. Readers may trace changes in usage in the *Oxford English Dictionary* and the *Dictionary of American English.* See also Hendrik Hartog, *Public Property and Private Power: The Corporation of the City of New York in American Law, 1730–1870* (Chapel Hill, N.C., 1983), p. 190.

4. The quotation is from James Willard Hurst, *Law and the Conditions of Freedom in the Nineteenth-Century United States* (Madison, 1956), p. 28. See also his *Law and Social Process in United States History* (Ann Arbor, 1960), pp. 234–53; Oscar Handlin and Mary F. Handlin, "Origins of the American Business Corporation," *Journal of Economic History* 5 (1945), 1–23; the same authors' *Commonwealth: A Study of the Role of Government in the American Economy— Massachusetts, 1774–1861* (New York, 1947); and E. Merrick Dodd, *American Business Corporations until 1860, with Special Reference to Massachusetts* (Cambridge, Mass., 1954).

5. *Trustees of Dartmouth College* v. *Woodward,* 17 U.S. 668 (4 Wheat.); James Kent, *Commentaries on American Law* (4 vols., Boston, 1826–30), 2:275. See also Frug, "City as Legal Concept," pp. 1101–9.

6. *People* v. *Morris*, 13 Wend. 325, 334–35, 337–38 (N.Y. 1835), discussed in Hartog, *Public Property and Private Power*, pp. 209–12.

7. Quotation from *Baker* v. *Boston*, 12 Pick. 183, 193 (Mass. 1831). See also *Gwynn* v. *City of Cincinnati*, 3 Ohio 24 (1827); and *Green* v. *Savannah*, 6 Ga. 1 (1849).

8. I am indebted to Hendrik Hartog for calling my attention to this important case. For its economic and political background, see Louis Hartz, *Economic Policy and Democratic Thought: Pennsylvania, 1776–1860* (Cambridge, Mass., 1948), pp. 113–28.

9. *Sharpless* v. *The Mayor of Philadelphia*, 21 Penn. St. 158 (1853). For reasons that remain unclear, the two dissenting opinions did not appear as part of the official court record. They reached print a year later. See *American Law Register*, old ser., 2 (1854), 27–43, 85–112.

10. The *Sharpless* case is so rich in opinion and ramifications that it deserves a thorough article or monographic treatment in its own right.

11. Lewis dissent, *American Law Register*, pp. 96–97.

12. Ibid., p. 107.

13. *Merriam* v. *Moody's Executors*, 25 Iowa 163 (1868); *Hunter* v. *City of Pittsburgh*, 207 U.S. 161 (1907); *City of Trenton* v. *State of New Jersey*, 262 U.S. 182 (1923). See also *Williams* v. *Mayor and City Council of Baltimore*, 289 U.S. 36 (1933).

14. Fred Bosselman, David Callies, and John Banta, *The Taking Issue* (Washington, D.C.: Council on Environmental Quality, 1973), p. 238; Andrew King, "Law and Land Use in Chicago: A Prehistory of Modern Zoning" (Ph.D. dissertation, University of Wisconsin—Madison, 1976), ch. 4; *Yates* v. *Milwaukee*, 10 Wall. (U.S.) 497, 505 (1870).

15. Useful secondary accounts of the rise of machine politics and reform reactions include Raymond A. Mohl, *The New City: Urban America in the Industrial Age, 1860–1920* (Arlington Heights, Ill., 1985), pp. 83–137; Seymour Mandelbaum, *Boss Tweed's New York* (New York, 1965); Zane L. Miller, *Boss Cox's Cincinnati: Urban Politics in the Progressive Era* (New York, 1968); William M. Maury, *Alexander "Boss" Shepherd and the Board of Public Works* (Washington, D.C., 1975); and Scott Greer (ed.), *Ethnics, Machines, and the American Urban Future* (Cambridge, Mass., 1981).

16. *Dictionary of American Biography*, vol. 3, pt. 1, p. 311. There exists no modern biography of John F. Dillon.

17. See Cooley opinion in *People ex rel. Le Roy* v. *Hurlbut*, 24 Mich. 44, 93 (1871); Amasa Eaton, "The Right to Local Self-Government" (pts. 1–5), *Harvard Law Review* 13 (1900), 441, 570, 638, and ibid. 14 (1900), 20, 116; Eugene McQuillin, *A Treatise on the Law of Municipal Corporations* (New York, 1911); John F. Dillon, *Commentaries on the Law of Municipal Corporations* (5th ed., Boston, 1911), sec. 98, pp. 154–56; and William Munro, *The Government of American Cities* (New York, 1923), p. 53. I am indebted to Gerald Frug, "City as Legal Concept," pp. 1113–15, for calling attention to several of these sources. See also Edwin A. Gere, "Dillon's Rule and the Cooley Doctrine: Reflections of the Political Culture," *Journal of Urban History* 8 (1982), 271–98.

18. Kent, *Commentaries* 2:239–40. See also Hartog, *Public Property and Private Power*, pp. 183–84 n. 14.

19. Dillon, *Treatise*, pp. 104, 101–2.

20. Ibid., pp. 217, 25, 82–83 n. 1.

21. Ibid., pp. 25–26. See also the brief discussion in Hartog, *Public Property and Private Power*, p. 224.

22. John F. Dillon, *The Laws and Jurisprudence of England and America* (New York, 1894), p. 16.

23. See Cooley's concurring opinion in *People ex rel. Le Roy v. Hurlburt*, 97–98; *City of Paterson v. The Society for Establishing Useful Manufactures*, 24 NJL 385 (1854); and the lengthy historical argument against the Dillon Rule by Eugene McQuillin, "Rise and Progress of Municipal Institutions," *Law of Municipal Corporations* (2d ed., New York, 1928), ch. 1. See also Hartog, *Public Property and Private Power*, pp. 220–21.

24. Dillon, *Treatise*, pp. 72, 101–5, 25. During the late nineteenth century, many a state legislature followed Dillon's line of reasoning and amended city charters at will, with or without the consent of the city itself. See Lawrence M. Friedman, *Contract Law in America* (Madison, 1965), p. 74; Frank Parsons, "Legal Aspects of Monopoly," in Edward M. Bemis (ed.), *Municipal Monopolies* (New York,1899), p. 433. For a recent challenge to the notion that city governments were the mere playthings of state legislatures, see Jon C. Teaford, "Special Legislation and the Cities, 1865–1900," *American Journal of Legal History*, 23 (1979), 189–212.

25. Dillon, *Commentaries* (4th ed., Boston, 1890), p. 28.

26. Among numerous historical accounts, see John F. Kasson, *Civilizing the Machine: Technology and Republican Values in America, 1776–1900* (New York, 1976); Ernest S. Griffith, *A History of American City Government: The Conspicuous Failure, 1870–1900* (New York, 1974); Paul Boyer, *Urban Masses and Moral Order in America, 1820–1920* (Cambridge, Mass., 1978); Robert Wiebe, *The Search for Order, 1877–1920* (New York, 1967); and John L. Thomas, *Alternative America: Henry George, Edward Bellamy, Henry Demarest Lloyd and the Adversary Tradition* (Cambridge, Mass., 1983). For an insightful corrective to the "conspicuous failure" thesis, see Jon C. Teaford, *The Unheralded Triumph: City Government in America, 1870–1900* (Baltimore, 1984).

27. These interpretations come from comprehensive examination of the various editions of Dillon's *Treatise* and other writings. They seem to me self-evident. Other scholars may disagree. For the quotations see: John F. Dillon, "Property—Its Rights and Duties in Our Legal and Social Systems," *American Law Review* 29 (1895), 173. In addition to secondary sources cited in note 26, see John G. Sproat, *"The Best Men": Liberal Reformers in the Gilded Age* (New York, 1968); and Frederic Cople Jaher, *The Urban Establishment: Upper Strata in Boston, New York, Charleston, Chicago, and Los Angeles* (Urbana, Ill., 1982).

28. Hartog, *Public Property and Private Power*, p. 263.

29. Among many discussions of the subject, see W. G. Hastings, "The Development of Law as Illustrated by the Decisions Relating to the Police Power of the State," *Proceedings of the American Philosophical Society* 39 (1900), passim; and Walter H. Hamilton, "The Path of Due Process of Law," in Leonard Levy (ed.), *American Constitutional Law: Historical Essays* (New York, 1966), pp. 131–54.

30. *Watertown v. Mayo*, 109 Mass. 315 (1872); *In re Commissioners of the Central Park*, 63 Barbour 282 (N.Y. 1872). See also *Brooklyn Park Commissioners v.*

Armstrong, 45 N.Y. 234 (1871). For citation of the urban cases, see *Shoemaker* v. *United States*, 147 U.S. 282 (1892).

31. *Harrison et al.* v. *The New Orleans Pacific Railways Co.*, 34 La. Ann. 462 (1882); *Fobes* v. *The Rome, Watertown & Ogdesburg R.R. Co.*, 121 NY 505 (1890); *Story* v. *New York Elevated R.R. Co.*, 90 NY 122 (1882); *John Reining et al., Respondents,* v. *The NY, Lackawana and Western Railway Company*, 128 NY 157 (1891); *Egerer* v. *The NY Central & Hudson R.R. Co.*, 130 NY 108 (1891). Summary discussion of the New York City elevated railway cases appears in Edward Quinton Keasbey, *The Law of Electric Wires in Streets and Highways* (Chicago, 1892), pp. 64–65.

32. *Rideout* v. *Knox*, 148 Mass. 368 (Mass. 1889). I do not intend to demean the importance of Holmes's distinctions, nor those of subsequent courts. A fine and often amorphous line separated aggressive government infringement of private property rights and genuine promotion of the public good through public works construction and planning efforts. From the standpoint of many urban leaders, however, the return of just compensation requirements raised new confusions about the limits of urban authority.

33. For general discussion see Clyde E. Jacobs, *Law Writers and the Courts: The Influence of Thomas M. Cooley, Christopher G. Tiedemann and John F. Dillon on American Constitutional Law* (Berkeley, 1954).

34. Readers may trace the evolution of these arguments through Cooley, *Constitutional Limitations*, esp. pp. 572ff.; Henry E. Mills, *A Treatise Upon the Law of Eminent Domain* (St. Louis, 1879); Christopher G. Tiedemann, *A Treatise on the Limitations of the Police Power in the United States, Considered from Both a Civil and Criminal Standpoint*; and his *A Treatise on the Law of Municipal Corporations in the United States* (New York, 1894); Keasbey, *The Law of Electric Wires*; Hastings, "The Development of Law"; and, of course, the writings of John F. Dillon. Qualifiers of or dissenters from the fundamental trends included Byron K. Elliott and William F. Elliott, *A Treatise on the Laws of Roads and Streets* (Indianapolis, 1890); Carman F. Randolph, *The Law of Eminent Domain in the United States* (Boston, 1894); and, especially, William P. Prentice, *Police Powers Arising Under the Law of Overruling Necessity* (New York, 1894).

35. Ernst Freund, *The Police Power: Public Policy and Constitutional Rights* (Chicago, 1904), pp. 6, 546–47, 25–26, 425, 362, 582, 591, 3.

36. Prentice, *Police Powers*, p. 8. Overview discussions of the police power and public health include H. Campbell Black, "The Police Power and the Public Health," *American Law Review* 25 (1891), 170–84; LeRoy Parker and Robert H. Worthington, *The Law of Public Health and Safety and the Powers and Duties of Boards of Health* (Albany, 1892); Prentice, *Police Powers*; James W. Garner, "Federal Activity in the Interest of Public Health," *Yale Review* 14 (August 1905), 181–225; Frank J. Goodnow, "Constitutional Foundations of Federal Public Health Powers," *American Journal of Public Health* 9 (1919), 561–66.

37. Tiedemann, *Municipal Corporations*, pp. 568, 565–66. See also Elliott and Elliott, *Roads and Streets*, pp. 363–64, 365, and cases cited therein. The most significant Supreme Court cases included *Munn* v. *Illinois*, 94 U.S. 113 (1876); *Stone* v. *Mississippi*, 101 U.S. 814 (1880); *New Orleans Gas Light Co.* v. *Drainage Commission*, 197 U.S. 453 (1905); and *Chicago, Burlington & Quincy Railway* v. *Drainage Commissioners*, 200 U.S. 561 (1906). At the same time, another influen-

tial case posed new due process limitations on the use of the police power. See *Lochner v. New York*, 198 U.S. 45 (1905).

38. For discussion of and lists of waterworks cases, see Tiedemann, *Municipal Corporations*, p. 449; and Dillon, *Commentaries* (4th ed., 1890), 2:828. See also Daniel H. Burnham and Edward H. Bennett, *The Plan of Chicago* (Chicago, 1909), especially the excellent addendum by Walter L. Fisher, "Legal Aspects of the Plan of Chicago."

39. For city street-use cases, among others, see the following: railroads—*Milburn et al. v. The City of Cedar Rapids & the Chicago, Iowa and Nebraska RR Co.*, 12 Iowa 246 (1861); *The People, et al. v. Kerr, et al.*, 27 N.Y. 188 (1863); street lighting, telephone and telegraph communication lines—Dillon, *Commentaries* (4th ed., 1890), 2:822ff.; *American Digest* 14 (decennial ed., 1897–1906); Keasbey, *The Law of Electric Wires*, pp. 7, 38, 49, 66–67, 86. On various aspects of building codes, restrictions, and regulations, see *Parker v. Nightengale*, 6 Allen 342 (Mass. 1863); *Rhodes et al. v. Dunbar et al.*, 57 Pa. St. Rep. 275 (Pa. 1868); *Wier's Appeal*, 74 Pa. St. Rep. 230 (Pa. 1873); *The City of Olympia v. C. B. Mann*, 1 Wash. St. 389 (Pa. 1890); *The City of St. Louis v. Russell*, 116 Mo. 248 (Mo. 1893); *Rochester v. West*, 164 NY 510 (N.Y. 1900); *American Digest* 14. For the Maryland case see *Commissioners of Easton v. Covey*, 74 Md. 262 (Md. 1891), and, subsequently, *Bostoch v. Sams*, 95 Md. 400 (Md. 1902). For the Boston case see *Attorney General v. Henry B. Williams and others*, 174 Mass. 476 (1899), and *Williams v. Parker*, 188 U.S. 491 (1903).

40. Readers interested in tracing the growing number of decisions will find the trade journals of the public health and municipal engineering professions invaluable sources. From the early 1880s on, those journals printed legal columns presenting and discussing urban cases from around the nation. Citations of those journals appear in the notes to Chapters 5, 6, 7, and 8 below. A useful contemporary overview of municipal regulations and improvements is John A. Fairlie, *Municipal Administration* (New York, 1901), esp. pt. 2, pp. 125–312. For discussion of "special legislation," see Teaford, "Special Legislation and the Cities, 1865–1900," pp. 189–212.

41. *Village of Euclid v. Ambler Realty Co.*, 272 U.S. 365 (1926). The most useful and thorough discussion of the case appears in Seymour I. Toll, *Zoned American* (New York, 1969), pp. 213–54.

42. Holmes to Pollock, 26 November 1922; 31 December 1922; Pollock to Holmes, 5 February 1923; all in Mark DeWolfe Howe (ed.), *Holmes-Pollock Letters: The Correspondence of Mr. Justice Holmes and Sir Frederick Pollock, 1874–1932* (2 vols., 2d ed., Cambridge, Mass., 1961), 2:106, 109, 111.

43. The other case was *Jackman v. Rosenbaum Co.*, 260 U.S. 22 (1922), discussed in Mark DeWolfe Howe (ed.), *Holmes-Laski Letters: The Correspondence of Mr. Justice Holmes and Harold J. Laski, 1916–1935* (Cambridge, Mass., 1953), p. 457. *Pennsylvania Coal Co. v. Mahon*, 260 U.S. 416 (1922).

44. *Pennsylvania Coal Co. v. Mahon*, 260 U.S. 417.

45. See the transcript of record, no. 31, for *Euclid* prepared during the Court's October 1926 term, pp. 1–6, 28–29, 146, hereafter cited as "Record." For a description of Euclid Avenue see Christopher Tunnard and Henry Hope Reed, *American Skyline* (New York, 1956), pp. 110–11.

46. "Record," pp. 6–11, 13–27, 167, 204.

47. Mel Scott, *American City Planning Since 1890* (Berkeley, 1969), p. 238; James Metzenbaum, *The Law of Zoning* (New York, 1930), p. 108.

48. "Record," pp. 167, 11, 40.

49. *Ambler Realty Co. v. Village of Euclid*, 297 Fed. 314 (D.C.N.D., Ohio, 1924).

50. Ibid., p. 316.

51. Ibid., pp. 309, 313. The case cited by Westenhaver was *Cleveland, etc. Ry. Co. v. Backus*, 154 U.S. 439 (1894).

52. *Village of Euclid v. Ambler Realty Co.*, "Motion for Leave to File Brief, Amici Curiae and Brief on Behalf of the National Conference on City Planning, the National Housing Association and the Massachusetts Federation of Town Planning Boards, Amici Curiae, Motion."

53. *Village of Euclid v. Ambler Realty Co.*, Supreme Court of the United States, October Term, 1926, No. 31, "Brief on Behalf of Appellants," p. 54; Ibid. "Brief and Argument for Appellee," pp. 38, 48, 78–79, 84; *Village of Euclid v. Ambler Realty Co.*, 272 U.S. 388.

54. Readers interested in the story of the about-face and the internal clash of philosophies among members of the Court will want to see Ray A. Brown, "Due Process of Law, Police Power, and the Supreme Court," *Harvard Law Review* 40 (1927), 943–44; Alfred Bettman, "The Decision of the Supreme Court of the United States in the Euclid Village Zoning Case," in his *City and Regional Planning Papers* (Cambridge, Mass., 1946), pp. 51ff.; Robert A. Walker, *The Planning Function in Urban Government* (Chicago, 1941), pp. 77–78; and Toll, *Zoned American*, pp. 229–53.

55. 272 U.S. 385, 386–87, 388, 390, 394.

56. Metzenbaum, *Law of Zoning*, p. 121; Toll, *Zoned American*, p. 242; Scott, *American City Planning*, p. 240; Norman L. Knauss, "768 Municipalities in United States Now Protected by Zoning Ordinances," *American City*, 40 (1929), 167.

57. Quoted in Russell VanNest Black, "Can Intelligent Zoning Be Done Without a Comprehensive City Plan?" *American City* 38 (1928), 108.

58. Lewis Mumford, "Botched Cities," *American Mercury*, 18 (1929), 147, 144, 148.

59. George H. Coffin, Jr., "To What Extent Should Business Areas Be Limited?" *Municipal and County Engineering* 81 (1926), 249.

60. 297 Fed. 312–13. The case to which he referred was *Buchanan v. Warley*, 245 U.S. 60 (1917), in which the Court invalidated a Louisville zoning ordinance that segregated the city into all-white and all-black residential districts. Racial justice was not the reason given by the Court; rather, it found that the ordinance hampered the constitutional right of white sellers to select their own buyers of property.

CHAPTER 5. THE UNHEALTHY CITY

1. Edward Everett Hale (ed.), *Joseph Tuckerman on the Elevation of the Poor* (Boston, 1874), pp. 89–90, 153. On Tuckerman see Daniel T. McColgan, *Joseph Tuckerman: Pioneer in American Social Work* (Washington, D.C., 1940); William

Ellery Channing, "A Discourse on the Life and Character of the Rev. Joseph Tuckerman, D.D.," in *Works of William Ellery Channing, D.D., with an Introduction, to Which Is Added THE PERFECT LIFE* (Boston, 1891), pp. 581, see also 578–97; Horace Mann, *The Massachusetts System of Common Schools: Being an Enlarged and Revised Edition of the Tenth Annual Report of the First Secretary of the Massachusetts Board of Education* (Boston, 1849), pp. 85–86. For broader discussion of the emergence of environmentalist attitudes during the pre–Civil War decades see Stanley K. Schultz, *The Culture Factory: Boston Public Schools, 1789–1860* (New York, 1973), ch. 9, "Poverty and the Urban Crisis."

2. Frederick L. Hoffman, "American Mortality Progress During the Last Half Century," in Mazyck P. Ravenel (ed.), *A Half Century of Public Health* (New York, 1921), pp. 94–117; E. H. Barton, "Report Upon the Sanitary Condition of New Orleans," in *Report of the Sanitary Commission of New Orleans on the Epidemic Yellow Fever of 1853* (New Orleans, 1854); Chicago Board of Health, *Reports of the Board of Health of the City of Chicago, 1867–69* (Chicago, 1870); *Proceedings and Debates of the Third National Quarantine and Sanitary Convention* (New York, 1859); Edward Meeker, "The Improving Health of the United States, 1850–1915," *Explorations in Economic History* 9 (1972), 353–73, esp. table 6, p. 370.

3. John L. Peyton, *Over the Alleghenies and Across the Prairies* (2d ed., London, 1870), p. 326; New York quotation from David W. Mitchell, *Ten Years in the United States: Being an Englishman's View of Men and Things in the North and South* (London, 1862), p. 146; Charleston quotation from *Report of the Committee of the City Council of Charleston, Upon the Epidemic Yellow Fever of 1858* (Charleston, 1859), pp. 19–20.

4. Quotation from Warren S. Tyron (ed.), *A Mirror for Americans: Life and Manners in the United States, 1790–1870, as Recorded by American Travelers* (3 vols., Chicago, 1952), 1:169–70. The most comprehensive survey of urban sanitation problems during the period remains George E. Waring, Jr. (comp.), *Report on the Social Statistics of Cities, Tenth Census of the United States, 1880* (2 vols., Washington, D.C., 1887). Useful historical accounts include Lawrence H. Larsen, "Nineteenth-Century Street Sanitation: A Study of Filth and Frustration," *Wisconsin Magazine of History* 52 (1969), 239–47; David R. Goldfield, "The Business of Health Planning: Disease Prevention in the Old South," *Journal of Southern History* 42 (1976), 557–70; Joel A. Tarr, "Urban Pollution—Many Long Years Ago," *American Heritage* 22 (October 1971), 65–69, 106; Martin A. Melosi," 'Out of Sight, Out of Mind': The Environment and the Disposal of Municipal Refuse, 1860–1920," *The Historian* 35 (1973), 621–40; and Melosi, "Refuse Pollution and Municipal Reform: The Waste Problem in America, 1880–1917," in Martin A. Melosi (ed.), *Pollution and Reform in American Cities, 1870–1930* (Austin, 1980), 105–33.

5. Jackson S. Schultz, esq., "The Utilization of Animal and Vegetable Refuse Substances in Our Large Cities," *The Sanitarian* 4 (1876), 261–67. At the time the author presented his solution, methods of refuse and garbage disposal that are more familiar to us today were being used in other American cities. See, for example, the discussion of Baltimore householders' use of two "garbage vessels"—one for ashes, the other for garbage—which city garbage carts periodically hauled away to dump in the countryside: Dr. C. A. Leas, "On the Sanitary Care and Utilization of Refuse in Cities," *Journal of the Franklin Institute* 67 (March 1874), 206–17.

6. Waring, *Social Statistics of Cities*, 1:126–27; 2:331–32, 326, 767, 558, 811, 320–21. For discussion of selling wastes to farmers and other usual methods of disposal, see Joel A. Tarr, "From City to Farm: Urban Wastes and the American Farmer," *Agricultural History* 49 (1975), 598–612; and Lawrence H. Larsen, *The Urban West at the End of the Frontier* (Lawrence, Kans., 1978), pp. 61–71.

7. B. A. Segur, "Privy Vaults and Cesspools," *Reports and Papers of the American Public Health Association* (hereafter *Reports of APHA*) 3 (1876), 185–87.

8. "Report of Committee on Disposal of Waste and Garbage," *Reports of APHA* 17 (1891), 90–119; and "Report of the Committee on the Disposal of Garbage and Refuse," ibid. 23 (1897), 206ff.

9. In addition to sources above, see Azel Ames, "The Removal and Utilization of Domestic Excreta," *Reports of APHA* 4 (1877), 70–75; Henry Robinson, "The Pail System," *Sanitary Engineer* 4 (15 March 1881), 179; R. Baumeister, *The Cleaning and Sewerage of Cities* (New York, n.d.), pp. 272–74; and for the Brooklyn example, Waring, *Social Statistics of Cities*, 1:484. See also "Sanitary Notes— Sewerage and Sewage," *Scientific American* 28 (28 June 1873), 405. For a summary of sanitarians' changing attitudes during the period, see William T. Sedgwick, *Principles of Sanitary Science and the Public Health* (New York, 1918), pp. 89–250.

10. Robert West Howard, *The Horse in America* (Chicago, 1965), pp. 237–38, and see "Clean Streets and Motor Traffic," *Literary Digest*, 5 September 1914, p. 413, for discussion of dead horses. For manure figures see Rudolph Hering and Samuel A. Greeley, *Collection and Disposal of Municipal Refuse* (New York, 1921), pp. 568–69.

11. The most useful contemporary account is John H. Griscom, *Uses and Abuses of Air* (New York, 1850). A useful historical discussion of air pollution is R. Dale Grinder, "The Anti-Smoke Crusades: Early Attempts to Reform the Urban Environment" (Ph.D. dissertation, University of Missouri-Columbia, 1973). See also Joel A. Tarr, "The Search for the Ultimate Sink: Urban Air, Land, and Water Pollution in Historical Perspective," *Records of the Columbia Historical Society of Washington, D.C.* 51 (1984), 9–10.

12. Horror stories about immigrant flats and tenement conditions emanated from every growing city during the years between 1840 and 1860. Typical were those detailing conditions in Boston. See *Report of the Committee on the Expediency of Providing Better Tenements for the Poor* (Boston, 1846); *Report of the Committee of Internal Health on Asiatic Cholera* (Boston, 1849); Dr. Josiah Curtis, "Brief Remarks on the Hygiene of Massachusetts, More Particularly on the Cities of Boston and Lowell," *Transactions of the American Medical Association* (hereafter *Transactions of AMA*) 2 (1849). Reviews of antebellum conditions appeared in later publications by the Massachusetts State Bureau of Labor: *Report of the Bureau of Statistics of Labor . . . 1871*, in *Massachusetts Senate Documents*, 1871, doc. no. 150, and *Third Annual Report of the Bureau of Statistics of Labor . . . 1872*, in *Massachusetts Senate Documents*, 1872, doc. no. 180. The quoted passages appear in *Report of the Committee of Internal Health*, pp. 13–14. For an interesting discussion of similar problems in New York, see Robert Ernst, *Immigrant Life in New York City 1825–1863* (New York, 1949), pp. 48–60.

13. For the text of the Metropolitan Health Bill, which granted to the new Board of Health all powers "for the purpose of preserving or protecting life or

health, or preventing disease," see New York *State Laws*, 89th sess., chap. 74, February 26, 1866, pp. 114–44. The composition of the board and the scope of its powers are described in John Duffy, *A History of Public Health in New York City, 1625–1866* (New York, 1968), ch. 24; and Duffy, *A History of Public Health in New York City, 1866–1966* (New York, 1974), ch. 1. On the early history of health boards, see *Transactions of AMA* 1–3 (1848–50), passim; John M. Toner, "Boards of Health in the United States," *Reports of APHA* 1 (1873), 499–521; Charles V. Chapin, "History of State and Municipal Control of Disease," in Ravenal, *Half Century of Public Health*, p. 137; Wilson G. Smillie, *Public Health Administration in the United States* (New York, 1940); and Howard D. Kramer, "Early Municipal and State Boards of Health," *Bulletin of the History of Medicine* (hereafter *BHM*) 24 (1950), 503–29.

14. The journalist's suggestion appeared in *Day-Book*, 8 December 1848. The Wood story comes from Stephen Smith, "The History of Public Health, 1871–1921," in Ravenal, *Half Century of Public Health*, p. 7. A "health warden" serving on the board (by occupation a saloonkeeper) proved the correctness of Wood's assertions. Asked to define "hygiene," his response was: "the vapor which rises from stagnant water."

15. Like most cities, Chicago had an on-again, off-again health board between the 1830s and the 1850s. For that city's experience see John H. Rauch, *A Sanitary History of Chicago from 1833 to 1870*, a Chicago Board of Health report (1867–69), pp. 11–25; and Herman N. Bundesen, "One Hundred Years of Public Health in Chicago 1840–1940," *Illinois Medical Journal* 77 (1940), 425–26. In Baltimore, as in most southern cities, the Board of Health convened only during the summer months, when the threat of epidemics was highest. Even then, the board's powers were limited to inspection and reporting about circumstances conducive to disease. See Baltimore Board of Health, *Report to the Mayor and City Council, December 30, 1860* (Baltimore, 1861), pp. 1–3. For the situation elsewhere see *Transactions of AMA* 1 (1848), 307; and Richard H. Shryock, "Origins and Significance of the Public Health Movement in the United States," *Annals of Medical History* 1 (1929), 646.

16. New York *Sun*, 30 July 1849. "Allopathy" was the method of treatment used by most "regular" physicians in which one sought to cure disease by producing a condition directly opposite to the effects of the illness; over the first half of the century, allopathic physicians generally employed such "heroic" treatments as bleeding and purging. "Homeopathy" referred to a system of treatment based on the principle that "like cures like"; in it physicians used small doses of medicine that, given to a healthy person, would produce the symptoms observed in the sick individual. For the Cincinnati situation see Thomas Carroll, "Observations on the Asiatic Cholera, as It Appeared in Cincinnati in 1849–50," *Cincinnati Lancet and Observer* 9 (1866), 299. For New Orleans see John Duffy (ed.), *The Rudolph Matas History of Medicine in Louisiana* (2 vols., Baton Rouge, 1958, 1962), 2:172–73. For Chicago see Rauch, *Sanitary History of Chicago*, pp. 54–120. For a discussion of the medical profession and boards of health in the South, see John Duffy, "Medical Practice in the Ante Bellum South," *Journal of Southern History* 25 (1959), 53–72; and Martha C. Mitchell, "Health and the Medical Profession in the Lower South, 1845–1860," ibid. 10 (1944), 424–46.

17. Childs is quoted in John Duffy, *The Healers: The Rise of the Medical Es-*

tablishment (New York, 1976), p. 187; Edward Jarvis, *Communications of the Massachusetts Medical Society* 8 (1847), 1.

18. For a valuable brief study of the politics of health boards in one city, see George Rosen, "Politics and Public Health in New York City," *BHM* 24 (1950), 441–61. For a typical attack on the ignorance of health boards, see D. F. C., "Report of the Board of Health of Philadelphia," *American Journal of the Medical Sciences*, 48 (1864), 213–14.

19. Among numerous contemporary discussions of these problems, see N. S. D., "National Medical Convention," *New York Journal of Medicine* 5 (1845), 418; M. Paine, "Medical Education in the United States," *Boston Medical and Surgical Journal* 29 (1843), 329–33; J. Marion Sims, *The Story of My Life* (New York, 1884), pp. 140–42; "Proceedings of the National Medical Convention," *New York Journal of Medicine* 9 (1847), 115. Secondary accounts include W. F. Norwood, *Medical Education in the United States Before the Civil War* (Philadelphia, 1944); Richard H. Shryock, *Medical Licensing in America, 1650–1965* (Baltimore, 1967); William G. Rothstein, *American Physicians in the Nineteenth Century: From Sects to Science* (Baltimore, 1972), pp. 63–121; and, for the situation in one growing city, Thomas Neville Bonner, *Medicine in Chicago, 1850–1950* (Madison, 1957), pp. 14–15.

20. Jacob Bigelow, "Discourse on Self-Limited Disease," *Medical Communications of the Massachusetts Medical Society* 5 (1835), 322; Bigelow, *Brief Expositions of Rational Medicine* (Boston, 1858); Austin Flint, *Essays on Conservative Medicine and Kindred Topics* (Philadelphia, 1874). See also Alex Berman, "The Heroic Approach in 19th-Century Therapeutics," *Bulletin of the American Society of Hospital Pharmacists* 11 (1954), 320–27; Charles E. Rosenberg, "The Therapeutic Revolution: Medicine, Meaning, and Social Change in Nineteenth-Century America," in Morris J. Vogel and Charles E. Rosenberg (eds.), *The Therapeutic Revolution: Essays in the Social History of American Medicine* (Philadelphia, 1979), pp. 3–25.

21. For an excellent discussion of Thomsonianism and homeopathy, see Rothstein, *American Physicians*, pp. 125–74. For the Cincinnati journal quotation, see John Duffy, *The Healers*, p. 187. Bartlett's observation comes from his "An Inquiry Into the Degree of Certainty in Medicine; and Into the Nature and Extent of Its Power Over Disease" (1848), excerpted in Gert H. Brieger (ed.), *Medical America in the Nineteenth Century: Readings from the Literature* (Baltimore, 1972), p. 118.

22. For discussion of the new germ theory of disease, see Chapter 6 below.

23. Lemuel Shattuck noted in 1849 that "the extent to which zymotic [contagious] diseases prevail is the great index of the public health; when the proportion is comparatively small, the condition of the public health is favorable; when large, it is unfavorable." But he went on to point out that endemic diseases, particularly consumption, were far more deadly, whatever public opinion might hold. "The occasional visit of the cholera, or some other epidemic disease, creates alarm and precautionary means are adopted for prevention. But where is the alarm and precaution against a more inexorable disease over which curative skill has little or no power?" *Report of a General Plan for the Promotion of Public and Personal Health, Devised, Prepared, and Recommended by the Commissioners Appointed Under a Resolve of the Legislature of Massachusetts, Relating to a Sanitary Survey of the State*

(Boston, 1850), pp. 92–98. Contemporaries customarily referred to this as the "Shattuck Report." For discussion of endemic and epidemic diseases, see Smillie, *Public Health*, pp. 120–66, 376–95; James A. Doull, "The Bacteriological Era (1876–1920)," in C.-E. A. Winslow et al. (eds.), *The History of American Epidemiology* (St. Louis, 1952).

24. Contemporary discussion of these issues may be found in Elisha Bartlett, *An Essay on the Philosophy of Medical Science* (Philadelphia, 1844); Thomas Carroll, "Observations on the Changes in the Practice of Medicine, Which Have Mostly Occurred Within the Last Twenty-five Years," *Cincinnati Medical Repository* 1 (1868); Bennett Dowler, "Researches Into the Types of Disease and Types of Therapy," *New Orleans Medical and Surgical Journal* 15 (1858); B. S. Woodworth, "Has There Been a 'Change of Type' in Inflammatory Diseases Within the Last Twenty Years; Or, In Other Words, Do Inflammations *Require* a 'Different' Treatment from That Pursued Fifteen or Twenty Years Ago?" *Chicago Medical Journal* 16 (1859); and R. E. Haughton, "On the Changes of Type of Disease," *American Journal of the Medical Sciences* 52 (1866). Secondary discussions of "heroic" therapies include Berman, "The Heroic Approach," pp. 321–27; Martin Kaufman, *Homeopathy in America: Rise and Fall of a Medical Heresy* (Baltimore, 1971), pp. 1–14; and Guenter Risse, "Calomel and the American Medical Sects During the Nineteenth Century," *Mayo Clinic Proceedings* 48 (1973), 57–64.

25. For a very useful survey of this issue, see John Harley Warner, " 'The Nature-Trusting Heresy': American Physicians and the Concept of the Healing Power of Nature in the 1850's and 1860's," *Perspectives in American History* 11 (1977–78), 289–324. J. Henry Clark, "Bloodletting in View of the Peculiarities of the Present Age," *Medical and Surgical Reporter* 11 (1858), 232–35, discusses the impact of social change on the physical constitution. For the British version of this concept, see William P. Alison, *Cases Illustrating the Asthenic Form of Internal Inflammation Now Common in This Country* (Edinburgh, 1852). I am indebted to Warner's article, pp. 304–5, for leading me to these sources. The quotation comes from: W. Taylor, "Changeability of Disease," Medical Association of the State of Alabama *Proceedings* (1852), 68–71.

26. Mann, "Physical Exercise," *Common School Journal* 7 (16 June 1845), 177–78; Warner, " 'Nature-Trusting Heresy,' " p. 305, quotes the Philadelphia physicians.

27. *Transactions of* AMA 2 (1849), especially reports on Concord, New Hampshire, Boston and Lowell, Massachusetts, and Baltimore, Maryland. An interesting addition to the environmental argument appears in the report on Concord (p. 448): "Both tea and coffee tend to enervate and derange the whole system and to produce an effeminate race."

28. For discussion of the theory and the growing debate about its validity, see M. P. Ravenel, "Endemic Diseases Vs. Acute Epidemics," *American Journal of Public Health* (hereafter *AJPH*) 10 (1920), 761–67; C.-E. A. Winslow, *The Conquest of Epidemic Disease* (Princeton, 1943); Smillie, *Public Health*, pp. 120–66; Phyllis Allen, "Etiological Theory in America prior to the Civil War," *Journal of the History of Medicine and Allied Sciences* 2 (1947), 489–520; Erwin H. Ackerknecht, "Anticontagionism Between 1821 and 1867," *BHM* 22 (1948), 562–93; and George Rosen, *A History of Public Health* (New York, 1958), pp. 103–8, 287–90.

29. Summaries of debates over the contagious nature of cholera appear in Sir Arthur Newsholme, *The Story of Modern Preventive Medicine* (Baltimore, 1929), pp. 83ff.; and Charles E. Rosenberg, *The Cholera Years: The United States in 1832, 1849, and 1866* (Chicago, 1962). Useful contemporary accounts include: C. L. Seeger, *A Lecture on the Epidemic Cholera . . .* (Boston, 1832); Bernard W. Byrne, *An Essay to Prove the Contagious Character of Malignant Cholera* (Baltimore, 1833); and "Report of the Committee on Practical Medicine and Epidemics," *Transactions of AMA* 3 (1850).

30. For a sampling of contemporary attacks on the quarantine system, see C. R. Gilman, *Hints to the People on the Prevention and Early Treatment of Spasmodic Cholera* (New York, 1832); *Southern Medical Journal* 3 (1839), 423; "Quarantine and Hygiene," *North American Review* 91 (1860), 438–91. For an overview of arguments against quarantine, see letter from Wilson Jewell to John H. Griscom in *Proceedings and Debates of the Third National Quarantine and Sanitary Convention*, pp. 3–4, and the "Report of the Committee on Quarantine" in the same volume. A brief history of the national conventions appears in Harold M. Cavins, "The National Quarantine and Sanitary Conventions of 1857 to 1860 and the Beginnings of the American Public Health Association," *BHM* 13 (1943), 404–26.

31. See Chapter 6 below for contemporary citations documenting the environmental arguments.

32. Alexander Stevens, "On the Communicability of Asiatic Cholera," *Transactions of the Medical Society of the State of New York* (1850), p. 33; Rosenberg, *Cholera Years*, p. 166.

CHAPTER 6. SANITIZING THE CITY

1. Jon Peterson, "The Impact of Sanitary Reform Upon American Urban Planning," *Journal of Social History* 13 (1979), 83–103.

2. For the meaning and connotations of "sanitary," see the *Oxford English Dictionary* and the *Dictionary of Americanisms*. [Edwin Chadwick], *Report from the Poor Law Commissioners on an Inquiry Into the Sanitary Condition of the Labouring Population of Great Britain* (London, 1842), bore no author's name, 'but the commissioners, eager to decline responsibility for conclusions about such unfamiliar matters, stated that the secretary had prepared it. Useful brief discussions of Chadwick's work include Sir John Simon, *English Sanitary Institutions* (London, 1897), pp. 183ff.; and M. E. M. Walker, *Pioneers of Public Health* (Edinburgh, 1930), pp. 71–86.

3. For examples of previous investigations, see Joseph Tuckerman, *On the Elevation of the Poor*, for Boston (N.P., c. 1830); Board of Guardians of the Poor of the City and Districts of Philadelphia, *Report of the Committee to Visit the Cities of Baltimore, New York, Providence, Boston, and Salem* (Philadelphia, 1827); and New York Society for the Prevention of Pauperism, *Report of a Committee on the Subject of Pauperism* (New York, 1818).

4. Memorial to the Legislature from the American Academy of Arts and Sciences, February, 1841; *First Annual Report . . . Relating to the Registry of Births, Marriages and Deaths in Massachusetts* (Boston, 1843), p. 25; John H. Griscom, *The Sanitary Condition of the Laboring Population of New York, with Suggestions*

for Its Improvement: A Discourse (with Additions) Delivered on the 30th December, 1844, at the Repository of the American Institute (New York, 1845), pp. 13–14 (hereafter referred to as the Griscom Report).

5. *Report of the Council of Hygiene and Public Health of the Citizens' Association of New York, Upon the Sanitary Condition of the City* (2d ed., New York, 1866; reprint ed., Arno Press, 1970), pp. xcvii, xlvii, xxxviii. For citations about contemporary attitudes toward the immorality of cities, see Chapter 1, n. 1, 14, 15.

6. For Shattuck see *DAB*, 9:33–34; Barbara Gutmann Rosenkrantz, *Public Health and the State: Changing Views in Massachusetts, 1842–1936* (Cambridge, Mass., 1972), pp. 14–36; and the Lemuel Shattuck Papers, Massachusetts Historical Society. The quotation is from Lemuel Shattuck, letter in *Fourth Annual Report to the Legislature Relating to the Registry and Returns of Births, Marriages and Deaths in Massachusetts, for the Year Ending April 30, 1845* (Boston, 1845), p. 99.

7. For Griscom see Duncan R. Jamieson, "Toward a Cleaner New York: John H. Griscom and New York's Public Health, 1830–1870" (Ph.D. dissertation, Michigan State University, 1971); John Duffy, *A History of Public Health in New York City, 1625–1866* (New York, 1968), pp. 302–14; and James H. Cassedy, "The Roots of American Sanitary Reform, 1843–47: Seven Letters from John H. Griscom to Lemuel Shattuck," *Journal of the History of Medicine and Allied Sciences* 30 (April 1975), 136–47.

8. For Waring see: *DAB*, 10:456–57; William Potts, "George Edwin Waring, Jr.," *Charities Review*, 8 (1898), 461–68; Albert Shaw, *Life of Col. George E. Waring, Jr.: The Great Apostle of Cleanliness* (New York, 1899); James H. Cassedy, "The Flamboyant Colonel Waring," *BHM* 26 (1962), 163–76; Richard Skolnik, "George Waring, Jr., Model for Reformers," *New York Historical Society Quarterly* 52 (1968), 354–78; and Martin V. Melosi, *Pragmatic Environmentalist: Sanitary Engineer George E. Waring, Jr.*, Public Works Historical Society (Washington, D.C., 1977).

9. For Richards see Edward T. James et al. (eds.), *Notable American Women, 1607–1950: A Biographical Dictionary* (3 vols., Cambridge, Mass. 1971), 3:143–46; Robert Clarke, *Ellen Swallow: The Woman Who Founded Ecology* (Chicago, 1973); and, among her many works, *Sanitation in Daily Life* (Boston, 1907) and *Euthenics: The Science of Controllable Environment* (Boston, 1912). For Kinnicutt see *DAB*, 10:419.

10. The *DAB* remains the best starting point to trace the careers of these and other individuals.

11. In addition to the *DAB*, brief biographical sketches of physicians and engineers involved in the sanitary movement appear in Howard A. Kelly and Walter Burrage (eds.), *Dictionary of American Medical Biography* (New York, 1928); Wilson G. Smillie, *Public Health: Its Promise for the Future* (New York, 1955), pp. 473–87; Leonard Metcalf and Harrison P. Eddy, *American Sewerage Practice* (4 vols., New York, 1914); and "Historic Review of the Development of Sanitary Engineering in the United States During the Past One Hundred and Fifty Years: A Symposium," *Proceedings* (of the American Society of Civil Engineers) 53 (1927), 1586–1648.

12. Griscom Report.

13. John Pintard, Wynant van Zant, and Edward Miller, *Report of Citizens' Committee on the Sanitary Conditions of New York City* (New York, 1806). Early

surveys detailing the unsanitary living conditions of the poor, included Josiah Quincy, *Remarks on Some of the Provisions of the Laws of Massachusetts Affecting Poverty, Vice, and Crime* (Cambridge, Mass., 1822); Mathew Carey,A *Plea for the Poor* (Philadelphia, 1837); New York Society for the Prevention of Pauperism, *Report.* Two useful secondary accounts are Blanche D. Coll, "The Baltimore Society for the Prevention of Pauperism, 1820–1822," *American Historical Review* 56 (1955), 77–87; and Benjamin J. Klebaner, "Public Poor Relief in America, 1790–1860" (Ph.D. dissertation, Columbia University, 1952).

14. Griscom Report, pp. 2–3.

15. Ibid., pp. 14, 15.

16. Ibid., p. 23; *Report of a General Plan for the Promotion of Public and Personal Health, Devised, Prepared and Recommended by the Commissioners Appointed Under a Resolve of the Legislature of Massachusetts, Relating to a Sanitary Survey of the State* (Boston, 1850), pp. 201–6, 280–82 (hereafter referred to as the Shattuck Report). For discussion of the general attitudes of Boston's elite toward immigrants, see Stanley K. Schultz, *The Culture Factory: Boston Public Schools, 1789–1860* (New York, 1973), pp. 209–51.

17. J. G. Pinkham, M.D., *The Sanitary Condition of Lynn, Including a Special Report on Diphtheria* (Boston, 1877), p. 58. For a similar, although earlier, comment from an Atlanta sanitarian, see F. D. Thurman, "Healthfulness of Atlanta," *Atlanta Medical and Surgical Journal* 3 (1858), 648–50.

Space limitations prohibit my listing all the sanitary surveys and discussion thereof that I examined. In addition to reports cited above in *Transactions of AMA*, see New York Association for Improving the Condition of the Poor, *First Report of a Committee on the Sanitary Condition of the Poor in the City of New York* (New York, 1853); *Report of the Council of Hygiene and Public Health of the Citizens' Association of New York* (1866) probably the most comprehensive of the nineteenth-century sanitary reports; Chicago Board of Health, *Reports of the Board of Health of the City of Chicago, 1867–69* (Chicago, 1870); Ross Winans, *Hygiene and Sanitary Matters: Selected, Prepared and Published by Ross Winans* (Baltimore, 1872); Charles E. Buckingham et. al., *Sanitary Condition of Boston* (Boston, 1875); Elisha Harris, "Report on the Public Health Service in the Principal Cities, and the Progress of the Sanitary Works in the United States," *Reports of APHA* 2 (1874–1875); and the same author's "The Public Health," *North American Review* 127 (1878), 444–55; *An Address from the Auxiliary Sanitary Association of New Orleans, to the Other Cities and Towns in the Mississippi Valley* (New Orleans, 1879); *First Annual Report of the Board of Health of the Taxing District of Shelby County, For the Year 1879* (Memphis, 1880); *Annual Reports of the Board of health of the City of Atlanta, 1880, 1882, 1888* (Atlanta, 1881, 1883, 1889); George Homan (ed.), "Sanitary Survey of Saint Louis," reprinted from *Transactions of the American Public Health Association* (Concord, N.H., 1885); Samuel C. Busey, "History and Progress of Sanitation of the City of Washington, and the Efforts of the Medical Profession in Relation Thereto," *The Sanitarian* 42 (1899), 205–16. Copies of these and scores of other sanitary reports may be found in the Library of Congress and in the Francis Loeb Library, Harvard School of Design. George E. Waring, Jr. (comp.), *Report on the Social Statistics of Cities, Tenth Census of the United States, 1880* (2 vols, Washington, D.C., 1887), contained sanitary reports of varying quality for 222 cities. A work by the health officer of Detroit provided a compendium of current information and misinformation derived from sanitary surveys of cities.

See O. W. Wight, A.M., M.D., *Maxims of Public Health* (New York, 1884). For an occasionally skeptical review of sanitarians' positions, see: F. L. Dibble, M.D., *Vagaries of Sanitary Science* (Philadelphia, 1893).

18. Among numerous sources see H. J. Parish, A *History of Immunization* (Edinburgh, 1965), pp. 42–45; and Thomas D. Brock (ed.), *Milestones in Microbiology* (Englewood Cliffs, 1961).

19. Concern about the impact of contagionist arguments on the sanitation crusade surfaced even earlier. See, for example, remarks made by the influential Boston doctor William Read, A *Letter to the Consulting Physicians of Boston* (Boston, 1866). But it was during the 1870s that sanitarians really began to debate the impact of recent evidence in support of contagionism and the germ theory. Among others see Austin Flint, "The Relations of Water to the Propagation of Fever," *Reports of APHA* 1 (1873), 164–72; J. S. Lynch, M.D., "The Prevention of Disease, with Especial Reference to Populous Neighborhoods and Municipal Governments," *The Sanitarian* 1 (1874), 449–58; and the first American publication, by the Massachusetts State Department of Health, of the English classic by John Simon, *Filth Diseases and Their Prevention* (Boston, 1876). Useful secondary accounts include James A. Doull, "The Bacteriological Era (1876–1920)," in Franklin H. Top (ed.), *The History of American Epidemiology* (St. Louis, 1952); Howard D. Kramer, "The Germ Theory and the Early Public Health Program in the United States," *BHM* 22 (1948), 233–47; Phyllis Allen Richmond, "American Attitudes Towards the Germ Theory, 1860–1880," *Journal of the History of Medicine* 9 (1954), 428–54; Edwin O. Jordan, "The Relations of Bacteriology to the Public Health Movement Since 1872," *AJPH* 11 (1921), 1042–47; and Dorothy Scanlon, "The Public Health Movement in Boston, 1870–1910" (Ph.D. dissertation, Boston University, 1956).

20. Frederick A. P. Barnard, "The Germ Theory of Disease and Its Relations to Hygiene," *Reports of APHA* 1 (1873), 86–87, and passim.

21. Jon C. Teaford, *The Unheralded Triumph: City Government in America, 1870–1900* (Baltimore, 1984), pp. 248–50.

22. Griscom Report, p. 15; Griscom to Shattuck, 25 April 1843, in Cassedy, "Roots of American Sanitary Reform," 141.

23. John Bell, *Report on the Importance and Economy of Sanitary Measures to Cities* (New York, 1859), p. 30; D. B. Eaton, "The Sphere and Method of Sanitary Administration in Cities: And How a Health Board Should Be Organized," *The Sanitarian* 1 (1873), 496–99. Henry I. Bowditch, first chairman of the Massachusetts State Board of Health, scattered similar warnings throughout his *Centennial Discourse on Public Hygiene in America* (Boston, 1877), and resigned from his position on the newly created (1879) Board of Health, Lunacy, and Charity because he viewed it as a tool of narrow, partisan politics. See Rosenkrantz, *Public Health and the State*, pp. 71–72.

24. John S. Billings, M.D., "Practical Sanitation—Presidential Address," *The Sanitarian* 9 (1881), 9–10, 13–14.

25. The most inclusive summation of the sewer socialists' views remains Frederic C. Howe, *The City: The Hope of Democracy* (1905; reprint ed., Seattle, 1967).

26. Griscom Report, p. 6; "Extracts from the 'Report on the Cholera in Boston in 1849,' " in Shattuck Report, p. 54; *Report of the Council of Hygiene and Public Health of the Citizens' Association of New York,* (1866) pp. lxxix, lxxxiii. For anal-

ysis of entrepreneurial capitalism at work in the real-estate market, see Sam Bass Warner, Jr., *Streetcar Suburbs: The Process of Growth in Boston, 1870–1900* (Cambridge, Mass., 1962); Eugene P. Moehring, *Public Works and the Patterns of Urban Real Estate Growth in Manhattan, 1835–1894* (New York, 1981); and Matthew Edel, Elliot D. Sclar, and Daniel Luria, *Shaky Palaces: Homeownership and Social Mobility in Boston's Suburbanization* (New York, 1984). The most useful discussion of laissez faire thought remains Sidney Fine, *Laissez Faire and the General-Welfare State: A Study of Conflict in American Thought, 1865–1901* (Ann Arbor, 1956; reprint ed., 1964).

27. Griscom Report, p. 23; Shattuck Report, pp. 292–93. The most recent, thorough, and analytically satisfactory account of the numerous reform campaigns of the period is Paul Boyer, *Urban Masses and Moral Order in America, 1820–1920* (Cambridge, Mass., 1978).

28. Biggs quoted in Smillie, *Public Health*, p. 373.

29. *Transactions of AMA* 2 (1849), 614, 474. Included among the reports in the previous year's volume was a "Memorial to the American Medical Association from the National Institute of Washington." In 1845 that scientific body had founded a hygiene committee that tried, unsuccessfully, to survey the nation's sanitary conditions. The "Memorial" attributed the lack of success to two factors: general apathy among medical men toward the subject of hygiene, and local boosters who insisted upon the healthfulness of their own communities while pointing a finger of blame at rival communities. The "Memorial" urged the AMA to appoint a permanent committee on hygiene and to try to persuade the states to establish a uniform system of registration of births, deaths, and marriages. The AMA took that advice, the result being the various sanitary reports printed in the 1849 volume. For further discussion of the early years of the AMA see Morris Fishbein, *History of the American Medical Association, 1847 to 1947* (Philadelphia, 1947).

30. Shattuck Report, pp. 20–21. The authors of the report devoted most of the remainder of their observations to these issues, including pages of extracts from English sanitary investigations. Shattuck noted (and today's reader can sense the "shock of discovery" underlying the statement) that "places may be found in the cities and towns of this State, as we shall show further on, that are scarcely to be paralleled in England. This fact will be developed to the astonishment of any one who makes the examination" (p. 157). For the Davis quotation see N. S. Davis, "On the Intimate Relation of Medical Science to the Whole Field of Natural Sciences," *Transactions* (of the Illinois State Medical Society) 4 (1853), 22.

31. Horace Bushnell, *Work and Play; or, Literary Varieties* (New York, 1864: reprint ed., 1871), pp. 318–19.

32. *Minutes of the Proceedings of the Quarantine Convention* (Philadelphia, 1857), p. 6–8.

33. *Proceedings and Debates of the Third National Quarantine and Sanitary Convention* (New York, 1859), pp. 17, 201. For a later rendition of Griscom's theme of educating the public as well as an index of the success of sanitarians in so doing, see J. Berrien Lindsley, "The People and the Public Health Movement— Address on State Medicine," *The Sanitarian* 29 (1892), 97–110.

34. Ibid., "Appendix E," pp. 645ff. Leading the battle against the model code was Dr. A. H. Stevens of New York City, a former president of the AMA and passionate champion of personal and local autonomy. In numerous respects, and par-

ticularly in its call for a state board of health and systematic recording of vital statistics, the "Sanitary Code for Cities" was a lineal descendant of the Shattuck Report. All told, the reports of the Committee on the Internal Hygiene of Cities filled several hundred pages of the total 728 pages of the volume and were a compendium of sanitarians' charges and investigations over the previous fifteen years.

35. *Proceedings and Debates of the Fourth National Quarantine and Sanitary Convention* (Boston, 1860), pp. 277–79. Bigelow, a prominent physician, botanist, and leading member of the Massachusetts Medical Society for the previous thirty years, was president of the 1860 convention. He deserves a modern biography. For biographical information see Walter L. Burrage, *A History of the Massachusetts Medical Society, With Brief Biographies of the Founders and Chief Officers, 1791–1922* (Norwood, Mass., 1923). On the formation of the Massachusetts State Board of Health, see Rosenkrantz, *Public Health and the State*, pp. 37–73.

36. For the formation of this organization see Stephen Smith, "Historical Sketch of the American Public Health Association," *Reports of APHA* 5 (1880), vii–liv; and M. P. Ravenel, "The American Public Health Association: Past, Present, Future," in Mazyck P. Ravenel (ed.), *A Half Century of Public Health* (New York, 1921), pp. 13ff. *The Sanitarian* began publication in 1873 and continued through 50 volumes until 1903, when it merged into *Popular Science Monthly*.

37. Robert D. Leigh, *Federal Health Administration in the United States* (New York, 1927), pp. 464ff.; Smillie, *Public Health*, pp. 331–39.

38. For the best brief discussion and guide to other sources, see Joel A. Tarr et al., "Water and Wastes: A Retrospective Assessment of Wastewater Technology in the United States, 1800–1932," *Technology and Culture* 25 (1984), 246–50. For quotations see May N. Stone, "The Plumbing Paradox: American Attitudes Towards Late Nineteenth-Century Domestic Sanitary Arrangements," *Winterthur Portfolio* 14 (1979), 289; and George C. Whipple, "The Training of Sanitary Engineers," *Engineering News* 68 (1912), 805–6.

39. Abraham Flexner, *Medical Education in the United States and Canada: A Report to the Carnegie Foundation for the Advancement of Teaching* (New York, 1910); Simon Flexner and James Thomas Flexner, *William Henry Welch and the Heroic Age of American Medicine* (New York, 1941); Donald Fleming, *William H. Welch and the Rise of Modern Medicine* (Boston, 1954).

40. See Gordon E. Gillson, *Louisiana State Board of Health: The Formative Years* (Baton Rouge, 1968); on that organization's ineffectiveness and politicized nature, the noted physician Stanford E. Chaille told the 1879 meeting of the Louisiana State Medical Society: "Louisiana has legislated on *paper* a State Board of Health and Vital Statistics; but in reality we have no state, merely a city, board of health, organized under laws which nobody except politicians (and a designing or an ignorant class of these) can possibly approve." Chaille, *Address on State Medicine and Medical Organization* (New Orleans, 1879). In addition to works cited above, see R. G. Paterson, *Historical Directory of State Health Departments in the United States of America* (Columbus, Ohio, 1939); and Samuel W. Abbott, *The Past and Present Condition of Public Hygiene and State Medicine in the United States* (Boston, 1900).

41. Griscom Report, p. 23; *North American Review* 73 (July 1851), 117–35.

42. Charles V. Chapin, *Municipal Sanitation in the United States* (Providence, R.I., 1901); Chapin, *Sources and Modes of Infection* (New York, 1912), p. 32.

43. Charles Eliot, "Welfare and Happiness," *Landscape Architecture* 1 (1911), 143–53.

CHAPTER 7. PROMOTING PUBLIC WORKS

1. Baltimore *Sun*, 24 April 1905.
2. Norman T. Newton, *Design on the Land: The Development of Landscape Architecture* (Cambridge, Mass., 1971), pp. 385–92.
3. The best sources for the ideas and activities of landscape architects are their own reports, articles, papers, addresses, and books. Few were shy about expressing themselves on paper. The works listed are the most readily accessible. The most comprehensive archive of landscape architecture materials, park plans, reports of parks commissions, and the like is the Francis Loeb Library at the Harvard School of Design.
    See Andrew Jackson Downing, *A Treatise on the Theory and Practice of Landscape Gardening* (New York, 1841), and his *Rural Essays*, ed. George W. Curtis (New York, 1881); Calvert Vaux, *Villas and Cottages* (New York, 1857); Frederick Law Olmsted, Jr., and Theodore Kimball (eds.), *Forty Years of Landscape Architecture: Being the Professional Papers of Frederick Law Olmsted, Senior* (2 vols., New York, 1928); Frederick Law Olmsted, "The Park at Birkenhead," *Horticulturalist* 6 (May, 1851), 224–28; Olmsted, *Public Parks and the Enlargement of Towns* (Cambridge, Mass., 1870); Olmsted, "The Justifying Value of a Public Park," *Journal of Social Science* 12 (1880), 147–64; Albert Fein (ed.), *Landscape Into Cityscape: Frederick Law Olmsted's Plans for a Greater New York City* (Ithaca, 1968); S. B. Sutton (ed.), *Civilizing American Cities: A Selection of Frederick Law Olmsted's Writings on City Landscapes* (Cambridge, Mass., 1971); Robert Morris Copeland, *The Most Beautiful City in America: Essay and Plan for the Improvement of the City of Boston* (Boston, 1872); Copeland and H. W. S. Cleveland, "A Few Words on the Central Park" (Boston, 1856); H. W. S. Cleveland, Collected Papers on Landscape Gardening, Center for Research Libraries, Chicago, Illinois; Cleveland, *Public Grounds in Chicago: How to Give Them Character and Expression* (Chicago, 1869); Cleveland, *Landscape Architecture as Applied to the Wants of the West* (Chicago, 1873); Cleveland, *Suggestion for a System of Parks and Parkways for the City of Minneapolis* (Minneapolis, 1883); Charles Eliot, "Parks and Squares of United States Cities," *Garden and Forest* 1 (October 1888), 412–13; Eliot, "The Necessity of Planning," ibid. 9 (1896), 342; Charles William Eliot, *Charles Eliot, Landscape Architect* (2 vols., Boston, 1903); John Nolen (ed.), *City Planning* (New York, 1915).
4. For examples see William Cullen Bryant, *Poetical Works*, ed. Parke Godwin (New York, 1883); Ralph Waldo Emerson, *Nature* (Boston, 1836); Thomas Cole, "Essay on American Scenery," *American Monthly Magazine* 7 (1836), 11. Useful secondary accounts include Roderick Nash, *Wilderness and the American Mind* (New Haven, 1967); Perry Miller, *Nature's Nation* (Cambridge, Mass., 1967); Charles Sanford, *The Quest for Paradise: Europe and the American Moral Imagination* (Urbana, Ill., 1961); James Callow, *Kindred Spirits: Knickerbocker Writers and American Artists, 1807–1855* (Chapel Hill, N.C., 1967); Roger Stein, *John Ruskin and Aesthetic Thought in America* (Cambridge, 1967).

5. For examples of the scenery album, see *The Scenery of the United States* (New York, 1855); N. P. Willis, *American Scenery* (2 vols., London, 1840); and *Homebook of the Picturesque* (New York, 1851); quotation from the last, pp. 7, 25. The most convenient and insightful presentation of the urban lithographs is John W. Reps, *Views and Viewmakers of Urban America: Lithographs of Towns and Cities in the United States and Canada, Notes on the Artists and Publishers, and a Union Catalog of Their Work, 1825–1925* (Columbia, Mo., 1984).

6. I have based these observations on materials in the Francis Loeb Library. For discussion by historians see Newton, *Design on the Land*, pp. 267–336; and Galen Cranz, *The Politics of Park Design: A History of Urban Parks in America* (Cambridge, Mass., 1982).

7. John H. Rauch, *Public Parks: Their Effects Upon the Moral, Physical, and Sanitary Conditions of the Inhabitants of Large Cities* (Chicago, 1869), p. 7.

8. Laura Wood Roper, *FLO: A Biography of Frederick Law Olmsted* (Baltimore, 1973), is a superb piece of work. Less satisfactory is Elizabeth Stevenson, *Park Maker: A Life of Frederick Law Olmsted* (New York, 1977). Other useful works on Olmsted include Albert Fein, *Frederick Law Olmsted and the American Environmental Tradition* (New York, 1969); Elizabeth Barlow, *Frederick Law Olmsted's New York* (New York, 1972); Leonard J. Simutis, "Frederick Law Olmsted, Sr.: A Reassessment," *Journal of the American Institute of Planners* 38 (1972), 276–84; Geoffrey Blodgett, "Frederick Law Olmsted: Landscape Architecture as Conservative Reform," *Journal of American History* 62 (1976), 869–89; and Cynthia Zaitzevsky, *Frederick Law Olmsted and the Boston Park System* (Cambridge, Mass., 1982).

On the suburban movement, including Olmsted's part in it, see Olmsted, Vaux, & Co., *Preliminary Report Upon the Proposed Suburban Village at Riverside, near Chicago* (New York, 1868); David Schuyler, "Public Landscapes and American Urban Culture, 1800–1870: Rural Cemeteries, City Parks, and Suburbs" (Ph.D. dissertation, Columbia University, 1979); and Kenneth T. Jackson, *Crabgrass Frontier: The Suburbanization of the United States* (New York, 1985), pp. 73–102.

9. Olmsted, *Public Parks and the Enlargement of Towns*, pp. 11, 18; see also his *A Consideration of the Justifying Value of a Public Park* (Boston, 1881).

10. Frederick Law Olmsted, "The Future of New York," *New York Tribune*, 28 December 1879; Olmsted, "Eighth Annual Report, 1868," *Annual Reports of the Brooklyn Park Commissioners, 1861–1873, Reprinted by Order of the Board . . . January 1873* (Brooklyn, 1873), pp. 155, 162. See also *Forty Years of Landscape Architecture* (reprint ed., Cambridge, Mass., 1973), p. 171.

11. Olmsted, Vaux & Co., *Preliminary Report in Regard to a Plan of Public Pleasure Grounds for the City of San Francisco* (New York, 1868), p. 17.

12. Olmsted, Vaux, & Co., *Preliminary Report . . . Riverside*, pp. 4–5; Olmsted, "Future of New York."

13. Cleveland, *Landscape Architecture*, esp. pp. 6, 14–18, 26–27, 31–38. Quotation from H. W. S. Cleveland, "Parks and Boulevards in Cities," *Lakeside Monthly* 7 (1872), 413. See also his *Public Parks, Radial Avenues, and Boulevards: Outline Plan of a Park System for the City of St. Paul, Comprised in Two Addresses Delivered Before the Common Council and Chamber of Commerce, June 24, 1872, and June 19, 1885* (St. Paul, 1885), and his "The Aesthetic Development of the

United Cities of St. Paul and Mineapolis, an Address Delivered . . . to the Minneapolis Society of Fine Arts" (Minneapolis, 1888).

14. Copeland and Cleveland, "A Few Words," p. 2.

15. Copeland, *The Most Beautiful City in America,* pp. 10–12, and passim.

16. Water supply is discussed in nineteenth-century local accounts as well as in more recent urban biographies and articles. Three reasonably comprehensive nineteenth-century accounts are Nathaniel J. Bradlee, *History of the Introduction of Pure Water Into the City of Boston, 1652–1868* (Boston, 1868), esp. pp. 8–42 for the period up to the 1840s; Fern L. Nesson, *Great Waters: A History of Boston's Water Supply* (Hanover, N.H., 1983); and Edward Wegman, *Water Supply of the City of New York, 1658–1895* (New York, 1896). The best modern overview remains Nelson M. Blake, *Water for the Cities: A History of the Urban Water Supply Problem in the United States* (Syracuse, 1956).

17. Snow's first analysis reached print as *On the Mode of Communication of Cholera* (London, 1849), with a more extensively documented edition appearing in 1854. Budd gathered the results of his investigations, on which he began reporting in 1856, and published them as *Typhoid Fever—Its Nature, Mode of Spreading, and Prevention* (London, 1874). The American Public Health Association reprinted this classic study in 1931. Flint attested to the impact of Budd's work on his own in "The Relations of Water to the Propagation of Fever," *Reports of APHA* 1 (1873), 164–72.

In 1859 the sanitarian John Bell expressed a conventional view when he noted: "Water in an average state of purity is indispensable for digestion and the elaboration of good blood, as on the contrary, if it be hard, and contaminated with vegetable or animal matters, it perpetually disorders digestion and gives rise to the innumerable secondary affections of the kidneys, skin, and nervous system, and an impairment of bodily strength and activity." *Report on the Importance and Economy of Sanitary Measures to Cities* (New York, 1859), p. 135. Allen Hazen, *Clean Water and How to Get It* (New York, 1907); George Whipple, *Typhoid Fever, Its Causation, Transmission, and Prevention* (New York, 1908); and William T. Sedgwick, *Principles of Sanitary Science and the Public Health* (New York, 1918) all discuss the acceptance of the importance of purifying water supplies.

18. See Blake, *Water for the Cities;* and John B. Blake, "Lemuel Shattuck and the Boston Water Supply," *BHM* 29 (1955), 554–62.

19. Committee report quoted in Blake, *Water for the Cities,* pp. 140–41. For the complete story of the new system, see pp. 121–71.

20. See Horace G. Wood, *A Practical Treatise on the Law of Nuisances in Their Various Forms: Including Remedies Therefor at Law and in Equity* (Albany, 1875), for discussion of legal rights and privileges; M. N. Baker (ed.), *The Manual of American Water-Works, 1897* (New York, 1897), for information on companies' practices; and Thomas M. Drowne, M.D., "The Newport Water Supply," *The Sanitarian* 28 (1892), 404, for quotation.

21. Baker, *Manual,* and the same author's *The Quest for Pure Water* (New York, 1948); Samuel W. Abbott, *Past and Present Condition of Public Hygiene and State Medicine in the United States* (Boston, 1900); C.-E. A. Winslow, *The Evolution and Significance of the Modern Public Health Campaign* (New Haven, 1923); J. J. Cosgrove, *History of Sanitation* (Pittsburgh, 1909); "Statistics of Cities," in *Bulletin* of the Department of Labor, no. 41 (Washington, D.C., 1902), pp. 1014–

23; U.S. Bureau of the Census, *Financial Statistics of Cities Having a Population of Over 30,000: 1910* (Washington, D.C., 1913), pp. 134–43. A factually useful and conceptually interesting piece comparing the histories of water and sewerage supplies in salt-water, fresh-water, major-river and minor-river cities is Louis P. Cain, "The Economic History of Urban Location and Sanitation" (MS. in author's possession). See also Letty Donaldson Anderson, "The Diffusion of Technology in the Nineteenth Century American City: Municipal Water Supply Investments" (Ph.D. dissertation, Northwestern University, 1980), an interesting and useful exposition based on a gravity-flow information model but marred by a curious hodgepodge of small factual errors.

22. The most useful primary source is G. P. Brown, *Drainage Channel and Waterway: A History of the Effort to Secure an Effective and Harmless Method for the Disposal of the Sewage of the City of Chicago and to Create a Navigable Channel Between Lake Michigan and the Mississippi River* (Chicago, 1894). A good brief secondary account is James C. O'Connell, *Chicago's Quest for Pure Water*, Public Works Historical Society (Washington, D.C., 1976). See also Randolph R. Isham, "A History of Sanitation in Chicago," *Journal of the Western Society of Engineers* 44 (1939), 227–40.

23. City of Detroit, Board of Water Commissioners, *Annual Reports, 1841–1874* (Detroit, 1842–75); City of Boston, Cochituate Water Board, *Annual Reports, 1855–1864* (Boston, 1855–65); J. T. Fanning, A Practical Treatise on Hydraulic and Water-Supply Engineering (New York, 1886), p. 625. For leading me to these and other sources, I am indebted to Joel A. Tarr, James McCurley, and Terry F. Yosie, "The Development and Impact of Urban Wastewater Technology: Changing Concepts of Water Quality Control, 1850–1930," in Martin V. Melosi (ed.), *Pollution and Reform in American Cities, 1870–1930* (Austin, 1980), pp. 59–82; and Joel A. Tarr and Francis Clay McMichael (eds.), *Retrospective Assessment of Wastewater Technology in the United States: 1800–1972* (Pittsburgh, 1977).

Given the poor quality of urban water supplies for much of the century, it is entirely possible that many Americans consumed beer, wine, and hard liquors for completely justifiable health reasons; alcohol was often safer than water. In addition to popular articles by physicians and sanitarians about the dangers of water sources during the period, consulting municipal engineers presented numerous reports that unfavorably compare the quality of water in American cities with that of European cities. For one example, among many, see James Pugh Kirkwood, *Report on the Filtration of River Waters, for the Supply of Cities, as Practised in Europe* (New York, 1869). The most useful recent survey of American drinking habits is W. J. Rorabaugh, *The Alcoholic Republic: An American Tradition* (New York, 1979), esp. the statistical data in the several appendices.

24. New York City figures, along with others, appear in Edgar W. Martin, *The Standard of Living in 1860* (Chicago, 1942), pp. 111–12. Among scant sources about the history of the water closet in the United States, see James J. Lawler, *Lawler's American Sanitary Plumbing* (New York, 1876); Glenn Brown, *Water Closets: A Historical, Mechanical and Sanitary Treatise* (New York, 1884); Lawrence Wright, *Clean and Decent: The Fascinating History of the Bathroom and the Water Closet* (New York, 1960); and May N. Stone, "The Plumbing Paradox: American Attitudes Towards Late Nineteenth-Century Domestic Sanitary Arrangements," *Winterthur Portfolio* 14 (1979), 284ff. Reaction to the water closet in the

White House cited in Daniel J. Boorstin, *The Americans: The Democratic Experience* (New York, 1973), p. 353.

25. City of Buffalo, *Sixth Annual Report of the City Water Works, 1874* (Buffalo, 1875), p. 47. The 1880 estimate appeared in Tarr, McCurley, and Yosie, "Development and Impact of Urban Wastewater Technology," p. 62.

There is no good historical discussion of the bathroom. Leads to attitudes about bathing appear in Harold Donaldson Eberlein, "When Society First Took a Bath," *Pennsylvania Magazine of History* 67 (1943), pp. 30–48; and Marilyn Thorton Williams, "The Municipal Bath Movement in the United States, 1890–1915" (Ph.D. dissertation, New York University, 1972). Dolores Hayden, *The Grand Domestic Revolution: A History of Feminist Designs for American Homes, Neighborhoods, and Cities* (Cambridge, 1981), and Gwendolyn Wright, *Building the Dream: A Social History of Housing in America* (New York, 1981), provide some insight into the broad social context of changing attitudes about the environment of the home. The degree to which sanitarians touted the bathroom and indoor plumbing as necessities of the healthful home can be traced through the pages of periodicals like that edited by G. P. Brown of Chicago—the *Sanitary News: Healthy Homes and Healthy Living: A Semi-Monthly Journal of Sanitary Science* which began publication in 1882, and through numerous articles in *The Sanitarian*, the journal of the American Public Health Association.

26. Henry I. Bowditch, *Public Hygiene in America* (Boston, 1877), pp. 103–4; "Early Sanitary History of Chicago, 1832–1874 and Sketch of the Early Drainage and Sewerage of Chicago, 1847–1879," MS in the City of Chicago Municipal Reference Library (n.p., n.d.); Samuel C. Busey, "History and Progress of Sanitation of the City of Washington and the Efforts of the Medical Profession in Relation Thereto," *The Sanitarian* 42 (1899), 205–16; George W. Rafter and M. N. Baker, *Sewage Disposal in the United States* (New York, 1894), pp. 169–86. Town of Pawtucket, Committee on Sewers, *Report, 1885* (Pawtucket, 1885), p. 15, quoted in Tarr, McCurley, and Yosie, "Development and Impact of Urban Wastewater Technology," p. 62.

27. "The Sewage Question," *Scientific American* 21 (24 July 1869), 57; Roberts Bartholow, M.D., *The Hygiene of Suburban Life: A Lecture Delivered at Clifton Hall, Suburb of Cincinnati, Friday Evening, March 29th, 1879* (Philadelphia, 1879), p. 18.

28. John H. Griscom, *The Sanitary Condition of the Laboring Population of New York* (New York, 1845), p. 52; John Bell, *Report on the Importance and Economy of Sanitary Measures to Cities* (New York, 1859), p. 35. A useful collection of primary sources is Barbara Rosenkrantz (ed.), *Sewering the Cities* (New York, 1977).

29. George E. Waring, Jr., *House-Drainage and Sewerage* (Philadelphia, 1878), p. 11.

30. The theory's antiquity is noted in George Preston Brown, *Sewer-Gas and Its Dangers, with an Exposition of Common Defects in House Drainage, and Practical Information Relating to Their Remedy* (Chicago, 1881), 146–47; Dr. Soyka, "On Sewer Gas as a Factor in the Spread of Epidemic Diseases," *Van Nostrand's Engineering Magazine* 27 (1882), 423; "Sewer Ventilation" *Sanitary News* 13 (20 April 1889), 291. The two works by Chadwick most widely read in the United States were *Report from the Poor Law Commissioners on an Inquiry into the Sanitary Condition of the Labouring Population of Great Britain* (London, 1842), and

Report on the Results of a Special Inquiry Into the Practice of Interment in Towns (U.S. ed., Philadelphia, 1845). For Murchison's evidence that sewer gas caused typhoid, see his *A Treatise on the Continued Fevers of Great Britain* (London, 1862), and C.-E. A. Winslow, "The Conveyance of Bacteria by Sewer Air," *American Journal of Public Hygiene* 19 (1909), 640ff. Familiar with Chadwick's writings, John H. Griscom emphasized the threat from gas emanating from sewers in *The Uses and Abuses of Air* (New York, 1850), pp. 76, 182–85. For Bell's discussion see his *Report*, pp. 43–65. Quotation is from Brown, *Sewer-Gas*, p. 146. The only adequate modern review of the sewer gas controversy is Deanna R. Springall, "The Sewer Gas Theory of Disease: A Period of Transition in Medical Etiology" (M.A. thesis, University of Wisconsin-Madison, 1977). Her work led me to many of the sources noted below.

31. "The Sewer-Gas Danger," *New York Times*, 27 January 1878, and "Dangers of Sewer Gas," ibid., 3 February 1878; Edward H. Janes, "Health of Tenement Populations and the Sanitary Requirements of Their Dwellings," *Reports of APHA* 2 (1876), 117ff., and other articles in that issue; A. L. Carroll, "Filth Diseases in Rural Districts," *Medical Record* 23 (1883), 617–19; J. W. Hughes, "Report of the Committee on Sanitation with Special Reference to Drainage, Plumbing and Ventilation of Public and Private Buildings," *Reports of APHA* 23 (1897), 400ff.

32. William Ripley Nichols, *Chemical Examinations of Sewer Air* (Boston, 1879); A. de Varona, *Sewer Gases, Their Nature and Origin and How to Protect Our Dwellings* (Boston, 1879); A. C. Abbott, "Chemical, Physical and Bacteriological Studies Upon Air Over Decomposing Substances, with Special Reference to Their Application to the Air of Sewers," *Transactions of the Congress of American Physicians and Surgeons* 3 (1894), 49. Typical of judgments that contemporaries had overestimated the dangers of sewer gas was Leonard P. Kinnicutt, "Sewer Air: Mistaken Ideas Regarding It," *Municipal Engineering* 17 (August 1899), 71–80. Quotation from *Sanitary Engineer* 6 (1882), 412.

Among a plethora of publications linking sewer gas and sewer air to specific diseases, see William H. Brewer, "The Gases of Decay and the Harm They Cause in Dwellings and Populous Places," *Reports of APHA* 3 (1877), 201ff.; "Sewer Gases and Their Evil Effects," *Plumber and Sanitary Engineer* 2 (1879), 208; C. W. Chamberlain, "Erysipelas and Sewer Gas," *Public Health* 1 (9 August 1879), 81–82; "Sewer Gases and Traps," *Sanitary Engineer* 5 (8 December 1881), 38; and "Sewer Gas and Insanity," *American Psychological Journal* 1 (1883–84), 310–11. As late as 1890 a popular journal could catalogue, in order of relative importance, symptoms and diseases directly attributable to sewer gas poisoning: "General lassitude, unrefreshing sleep, uncomfortable heavy-headedness, morning headache, sticky saliva, bad taste in the mouth, poor appetite for breakfast, nausea on first rising, feebleness, pasty-furred tongue, 'malaria,' relaxed throat, elongated uvula, ulcerated tonsils, laryngitis, sticky and inflamed eyes, feverishness, disturbed sleep, 'nervousness,' dyspepsia, irregular action of the bowels and kidneys, diarrhoea, typhoid fever, diphtheria, erysipelas, puerperal fever, pyaemia, septicaemia and death—the post-mortem sign—and this . . . is the only symptom recognized as being of sufficient importance to base inquiry upon." *Scientific American* 62 (29 November 1890), 344.

33. Discussion of sewer gases as germ carriers appeared in, among others,

Brown, *Sewer-Gas*, pp. 98–99; Henry Hun, "Sewer-Gas Poisoning," *Medical News* 51 (20 August 1887), 197–203; and Henry O. Marcy, "The Recent Advances of Sanitary Science—The Relation of Micro-Organisms to Disease," *Journal of the American Medical Association* 1 (1883), 494ff. Among numerous technical schemes for the elimination of sewer gases, see George E. Waring, Jr., *Earth Closets and Earth Sewage* (New York, 1870); Frank H. Hambleton, "A Plea for Sanitary Engineering—A Report on Efficient House Connections with Sewers and the Protection of Houses Against Sewer Gas," *Reports of APHA* 2 (1876); "The Discussion of the Academy of Medicine on Plumbing," *Sanitary Engineer* 5 (1882), 338–39; and "Sewer Gas Prevention in Houses," *Municipal Engineering* 13 (August 1897), 91.

34. Frank H. Hamilton, "Sewer-Gas," *Popular Science Monthly* 22 (November 1882), 1–20; John Mitchell, "Plumbing in Sanitation," *Reports of APHA* 20 (1894), 336–39, reviewed some of the licensing legislation. Quotation from Andrew Young, "The Relations of the Plumbers and the Physicians," ibid. 17 (1891), 48.

35. *Sanitary Engineer* 7 (1883), 314.

36. Sources for this and the previous paragraph include "Early Sanitary History of Chicago, 1832–1874"; George E. Waring, Jr., "Sanitary Drainage of Houses and Towns," *Atlantic Monthly* 36 (1875), 537–53; Bowditch, *Public Hygiene in America*, pp. 103–9; Rafter and Baker, *Sewage Disposal in the United States*, pp. 169–86; Busey, "History and Progress of Sanitation of the City of Washington," pp. 205–16; Charles V. Chapin, *Municipal Sanitation in the United States* (Providence, 1901), pp. 172–92; Leonard Metcalf and Harrison P. Eddy, *American Sewerage Practice* (3 vols., New York, 1914), 1: "Design of Sewers"; and Richard Shelton Kirby and Philip Gustave Laurson, *The Early Years of Modern Civil Engineering* (New Haven, 1932), pp. 185–239.

37. Tarr, McCurley, and Yosie, "Development and Impact of Urban Wastewater Technology," p. 64; and Tarr and McMichael, *Retrospective Assessment of Wastewater Technology*, ch. 2.

38. Waring, *House-Drainage*, p. 11; Waring, *Social Statistics of Cities*, 1:570–71; Bowditch, *Public Hygiene in America*, pp. 103–4; Eliot C. Clarke, *Main Drainage Works of the City of Boston* (Boston, 1885).

39. Brown, *Drainage Channel and Waterway*, pp. 28–29, 49, 50; *Biographical Sketches of the Leading Men of Chicago* (Chicago, 1868), p. 192; Louis P. Cain, "Raising and Watering a City: Ellis Sylvester Chesbrough and Chicago's First Sanitation System," *Technology and Culture* 13 (1972), 353–56; quotation from Brown, *Drainage Channel and Waterway*, p. 53. See also O'Connell, *Chicago's Quest*, pp. 3–4.

40. *Report and Plan of Sewerage for the City of Chicago, Illinois* (Chicago, 1855). For the story of the later canal, see Louis. P. Cain, "Unfouling the Public's Nest: Chicago's Sanitary Diversion of Lake Michigan Water," *Technology and Culture* 15 (1974), 594–613; and Cain, *Sanitation Strategy for a Lakefront Metropolis: The Case of Chicago* (DeKalb, Ill., 1978).

41. R. Isham Randolph, "A History of Sanitation in Chicago," *Journal of the Western Society of Engineers*, 44 (1939), 229; Workers of the Writer's Program, WPA in Illinois for Board of Education, "Up From the Mud: An Account of How Chicago's Streets and Buildings Were Raised" (Chicago, 1941).

42. For details see Cain, "Raising and Watering a City," pp. 361–70; O'Connell, *Chicago's Quest*, pp. 4–5. Chesbrough's recommendations for further projects came as a result of the Board of Sewerage Commissioners' sending him to study

sewer systems in Europe. See his *Chicago Sewerage: Report of the Results of Examinations Made in Relation to Sewerage in Several European Cities, in the Winter of 1856–57* (Chicago, 1858).

43. *Journal of the American Society of Civil Engineers* 15 (November 1889), 161–62. During the immediate post–Civil War years, engineers in other cities emulated Chesbrough's work: Providence in 1869, New Haven in 1872, Fall River, Lawrence, and Boston during the mid-1870s. See Rafter and Baker, *Sewage Disposal in the United States,* pp. 177–85.

44. U.S. Bureau of the Census, *Statistics of Cities Having a Population of Over 30,000: 1905* (Washington, D.C., 1907), p. 104; Arthur Reynolds, "Three Chicago and Illinois Public Health Officers: John H. Rauch, Oscar C. DeWolf, and Frank W. Reilly," *Bulletin of the Society of Medical History of Chicago* 1 (August 1912), 87–134; John H. Rauch, *The Sanitary Problems of Chicago, Past and Present* (Chicago, 1879), pp. 13–14.

45. Among surveys of European practices cited most often by other engineers, sanitarians, and engineering periodicals, see Chesbrough, *Report*; Julius W. Adams, *Report of the Engineer to the Commissioners of Sewerage of the City of Brooklyn, Upon the General Drainage of the City* (Brooklyn, 1859); *Report on Sewerage in the City of Providence, Made by the Water Commissioners as a Committee Constituted by the Board of Aldermen to Construct Certain Sewers, Transmitting a Report on the Subject Made to Them by J. Herbert Shedd, Chief Engineer of the Providence Water Works. February, 1874* (Providence, 1874), City doc. 56; "The Sewerage of Boston: A Report by a Commission, Consisting of E. S. Chesbrough, C.E., Moses Lane, C.E., Charles F. Folsom, M.D.," *Boston City Documents, 1876* (Boston, 1876), City Doc. no. 3; *U.S. Congress, Senate, Miscellaneous Documents,* "Letter from the Consultng Engineer of the District of Columbia Addressed to the Committee on the District of Columbia, Submitting a Plan for the Improvement of the System of Sewerage in Said District," 45th Cong., 3d sess., 3 December 1878, Mis. Doc. no. 13, pp. 1–40; Julius W. Adams, *Sewers and Drains for Populous Districts, with Rules and Formulae for the Determination of Their Dimensions Under All Circumstances* (New York, 1880); Rudolph Hering, "Reports of an Examination Made in 1880 of Several Sewerage Works in Europe," *Annual Report of the National Board of Health, 1881* (Washington, D.C., 1882); and *Proposed Plan for a Sewerage System, and for the Disposal of the Sewage of the City of Providence: By Samuel M. Gray, City Engineer* (Providence, 1884), City Doc. no. 25.

For discussion of whether health or wealth was the best reason to sewer cities, see George E. Waring, Jr., *Drainage for Health and Draining for Profit* (New York, 1867); Max Von Pettenkofer, "The Value of Health to a City," *Sanitarian* 4 (January 1876), 17–23; J. N. DeHart, M.D., *Practical Hygiene, As it Relates to a Proper Water Supply, and the Defective Sewage of Cities and Towns, Hospitals and Asylums* (Chicago, 1879); and J. S. Billings, "Sewage Disposal in Cities," *Harper's New Monthly Magazine* 71 (1885), 579ff. See also Joel A. Tarr, "The Separate vs. Combined Sewer Problem: A Case Study in Urban Technology Design Choice." *Journal of Urban History* 5 (1979), 308–33. For interesting case studies of one city's experiences, see George P. Gregory, "A Study in Local Decision Making: Pittsburgh and Sewage Treatment," *Western Pennsylvania Historical Magazine* 57 (1974), 25–42; and Mark Tierno, "The Search for Pure Water in Pittsburgh: The Urban Response to Water Pollution, 1893–1914," ibid 60 (1977), 23–36.

For statistics see: U.S. Bureau of the Census, *Financial Statistics of Cities Hav-*

ing a Population of Over 30,000: 1910 (Washington, D.C., 1913), pp. 134–43. See also Edward Meeker, "The Improving Health of the United States, 1850–1915," *Explorations in Economic History* 9 (1972), 353–73, esp. table 6, p. 370; Meeker, "The Social Rate of Return on Investment in Public Health, 1880–1910," *Journal of Economic History* 34 (1974), 392–421; Gretchen A. Condran and Eileen M. Crimmins-Gardner, "Public Health Measures and Mortality in U.S. Cities in the Late Nineteenth Century," *Human Ecology* 6 (March 1978), 27–54; and Crimmins and Condran, "Mortality Variation in U.S. Cities in 1900," *Social Science History* 7 (Winter 1983), 31–59.

46. "Report of the Massachusetts Drainage Commission, 1884–85," excerpted in Rafter and Baker, *Sewage Disposal in the United States*, p. 115. For discussion of several cities' special service districts see Louis P. Cain, "The Search for an Optimum Sanitation Jurisdiction: The Metropolitan Sanitary District of Greater Chicago: A Case Study," *Essays in Works History* 10 (1980), 20–23.

47. Chapin, *Municipal Sanitation*, pp. 296–97.

48. U.S. Bureau of the Census, *Bulletin Number 100, Social Statistics of Cities, 1890* (Washington, D.C., 1891), pp. 5–16. The most scholarly and insightful discussion of streets and street paving, among other subjects, is Clay McShane, "American Cities and the Coming of the Automobile, 1870–1910" (Ph.D. dissertation, University of Wisconsin-Madison, 1975). See also his article, "Transforming the Use of Urban Space: A Look at the Revolution in Street Pavements, 1880–1924," *Journal of Urban History* 5 (1979), 288ff. I am indebted to Professor McShane, presently at Northeastern University in Boston, for instructing me in the vital, albeit arcane, subject of paving, central to any account of city planning thought and practice.

49. The most useful brief discussion of this problem is Martin V. Melosi, "Refuse Pollution and Municipal Reform: The Waste Problem in America, 1880–1917," in Melosi (ed.), *Pollution and Reform*, pp. 105–33.

50. Ladies' Health Protective Association, *Memorial of the New York Ladies' Health Protective Association, to the Hon. Abram S. Hewitt, Mayor of New York, on the Subject of Street-Cleaning* (New York, 1887), pp. 4, 5; Suellen M. Hoy, " 'Municipal Housekeeping': The Role of Women in Improving Urban Sanitation Practices, 1880–1917," in Melosi, *Pollution and Reform*, pp. 173–98, led me to this source.

51. Over the latter third of the nineteenth century, articles on refuse disposal and street-cleaning technologies regularly appeared in popular magazines like *Harper's Weekly, Scientific American, North American Review, Forum,* and *Popular Science,* in public health journals like *The Sanitarian,* and in such professional journals as *Engineering News.* The best summaries of concerns, practices, and technological knowledge remain William Mayo Venable, *Garbage Crematories in America* (New York, 1906); George A. Soper, *Modern Methods of Street Cleaning* (New York, 1907); William F. Morse, *The Collection and Disposal of Municipal Waste* (New York, 1908); and Rudolph Hering and Samuel A. Greeley, *Collection and Disposal of Municipal Refuse* (New York, 1921). For Waring's estimate see George E. Waring, Jr., "The Relation of Street Cleaning to Good Paving," *Engineering Magazine* 12 (1897), 781–85.

52. McShane, "American Cities and the Coming of the Automobile," pp. 101–4. American and European attitudes about the uses of city streets are com-

pared by François Bedarida and Anthony R. Sutcliffe, "The Street in the Structure and Life of the City: Reflections on Nineteenth-Century London and Paris," *Journal of Urban History* 6 (1980), 379–96.

53. John F. Dillon, *Treatise on the Law of Municipal Corporations* (Chicago, 1872), p. 481; Victor Rosewater, *Special Assessments: A Study in Municipal Finance* (New York, 1883), pp. 9–25; N. P. Lewis, "Some Observations on General Taxation and Special Assessments," *American Society for Improvements Proceedings* 4 (1901), 132–33.

54. "Appendix II: Street Paving Statistics," p. 304 in McShane, "American Cities and the Coming of the Automobile"; John L. MacAdam, *Road Making* (London, 1823); Q. A. Gilmore, *A Practical Treatise on Roads, Streets and Pavements* (New York, 1876), pp. 88–103. For problems of maintenance and cleaning, see George W. Tillson, *Street Pavements and Paving Materials* (New York, 1901), pp. 6–13.

55. The best brief discussion is McShane, "American Cities and the Coming of the Automobile," pp. 246–300: "Appendix I: The Technology of Street Paving." For contemporary discussion of the Nicholson system, see Samuel Nicholson, *The Nicholson Pavement* (Boston, 1859); and Frank G. Johnson, *The Nicholson Pavement and Pavements Generally* (New York, 1867).

56. William Glazer, *Peculiarities of American Cities* (Philadelphia, 1884), p. 164; Howard H. Gross, "The Evolution of Street Paving in Chicago," *Municipal Journal and Engineer* 11 (1901), 206–7.

57. Gilmore, *A Practical Treatise*, pp. 175–92; George W. Tillson, "Asphalt and Asphalt Pavements," in Arthur H. Blanchard (ed.), *American Highway Engineers Handbook* (New York, 1919), pp. 224, 234–35; Bernard Bienfield, "The Origin and History of Asphalt," *Municiapl Engineering* 12 (February 1897), 79–80; E. P. North, "The Construction and Maintenance of Roads," *Transactions of the American Society of Civil Engineers* 8 (1897), 95–105.

58. Joseph Rock Draney, "Asphalt—Origin, History, Development—Its Relation to Petroleum," *Americana* 33 (1939), 1–31; Herbert Abraham, *Asphalts and Allied Substances* (New York, 1929), pp. 1–72; Edwin J. Barth, *Asphalt: Science and Technology* (New York, 1962), pp. 1–8; Gilmore, *A Practical Treatise*, pp. 227–32; William Pierce Judson, *City Roads and Pavements* (New York, 1902), pp. 19–21.

59. H. Wager Halleck, *Bitumen: Its Varieties, Properties and Uses* (Washington, D.C., 1841). For a brief end-of-the-century overview of the changing functions of streets in the nation's largest city see: J. F. Harder, "The City's Plan," *Municipal Affairs* 2 (1898), 24–45.

60. For example, see "The Future of Great Cities," *Nation* (1866), 232; Robert Moore, "Street Pavements," *Engineering News* 3 (6 May 1876), 146; Seth Low, "The Government of Cities in the United States," *Century Magazine* 42 (1891), 731ff.; Samuel Whinery, "The Effect of Street Paving on the Abutting Property," *Engineering Record* 25 (1892), 418; quotation from Nelson P. Lewis, "From Cobblestone to Asphalt and Brick," *Municipal and Paving Engineering* 10 (March, 1896), 234–35.

61. Among other sources see Citizens Association for the Improvements of the Streets and Roads of Philadelphia, *First Annual Report* (Philadelphia, 1871); John H. Sargeant, "Street Pavement—Past, Present, and Future," *Journal of the Association of Engineering Societies* 6 (1887), 331; Lewis M. Haupt, "Municipal Engi-

neering—A Study of Street Pavements," *Journal of the Franklin Institute* 128 (1889), 458ff.; George N. Bell, C.E., "Public Streets and Highways," *Sanitarian* 28 (1892), 386–94; David Molitor, "Municipal Public Improvements and the Laws Governing Them," *Municipal Engineering* 13 (1897), 331–35; "Municipal Co-operation: Possible Substitute for Municipal Consolidation," *Engineering News* 41 (16 February 1899), 104–6.

62. Lewis M. Haupt, "On the Best Arrangement of City Streets," *Journal of the Franklin Institute* 103 (1877), 252; Francis V. Greene, "Construction and Care of Streets," *Engineering and Building Record* 21 (1 March 1890), 196.

CHAPTER 8. THE ENGINEERED METROPOLIS

1. Charles V. Chapin, *Municipal Sanitation in the United States* (rev. ed., Providence, 1901), p. 297.

2. Raymond H. Merritt, *Engineering in American Society, 1850–1875* (Lexington, Ky., 1969), pp. 136–76; and, for the pre–Civil War experience, Daniel Calhoun, *The American Civil Engineer: Origins and Conflict* (Cambridge, Mass., 1960). Quotation from *Engineering News* 4 (7 July 1877), 173.

3. Samuel C. Busey, "History and Progress of Sanitation of the City of Washington and Efforts of the Medical Profession in Relation Thereto." *The Sanitarian* 42 (1899), 205–16; Constance McLaughlin Green, *Washington, Village and Capital, 1800–1878* (Princeton, 1962), pp. 241–60; M. L. Holman, "Historical Aspects of the St. Louis Water Works," *Journal of the American Engineering Society* 14 (1895), 1–9; A. L. Anderson, "The Sanitary Conditions of the Cincinnati Sewer," *Engineering News* 5 (November 14, 21, 1878), 324, 372; Arthur S. Hobby, "The Sewerage of Cincinnati," ibid., (November 28, 1878) pp. 377–78; Melvin G. Holli, *Reform in Detroit: Hazen S. Pingree and Urban Politics* (New York, 1969), pp. 26–27.

4. Sources for this and the previous two paragraphs include "The Better Water Supply of Northeastern New Jersey," *Engineering News and American Railway Journal* 19 (1888), 230–31; *Newark Aqueduct Board v. City of Passaic*, Court of Chancery of New Jersey, 22 July 1889, reprinted in George W. Rafter and M. N. Baker, *Sewage Disposal in the United States* (New York, 1894), pp. 579–85; Commonwealth of Massachusetts, *Acts of 1889* (Boston, 1890), ch. 439; *First Annual Report of the Board of Metropolitan Sewerage Commissioners* (Boston, 1890); "Troy, N.Y.," *Engineering News* 4 (November 3, 1877), 359–69; "Municipal Co-operation a Possible Substitute for Consolidation," ibid. 41 (February 16, 1899), 104–6; Paul Studenski, *The Government of Municipal Areas in the United States* (New York, 1930), pp. 33–34, 49–59, 105–13. On extra-municipal powers see, among others, Nelson Tibbs, "The Sanitary Protection of the Watershed Supplying Water to Rochester, N.Y.," *Engineering News and American Railway Journal* 19 (April 28, 1888), 531; Olmsted, Vaux & Co., *Report on the Parkway Proposed for the City of Brooklyn* (Brooklyn, 1868); "How to Subdivide Land in Illinois," *Engineer and Surveyor* 1 (1874), 4; and for a general discussion of the broad context, Mel Scott, *American City Planning Since 1890* (Berkeley, 1969), pp. 110–269.

5. On the organization of their own offices and boards of administration, see a lengthy series of articles in *Engineering News* from 6 January through 25 Decem-

ber 1886; the March 1893 issue of the *Journal of the Association of Engineering Societies*; Albert F. Noyes, "Organization and Management of a City Engineer's Office," ibid. 13 (October 1894), 541ff. On budgetary and tax policies, see David Molitor, "Municipal Public Improvements and the Laws Governing Them," *Municiapl Engineering* 13 (1897), 331–36; August Herrman, "Rates of Taxation in the Larger Cities of the United States," *Proceedings of the American Society for Municipal Improvements* 5 (1898), 3–27.

6. Information about the legal training of engineers appears in American Society of Civil Engineers, *A Biographical Dictionary of American Civil Engineers* (New York, 1972). For the Boston and Chicago examples, see *Engineering News* 6 (10 January 1878); *Sanitary News* 6 (10 October 1885); and James C. O'Connell, *Chicago's Quest for Pure Water*, Public Works Historical Society (Washington, D.C., 1976), p. 17.

7. *Biographical Dictionary of American Civil Engineers*, pp. 23–24; Calhoun, *American Civil Engineer*, pp. 68–78.

8. Charles W. Eliot, "One Remedy for Municipal Misgovernment," *Forum* 12 (1891), 153–68; John Ficklen, "The Municipal Condition of New Orleans," *Proceedings of the Second National Conference on Good City Government* (1894); "Municipal Reports," *Municipal Engineering* 17 (1900), 56–58; and, on civil service protection, "Engineers as Commissioners of Public Works," *Engineering News and American Railway Journal* 31 (1 February 1894), 82; and A. Marston and G. W. Miller, "The Methods of Choosing City Engineers," *Engineering Record* 47 (21 December 1903), 198–99.

9. For general discussion of engineers' careers, see Merritt, *Engineering in American Society*, pp. 88–109, 136–76.

10. For example, see "European Systems of Sewerage," *Engineering News* 9 (28 January 1882), 33–35; "Municipal and Sanitary Engineering in the City of London," *Engineering News and American Contract Journal* 16 (August 21, 28, 1886), 122–23, 134–35; L. M. Haupt, "The Growth of Cities as Exemplified in Philadelphia," *Proceedings of the Engineering Club of Philadelphia* 4 (1884), 148–75; Robert Gilliam, "Work for Our Engineers' Club," *Journal of the Association of Engineering Statistics* 11 (1893), 305–13; and "St. Louis Boulevards in the Business District," ibid. 12 (1894), 190. For the Chesbrough and Hering reports, among others, see Ellis S. Chesbrough, *Chicago Sewerage: Report of the Results of Examinations Made in Relation to Sewerage in Several European Cities, in the Winter of 1856–57* (Chicago, 1858), and Rudolph Hering, "Reports of an Examination Made in 1880 of Several Sewerage Works in Europe," *Annual Report of the National Board of Health, 1881* (Washington, D.C., 1882). See discussion of these reports *supra*, Chapter 7.

11. *Journal of the Association of Engineering Societies* 12 (1893), 443; John N. Olmsted, "Relation of the City Engineer to Public Parks," ibid. 13 (1894), 595. See also the series of articles titled "Municipal Government with Especial Reference to the Management of Public Works," ibid. 11 (1892), 123–75; Karwiese quotation from *U.S. Congress, Senate, Miscellaneous Documents*, "Letter from the Consulting Engineer of the District of Columbia Addressed to the Committee on the District of Columbia, Submitting a Plan for the Improvement of the System of Sewerage in Said District," 45th Cong., 3d sess., 3 December 1878, Mis. Doc. no. 13, p. 3.

12. Quotation from Eugene P. Moehring, "Public Works and Urban History: Recent Trends and New Directions," in *Essays in Public Works History*, no. 13 (Public Works Historical Society: Chicago, 1982), p. 3. For examples of collaboration between machines and engineers see Geoffrey Giglierano, "The City and the System: Developing a Municipal Service, 1800–1915," *Cincinnati Historical Society Bulletin*, 35 (1977), 223–47; and Eugene P. Moehring, *Public Works and the Patterns of Real Estate Growth in Manhattan, 1835–1894* (New York, 1981).

The apparent political neutrality of engineers is a subject worthy of more detailed investigation than undertaken here. A careful examination of the topic would not only shed light on the engineers and their relationship to city development, but, more important, inform us about the larger role played by professionals in the determination of public policies. Until recently, historians have tended to ignore this topic. For an interesting historical examination of the subject, see Burton J. Bledstein, *The Culture of Professionalism: The Middle Class and the Development of Higher Education in America* (New York, 1976). The most satisfactory writings on the subject have come from political scientists and sociologists. Readers wanting to pursue the subject will profit from beginning with Karl W. Deutsch, *The Nerves of Government: Models of Political Communication and Control* (new ed., New York, 1966), and Harold L. Wilensky, *Organizational Intelligence: Knowledge and Policy in Government and Industry* (New York, 1967).

13. Noyes, "Organization and Management of a City Engineer's Office," p. 544.

14. The term "elite" "refers first of all to a minority of individuals designated to serve a collectivity in a socially valued way. . . . Socially significant elites are ultimately responsible for the realization of major social goals and for the continuity of the social order." Furthermore, "only certain leadership groups have a general and sustained social impact. . . . We refer to these groups as *strategic elites* . . . who comprise not only political, economic, and military leaders, but also moral, cultural, and scientific ones. Whether or not an elite is counted as strategic does not depend on its specific activities but on the scope of its activities, that is, on how many members of society it directly impinges upon and in what respects." Suzanne Keller, *Beyond the Ruling Class: Strategic Elites in Modern Society* (New York, 1963), pp. 4, 20.

15. Benjamin Ward Richardson, "Hygeia—A City of Health: A Presidential Address Delivered Before the Health Department of the Social Science Association . . . October, 1875" (London, 1876). Richardson's work was widely read in the United States. See the reprint of most of the address as "Modern Sanitary Science—A City of Health," *Van Nostrand's Eclectic Engineering Magazine* 14 (January 1876), 31–44; and "A City of Health," *The Sanitarian* 4 (1876), 24–30, 68–76. Many of the same notions appeared years later in a piece by Richard Wheatley, "Hygeia in Manhattan," *Harper's Magazine* 94 (1896–97), and in Hollis Godfrey, *The Health of the City* (Boston, 1910), of which 8 (out of 10) chapters had already appeared in "more or less abbreviated form" in the *Atlantic Monthly*. In 1874 the Boston physician Edward Jarvis had anticipated Richardson in calling for control by government-appointed sanitary engineers of the layout of prospective cities. See his *Political Economy of Health* (Boston, 1874). For brief historical discussion of Richardson, see James H. Cassedy, "Hygeia: A Mid-Victorian Dream of a City of Health," *Journal of the History of Medicine and Allied Sciences* 17 (1962), 217–29.

For Waring's views see Albert Shaw, *Life of Col. Geo. E. Waring, Jr., the Great Apostle of Cleanliness . . . and A.D., 1997—A Prophecy by Colonel George E. Waring, Jr.* (New York, 1899); J. M. Gregory, "The Hygiene of Great Cities," *Engineering News* 7 (10 January 1880), 17.

16. *New Orleans Times-Democrat*, 19 April 1894; J. N. Olmsted, "Relation of the City Engineer to Public Parks," pp. 594–95.

17. Walter Muir Whitehill, *Boston: A Topographical History* (Cambridge, Mass., 1968), pp. 141–73; Norman T. Newton, *Design on the Land: The Development of Landscape Architecture* (Cambridge, Mass., 1971), pp. 290–306; Lawrence J. Friedman, *A History of American Law* (New York 1973), p. 397.

18. For initiation and progress of the plan, see Board of Commissioners of the Department of Parks for the City of Boston, *Seventh Annual Report for the Year 1881* (Boston, 1882), pp. 1–28 and subsequent reports through 1886. The quotation is from the 1881 report, p. 26.

19. The series of reports were: *Preliminary Report of the Landscape Architect and the Civil and Topographical Engineer, Upon the Laying Out of the Twenty-third and Twenty-fourth Wards, and Report of the Landscape Architect and the Civil Topographical Engineer, Accompanying a Plan for Laying Out That Part of the Twenty-fourth Ward, Lying West of Riverdale Road* (New York, 1876); *Report of the Civil and Topographical Engineer and the Landscape Architect, Accompanying a Plan for Local Steam Transit Routes in the Twenty-third and Twenty-fourth Wards* (New York, 1877); and *Communication for the Landscape Architect and the Civil and Topographical Engineer, in Relation to the Proposed Plan for Laying out the Central District of the Twenty-third and Twenty-fourth Wards, Lying East of Jerome Avenue and West of Third Avenue and the Harlem Railroad* (New York, 1877). See also E. B. Van Winkle, "Drainage of the Twenty-third and Twenty-fourth Wards, This City," *Engineering News* 8 (18, 20 August 1881), 321–27, 337–49; S. S. Haight, "Surveying, Laying out and Monumenting the New Wards of New York," ibid. (5 March 1881), p. 96. The official description of the Croes-Olmsted plans as "a hazardous experiment" is in "Report of Commissioner Stebbins Upon the Plans for Laying Out That Part of the Twenty-fourth Ward Lying West of Riverdale Road," *Board of the Department of Public Parks* (New York, 1877), Doc. no. 74.

20. For discussion of some of these plans, see Newton, *Design on the Land*, pp. 307–36. This generalization rests upon scrutiny of scores of park planning and park board reports, many in the author's possession and more available in the Francis Loeb Library, Harvard School of Design.

21. L. M. Haupt, "Rapid Transit," *Proceedings of the Engineering Club of Philadelphia* 4 (1884), 135–38, which appears to have been modeled on an 1875 survey of rapid transit in New York City undertaken by the American Society of Civil Engineers, published as "Rapid Transit and Terminal Freight Facilities," *ASCE Transactions* 4 (1875), 1–80; Haupt, "The Growth of Cities as Exemplified in Philadelphia," pp. 148–75; the Hering article is in *Proceedings of the Engineering Club of Philadelphia* 2 (1880), 36–50. Among others, see also J. J. Flinn, *Chicago* (Chicago, 1891), pt. 2, on water, sewerage, and population; Rudolph Hering, "Sewerage System of Atlanta," *Engineering Record* 35 (1891), 294ff.; L. M. Hastings, "Some Problems in Municipal Engineering," *Journal of the Association of Engineering Societies* 9 (1891), 549ff.; "Civil Engineering," *Engineering Magazine* 3 (1892), 418–20; George H. Benzenberg, "Sewage of Milwaukee," *Engineering*

Record 37 (1893), 219ff.; J. Stubben, "Practical and Aesthetic Principles for the Laying Out of Cities," *Transactions of the American Society of Civil Engineers* 29 (1893), 718ff.; William Paul Gerhard, "The Laying Out of Cities and Towns," *Journal of the Franklin Institue* 140 (August 1895), 90–99; and Albert F. Noyes, "The Massachusetts Metropolitan Water Suppply," *Journal of the New England Water Works Association* 10 (1895), 117ff.

22. U.S. Bureau of the Census, *Eleventh Census of the United States, 1890: Report on Vital and Social Statistics*, 2:2–99, for population and urban mortality figures. For a useful discussion of Newark, see Stuart Galishoff, *Safeguarding the Public Health: Newark, 1895–1918* (Westport, Conn., 1975), esp. pp. 3–13.

23. W. L. Fairbanks, *A Statistical Analysis of the Population of Maryland* (Baltimore, 1931), pp. 104–19. For a perceptive summary of the impact of annexation on nineteenth-century urban America, see Kenneth T. Jackson, "Metropolitan Government Versus Suburban Autonomy: Politics on the Crabgrass Frontier," in Kenneth T. Jackson and Stanley K. Schultz (eds.), *Cities in American History* (New York, 1972), pp. 442–62.

Readers interested in pursuing the story of Baltimore in greater depth will profit from Carrol D. Wright, *The Slums of Baltimore, Chicago, New York, and Philadelphia* (Washington, D.C., 1894); Clayton Colman Hall (ed.), *Baltimore: Its History and Its People*, Vol. 1 (Baltimore, 1912); Jacob Hollander, *The Financial History of Baltimore* (Baltimore, 1899); Leonard Owens Rea, *The Financial History of Baltimore, 1900–1926* (Baltimore, 1929); Frederick P. Stieff (ed.), *The Government of a Great American City* (Baltimore, 1935); William T. Howard, *Public Health Administration and the Natural History of Disease in Baltimore, Maryland, 1797–1920* (Washington, D.C., 1924); Charles Hirschfield, *Baltimore, 1870–1900: Studies in Social History* (Baltimore, 1941); James B. Crooks, *Politics and Progress: The Rise of Urban Progressivism in Baltimore, 1895 to 1911* (Baton Rouge, 1968); and Alan D. Anderson, *The Origin and Resolution of an Urban Crisis: Baltimore, 1890–1930* (Baltimore, 1977).

24. In addition to sources cited *supra*, see Daniel C. Gilman, "Baltimore," *St. Nicholas* 20 (1893), 723–33; and U.S. Bureau of the Census, *Vital Statistics of District of Columbia and Baltimore, Covering Period of Six Years Ending May 31, 1890* (Washington, D.C., 1893), pp. 55–62. On the Negro population see ibid., pp. 72–73; U.S. Bureau of the Census, *Negroes in the United States*, Bull. 8 (Washington, D.C., 1904), pp. 230–32; and Howard, *Public Health Administration*, p. 26.

25. John H. Gregory et al., *Report to the Public Improvement Commission of Baltimore on Future Sources of Water Supply* (Baltimore, 1934), pp. 8–27; Nelson M. Blake, *Water for the Cities: A History of the Urban Water Supply Problem in the United States* (Syracuse, 1956), pp. 219–47. For filtration and purification statistics, see U.S. Public Health Service, *Public Health Bulletin No. 164: Municipal Health Department Practice for the Year 1923 Based Upon Surveys of the 100 Largest Cities in the United States* (Washington, D.C., 1926), pp. 474–75.

26. Calvin W. Hendrick, "Sewerage System," in Hall, *Baltimore*, 1:423–27; *Sewerage Commission Report, 1906* (Baltimore, 1906), pp. 16–17.

27. *Sewerage Commission Report, 1906*, p. 17; *Report of the Sewerage Commission of the City of Baltimore* (Baltimore, 1897), pp. 16–22. H. L. Mencken recalled of his youth in the Baltimore of the 1880s: "The legend seems to prevail that there were no sewers in Baltimore until after the World War, but that is something of an

exaggeration. Our house in Hollins street [one of the best neighborhoods in the city] was connected with a private sewer down the alley in the rear as early as I have any recollection of it, and so were many other houses, especially in the newer parts of the town. . . . All the sewers of Baltimore, whether private or public, emptied into the Back Basin in those days. . . . As a result it began to acquire a powerful aroma every Spring, and by August smelled like a billion polecats." H. L. Mencken, *Happy Days: 1880–1892* (New York, 1940), pp. 69–70.

28. *Report of the Sewerage Commission* (1897), pp. 16–18.

29. Quotation from the 1895 report of the commissioner of health, reprinted ibid., p. 20.

30. Ibid., pp. 24–88; *Second Report of the Sewerage Commission of the City of Baltimore* (Baltimore, 1899), pp. 7–40; Crooks, *Politics and Progress*, pp. 132–37.

31. Anderson, *Origin and Resolution of an Urban Crisis*, pp. 69–72.

32. Crooks, *Politics and Progress*, pp. 127–54.

33. Frederic C. Howe, *The City: The Hope of Democracy* (1905; reprint ed, Seattle, 1967), pp. 50, 127, 131, 182. For historians' discussion of reformers' ambitions, see, among others, Samuel Haber, *Efficiency and Uplift* (Chicago, 1964); Ernest S. Griffith, *A History of American City Government: The Progressive Years and Their Aftermath, 1900–1920* (New York, 1974), chs. 1–11; Samuel P. Hays, "The Changing Political Structure of the City in Industrial America," *Journal of Urban History* 1 (1974), 6–38; Robert Wiebe, *The Search for Order, 1877–1920* (New York, 1967), pp. 164–95; and Martin J. Schiesl, *The Politics of Efficiency: Municipal Administration and Reform in America: 1880–1920* (Berkeley, 1977).

34. John Nolen, "City Making," *American City* 1 (1909), 19.

35. Frederic C. Howe, *The Confessions of a Reformer* (1925; reprint ed., New York 1967), pp. 113–14.

36. On the planning profession see Scott, *American City Planning*; Roy Lubove, *The Progressives and the Slums: Tenement House Reform in New York City, 1890–1917* (Pittsburgh, 1962), pp. 217–45; Lubove, *The Urban Community: Housing and Planning in the Progressive Era* (Englewood Cliffs, N.J., 1967), pp. 1–22; John L. Hancock, "Planners in the Changing American City, 1900–1940," *Journal of the American Institute of Planners* 33 (1967), 290–304; and Thomas S. Hines, *Burnham of Chicago: Architect and Planner* (New York, 1974). On the profession of city manager, and its cousin the city commission, see Harry Aubrey Toulmin, Jr., *The City Manager: A New Profession* (New York, 1915); Leonard D. White, *The City Manager* (Chicago, 1927); Clarence E. Ridley and Orin F. Nolting, *The City-Manager Profession* (Chicago, 1934); John Porter East, *Council-Manager Government: The Political Thought of Its Founder, Richard S. Childs* (Chapel Hill, 1965); Richard J. Stillman II, *The Rise of the City Manager: A Public Professional in Local Government* (Albuquerque, 1974); and Bradley Robert Rice, *Progressive Cities: The Commission Government Movement in America, 1901–1920* (Austin, 1977).

37. U.S. Congress, Senate, Documents, "City Planning," 61st Cong., 2d sess., 1910, Doc. no. 422, pp. 75, 61, 59, 66.

38. Ibid., p. 78.

39. Nelson P. Lewis, *The Planning of the Modern City: A Review of the Principles Governing City Planning* (New York, 1916); George B. Ford and Ralph F. Warner, *City Planning Progress* (Washington, D.C., 1917), iii; Scott, *American City Planning*, pp. 163–64, 228.

40. Delos F. Wilcox, "The Municipal Program," *Proceedings of the Chicago*

Conference for Good City Government and the Tenth Annual Meeting of the National Municipal League (Philadelphia, 1904), pp. 187–88.

41. Herman G. James, "The City Manager Plan, the Latest in American City Government," *American Political Science Review* 8 (1914), 611–12. For a brief summary of contemporary arguments pro and con, see Schiesl, *The Politics of Efficiency*, pp. 171–88.

42. Henry Oyen, "A City with a General Manager," *World's Work* 23 (1911), 220–23; John Crosby, "Municipal Government Administered by a General Manager—The Staunton Plan," *Annals of the American Academy of Political and Social Science* 38 (1911), 880–82; Schiesl, *Politics of Efficiency*, pp. 174–78.

43. Arch Mandel and Wilbur H. Cotton, "Dayton's Sixteen Years of City Manager Government: An Appraisal of a Popular Venture,"*National Municipal Review* 19 (1930), 497–509; Harrison Gray Otis, "The City Manager Movement," *National Municipal Review* 19 (March 1920), 195–98; White, *City Manager*, pp. 74–76; Chester E. Rightor, *City Manager in Dayton* (New York, 1919).

44. Griffith, *A History of American City Government: The Progressive Years*, pp. 167–69.

45. Lewis, *Planning of the Modern City*, p. 415; Toulmin, *The City Manager*, pp. 78–81; "City Manager Plan Widely Endorsed," *Engineering News-Record*, 85 (7 October 1920), 703; Stillman, *Rise of the City Manager*, pp. 38–39; Harold Stone, Don K. Price, and Kathryn H. Stone, *City Manager Government in the United States: A Review After Twenty-five Years* (Chicago, 1940), p. 57.

THE AFFAIR OF THE FAIR

1. Candace Wheeler, "A Dream City," *Harper's New Monthly Magazine* 86 (1893), 833. There are many contemporary collections of photographs and drawings of the Fair. See, for example, *Glimpses of the World's Fair: A Selection of Gems of the White City Seen Through a Camera* (Chicago, 1893). See also David F. Burg, *Chicago's White City of 1893* (Lexington, Ky., 1976); and R. Reid Badger, *The Great American Fair: The World's Columbian Exposition and American Culture* (Chicago, 1979).

2. Augustus Saint-Gaudens to Daniel Burnham, quoted in Charles Moore, *Daniel H. Burnham, Architect, Planner of Cities* (2 vols., Boston, 1921), 1:47; Louis Henry Sullivan, *The Autobiography of an Idea* (reprint ed. New York, 1956), p. 325; Henry Adams, *The Education of Henry Adams*, ed. Ernest Samuels (Boston, 1973), p. 343.

3. Rossiter Johnson (ed.) *A History of the World's Columbian Exposition Held in Chicago in 1893*, 1 (New York, 1897), 135.

4. *Chicago Tribune*, 1 November 1893. See also, for example, Henry Van Brunt, "The Columbian Exposition and American Civilization," *Atlantic Monthly* 71 (1893), 582–83; Julian Hawthorne, "A Description of the Inexpressible," *Lippincott's Monthly Magazine* 51 (1893), 496–503; and Hjalmar H. Boyesen, "A New World Fable," *The Cosmopolitan* 16 (1893), 178. On the Fair as the starting point of modern American city planning, in addition to references in Preface, n. 2, see Maurice F. Neufeld, "The Contribution of the World's Columbian Exposition of 1893 to the Idea of a Planned Society in the United States: A Study of Adminis-

trative, Financial, Esthetic, Social and Intellectual Planning" (Ph.D. dissertation, University of Wisconsin, 1935); and John M. Gaus, *The Education of Planners* (Cambridge, Mass., 1943). Quotation from John W. Reps, *The Making of Urban America: A History of City Planning in the United States* (Princeton, 1965), p. 498. See also Thomas S. Hines, *Burnham of Chicago: Architect and Planner* (New York, 1974), p. 141.

5. George Kriehn, "The City Beautiful," *Municipal Affairs* 3 (1899), 594; John W. Reps, *Monumental Washington: The Planning and Development of the Capitol Center* (Princeton, 1967); Mel Scott, *American City Planning Since 1890* (Berkeley, 1969), pp. 43–109. On the National Conference on City Planning see Chapter 8.

6. Daniel H. Burnham and Edward H. Bennett, *Plan of Chicago* (Chicago, 1909), p. 108.

7. See arguments advanced by C. L. Eshelman, "Modern Street Lighting," *American City* 6 (1912), 46–47. The quotation comes from Howard Strong, "The Street Beautiful in Minneapolis," *American City* 9 (1913), 229. Citations for both articles came from an engaging piece by Mark J. Bournan, "Luxury and Control: The Urbanity of Street Lighting in Nineteenth-Century Cities," *Journal of Urban History* 14 (1987), 7–37.

8. Paul Boyer, *Urban Masses and Moral Order in America, 1820–1920* (Cambridge, Mass., 1978), p. 264 (see especially pp. 189–283 for a broad-ranging discussion of Progressivism and the city); Hines, *Burnham of Chicago*, p. 138.

9. City engineer Nelson P. Lewis quoted the alderman in his seminal text, *The Planning of the Modern City* (New York 1916), p. 9.

10. Robert Fleming Gourlay, *Plans for Beautifying New York and for Enlarging and Improving the City of Boston: Being Studies to Illustrate the Science of City Building* (Boston, 1844), p. 17. Historians have forgotten Gourlay as a pioneering city planner. Walter Muir Whitehill, in his superb *Boston: A Topographical History* (Cambridge, Mass., 1968) mentions him, but the only "modern" studies of this important man are Janet Carnochan, "Robert Gourlay," *Publications of the Niagara Historical Society*, no. 18 (1909), 35–47; and Fletcher Steele, "Robert Fleming Gourlay, City Planner," *Landscape Architecture* 6 (October 1915), 1–14.

11. Gourlay, *Plans*, pp. 19–20, 30, 35, 37; quotation on p. 16.

12. Among a number of useful works, the most impressive is Jon C. Teaford, *The Unheralded Triumph: City Government in America, 1870–1900* (Baltimore, 1984).

13. Christine Meisner Rosen, *The Limits of Power: Great Fires and the Process of City Growth in America* (New York, 1986), p. 328. Although Rosen argues that pluralistic politics slowed the pace of change, she admits that many of the actions of various classes of urbanites mediated their conflicts in the political arena and helped force reform, if not at a gait she admires. My emphasis on social and cultural change that encouraged physical and legal change amends rather than attacks her conceptually satisfying and narratively rewarding discussion of the barriers to environmental reform.

14. William Tudor, *Letters on the Eastern States* (Boston, 1821), excerpted in Bayrd Still, *Urban America: A History with Documents* (Boston, 1974), pp. 72–73.

15. Arthur H. Grant, "The Conning Tower," *American City* 1 (1909), 20; Charles Zueblin, *American Municipal Progress* (New York, 1916), pp. 398–99.

INDEX

[Author's note: Except for principal usages, I have not indexed the following words that recur throughout the book: city; culture; engineer; engineering; industrialization; law; plan; planning; sanitarian; sanitary; sewers; streets; technology; transit; transportation; urban; urbanization; utopia; water supplies]